Early Learning of Modern Foreign Languages

SECOND LANGUAGE ACQUISITION
Series Editor: Professor David Singleton, *Trinity College, Dublin, Ireland*

This series brings together titles dealing with a variety of aspects of language acquisition and processing in situations where a language or languages other than the native language is involved. Second language is thus interpreted in its broadest possible sense. The volumes included in the series all offer in their different ways, on the one hand, exposition and discussion of empirical findings and, on the other, some degree of theoretical reflection. In this latter connection, no particular theoretical stance is privileged in the series; nor is any relevant perspective – sociolinguistic, psycholinguistic, neurolinguistic, and so on – deemed out of place. The intended readership of the series includes final-year undergraduates working on second language acquisition projects, postgraduate students involved in second language acquisition research, and researchers and teachers in general whose interests include a second language acquisition component.

Full details of all the books in this series and of all our other publications can be found on http://www.multilingual-matters.com, or by writing to Multilingual Matters, St Nicholas House, 31–34 High Street, Bristol BS1 2AW, UK.

SECOND LANGUAGE ACQUISITION
Series Editor: David Singleton

Early Learning of Modern Foreign Languages

Processes and Outcomes

Edited by

Marianne Nikolov

MULTILINGUAL MATTERS
Bristol • Buffalo • Toronto

Library of Congress Cataloging in Publication Data
A catalog record for this book is available from the Library of Congress.
Early Learning of Modern Foreign Languages: Processes and Outcomes/Edited by
Marianne Nikolov.
Second language acquisition
Includes bibliographical references.
1. Second language acquisition--Age factors. 2. Second language acquisition--Research.
3. Bilingualism in children. I. Nikolov, Marianne.
P118.2.E16 2009
418.0071–dc22 2009001467

British Library Cataloguing in Publication Data
A catalogue entry for this book is available from the British Library.

ISBN-13: 978-1-84769-146-0 (hbk)
ISBN-13: 978-1-84769-145-3 (pbk)

Multilingual Matters
UK: St Nicholas House, 31–34 High Street, Bristol BS1 2AW, UK.
USA: UTP, 2250 Military Road, Tonawanda, NY 14150, USA.
Canada: UTP, 5201 Dufferin Street, North York, Ontario M3H 5T8, Canada.

The policy of Multilingual Matters/Channel View Publications is to use papers
that are natural, renewable and recyclable products, made from wood grown in
sustainable forests. In the manufacturing process of our books, and to further
support our policy, preference is given to printers that have FSC and PEFC Chain
of Custody certification. The FSC and/or PEFC logos will appear on those books
where full certification has been granted to the printer concerned.

Typeset by Techset Composition Ltd., Salisbury, UK.
Printed and bound in Great Britain by Short Run Press Ltd.

Contents

Contributors

John Harris is Senior Lecturer in Psycholinguistics and Director of Research in the School of Linguistic, Speech and Communication Sciences in Trinity College Dublin. He has conducted research on bilingualism, second-language learning, immersion and minority languages. He has been the principal investigator in nearly all national monitoring and evaluation studies of the teaching and learning of spoken Irish and modern European languages at primary level in Ireland in recent years.

Denise O'Leary joined the School of Linguistics, Speech and Communication Sciences, Trinity College Dublin in 2004 as a Lecturer in Psycholinguistics. Prior to this she had been working in the Linguistics Institute of Ireland (Institiúid Teangeolaíochta Éireann) as a Research Officer in the Psycholinguistics Department. It was here in 2001 that she began working with Dr Harris on the evaluation of the Modern Languages in Primary Schools Initiative. She has taught modern languages in first, second and third level education.

Janet Enever is senior lecturer at London Metropolitan University where she is Project Director for a three year European Commission-funded research study, *Early Language Learning in Europe (ELLiE)*. She coordinates the MA Primary ELT: Policy and Practice, contributes to the MA TESOL programme and supervises PhD students. Her main research and consultancy interests are primary language policy and practice and the impact of globalisation on language provision.

Zrinka Jelaska is professor at the Deptartment of Croatian (University of Zagreb) and the chief editor of the linguistic journal *LAHOR*, teaches courses on linguistics, phonology, semantics (synonymies, colour names), L2 development, Croatian as L1 and L2, and language assessment. She was Fulbright lecturer of Croatian in the USA and in Germany. She published six books, 17 book chapters and more than hundred articles.

Lidija Cvikić is a research fellow at the University of Zagreb, Department of Croatian. Her first degree is in Croatian language and literature; presently, she is a PhD student of linguistics at her home university. Her research focuses on Croatian as a second and foreign language, and the acquisition of second language grammar and vocabulary. She has been teaching Croatian as L2 at the University School of Croatian Language and Culture, University of Zagreb for many years. She also spent two academic years at Indiana University, Bloomington as a visiting instructor for the Croatian language.

Thomaï Alexiou, PhD, comes from Kastoria, Greece. She holds a BA in Pre-school Education, an MA in TEFL from the University of Kent and a PhD in Applied Linguistics from the University of Wales Swansea. She has been teaching English for 10 years in Greece and Britain and she has published several articles throughout Europe. Her research interests concern pedagogy and the methodology of teaching languages while her expertise is on cognitive development and aptitude of young language learners. She is currently a lecturer at the Department of English Language and Literature at Aristotle University in Thessaloniki.

Kata Csizér is an Assistant Professor at the Department of English Applied Linguistics, School of English and American Studies, Eötvös Loránd University, Budapest. She holds a PhD in Language Pedagogy and her main field of research interest focuses on the sociopsychological aspects of second language learning and teaching as well as second and foreign language motivation. She has published over 30 academic papers on L2 motivation and related issues and a book titled *Motivation, Language Attitudes and Globalisation* (2006, Multilingual Matters, co-authored by Zoltán Dörnyei and Nóra Németh).

Judit Kormos is a Senior Lecturer at the Department of Linguistics and English Language, Lancaster University. She formerly worked at Eötvös Lorand University, Budapest. Together with Kata Csizér, she has conducted several research projects on the motivation of Hungarian language learners. She has published a number of papers on the psychological aspects of second language acquisition and is the author of the book *Speech Production and Second Language Acquisition* (2006, Lawrence Erlbaum).

Jelena Mihaljević Djigunović is a full professor and Head of SLA and TEFL Section at Zagreb University. Her main research interests focus on affective learner variables, the age factor and on teaching young learners. Her publications include two research books, several edited volumes that she co-edited, and over 80 research papers. She has participated in several international projects on language learning and teaching.

Marianne Nikolov is a professor of English Applied Linguistics at the University of Pecs, Hungary. Her research interests include early learning and teaching of modern languages, assessment of processes and outcomes in language education, individual differences, and language policy. She used to teach groups of English learners for eight years (ages 6–14). Her studies have been published in international and Hungarian journals, edited volumes and a monograph.

Ion Drew is Associate Professor of English at the Department of Cultural Studies and Languages, Faculty of Arts and Education, The University of Stavanger, Norway. He has been involved in EFL in Norway since 1976 at different levels: adult education, secondary school and higher education. His main fields of teaching and research are second language acquisition, second language literacy development, teacher training and second language teaching methodology.

Renata Šamo teaches EFL and English language instructional methodology (with a special emphasis on teaching English to young learners) at the University of Juraj Dobrila, Pula (Croatia), and ESP at the Polytechnic of Rijeka (Croatia). She has taught at primary, secondary and tertiary levels. She has mostly written on L2 reading for professional journals, presented papers and workshops throughout Croatia and abroad. She obtained her PhD from the University of Zagreb.

Eleni Griva, PhD, is a Lecturer at the Department of Primary Education of the University of Western Macedonia in Greece. She teaches courses on Methodology of teaching a second/foreign language, bilingualism and language learning strategies. She has published several articles in Greek and international journals, and she has participated in many European and international conferences.

Helen Tsakiridou, PhD, is currently Assistant Professor of Applied Statistics and Educational Research at the Department of Primary Education, University of Western Macedonia, Greece. Her research interests include educational research in preschool, primary and tertiary education. She has published several papers in Greek and international journals on these issues.

Ioanna Nihoritou is a teacher in primary education. She is particularly interested in the field of language learning and teaching. She has participated in some conferences and research projects related to learning and teaching second/foreign languages.

Vanda Marijanovic is a Research and Teaching Assistant in the Language Sciences Department at the University of Poitiers, affiliated to the Interdisciplinary Research Unit OCTOGONE – J. Lordat (Toulouse). She has an MA degree in Foreign Language Teaching/Learning and Linguistics.

Nathalie Panissal, PhD, is a full-time Lecturer at the Psychology Department at the University of Toulouse – Le Mirail, an associated Member of the Interdisciplinary Research Unit OCTOGONE – J. Lordat, a Teacher Trainer at the IUFM (University Institute of Teacher Training) Toulouse Midi-Pyrénées and a researcher in Didactics at the ERTE 64, a research team interested in didactic interactions.

Michel Billières, PhD, is a Reader at the Language Sciences Department at the University of Toulouse – Le Mirail and Director of the Laboratory Jacques-Lordat (member of Interdisciplinary Research Unit OCTOGONE). His principal research area is cognitive didactics. Specialising in the Verbotonal Method of Phonetic Speech Correction, his research concerns phonological deafness, memorisation and speech sound production.

Ilona Huszti has taught in higher education for 11 years in Beregszász, the Ukraine, where she teaches Methodology of Teaching English to Young Learners to English major students. Her research interests include teacher training, and teaching and researching reading skills. She received her PhD at ELTE University, Budapest, Hungary in 2008. Her doctoral research focuses on the macro and micro levels of reading miscues and the use of oral reading in the language classroom.

Márta Fábián is an English teacher and teacher trainer. She teaches practical grammar classes to English major students. She has conducted research into the teaching of EFL in Transcarpathian Hungarian schools. She is the co-author of a textbook for young learners *English with You and Me*. Her research interest is TEYL. She is currently a doctoral student at the University of Pannonia, Hungary.

Erzsébet Báranyné Komári is a teacher of the Ukrainian language and she has taught in tertiary education for 10 years. She is doing her PhD at ELTE University, Budapest, Hungary, in Slav Linguistics on the analysis of Hungarian loanwords in Ruthenian dialects of Transcarpathia. She is also interested in teaching Ukrainian in the Hungarian schools of Transcarpathia and has carried out research into this area investigating the learners' general knowledge of Ukrainian.

Andrea Orosz graduated from the University of Pécs. She worked as a school-based teacher trainer at the Primary School affiliated to the University of Szeged for six years. She is currently a lecturer at the Department of English, University of Szeged, Hungary and a doctoral student at the Swansea University, UK. She teaches courses on Methodology of English Language Teaching, Learning and Teaching Vocabulary in English and English Language Practice. Her main research interests include English vocabulary acquisition in a state primary and secondary school context. She is member of the M4 Vocabulary Research Group in Britain.

Magdalena Szpotowicz, PhD, is a senior lecturer at the Centre for Foreign Language Teacher Training and European Education, University of Warsaw, Poland. Her research interests include early foreign language acquisition, foreign language policy changes and young learner teacher development. She authored and co-authored English coursebooks for primary children published by Oxford University Press, school curricula, training and research papers published locally and abroad. Since 2006 she has been involved in a multinational longitudinal study *Early Language Learning in Europe*.

Jing Peng, PhD, works at the Foreign Language College of Chongqing University, China. She teaches courses on curriculum design and teaching theory to MA students. Her main interests are teacher education, classroom research, young learners' development and materials design.

Lili Zhang is a lecturer at the School of Foreign Languages, Southwest University, China. Her research area includes teaching English for young learners, English and American literature and teaching English to college students.

Krisztina Nagy was trained as a primary school teacher in her native Hungary and taught there for five years. Then, she trained in London to use the Montessori Method and taught for three years in a Montessori school. Subsequently she did a course in Scotland on teaching children with learning difficulties, and worked as a learning support teacher. She has completed an MA course at Stirling University on Teaching English as a Foreign Language and is following this up with her doctoral research. She has presented papers at various conferences on language learning in primary schools. Her creative spirit is expressed in her use of new, interesting materials for carrying out research.

Introduction

I vividly remember my very first conference presentation almost three decades ago. After it, a senior member of the audience, an established figure in applied linguistics, congratulated me and asked, 'Why do you research young learners?' He suggested finding a more appropriate area. Since then, the world has definitely changed, as chapters in this edited volume illustrate.

These days, foreign language programmes tend to start at an increasingly early stage not only in Europe (Eurydice, 2005: 28), but the same trend is observable on other continents as well. This worldwide increase in early language learning (ELL) in public education has resulted in a growing number of empirical studies. These developments are well documented in publications of small-scale research projects usually focusing on a particular aspect of ELL (e.g. studies in Moon & Nikolov, 2000; Nikolov, 2002; Nikolov & Curtain, 2000; Nikolov *et al.*, 2007), large-scale longitudinal national projects (e.g. in Spain by García Mayo & García Lecumberri, 2003; Muñoz, 2006; in Ireland by Harris & Conway, 2002; Harris *et al.*, 2006) and recent state-of-the-art reviews (e.g. Edelenbos *et al.*, 2007; Nikolov & Mihaljević Djigunović, 2006).

Despite the widely spread practice of offering modern languages to young learners at an increasingly early age, few publications focus on what is available to children in different contexts and classrooms, on processes and outcomes, and emerging issues. This edited volume aims to fill this gap by showing how in a number of contexts early access to modern languages varies, how young children progress and benefit from an early exposure to modern languages in different educational contexts, and how affective, cognitive, social, linguistic and classroom-related factors interact in the processes. The book documents the state of the art in researching young language learners by exploring different approaches to early modern language learning and offering both large-scale and narrowly-focused empirical studies.

The world wide spread of ELL is often seen as the outcome of English becoming the lingua franca (e.g. Graddoll, 2006). A special strength of the volume is the range of languages: although English is the most widely learnt foreign language, chapters in the book focus on a variety of target languages: Croatian, French, English, German, Italian, Spanish and Ukrainian. As for the contexts where the empirical studies were conducted, they range from China, to Croatia, Greece, Hungary, Ireland, Norway, Poland, the Ukraine and the UK. In these countries the status of the target language is a foreign, second or third language on a continuum where divisions are hard to identify. As readers will see, an additional strength of the book is that the studies represent a variety of research methods: enquiries apply qualitative, quantitative and mixed methods. Also, some of the chapters give an account of research applying triangulation.

The Structure of the Book

The 16 chapters in the book are arranged into five sections. The first three chapters outline the larger picture. In the first chapter John Harris and Denise O'Leary discuss a large-scale long-term project, the Modern Languages in Primary Schools Initiative, in the bilingual context of Ireland, where the aim is to achieve language diversity by making four European languages available to children. The second chapter, authored by Janet Enever, explores resistance to implementation of early modern language programmes in the UK by analysing empirical data collected in one city in two phases. In a very different context, Zrinka Jelaska and Lidija Cvikić discuss young learners' competences in Croatian, a second language for minority children living inside and outside Croatia.

The four chapters in the second section focus on narrower areas as they examine how cognitive, affective, socio-economic and classroom-related factors interact with one another. Participants in the first study were Greek pupils learning English. Thomaï Alexiou administered an aptitude test to them and examined how different components of the aptitude measure contributed to young learners' development over time. Results of a nationwide survey are reported in the next chapter on Hungarian learners studying English and German. Kata Csizér and Judit Kormos examine the relationship between language learning motivation and cross-cultural contact. A different method is applied to explore young learners' motivation in a study conducted by Jelena Mihaljević Djigunović: she provides insights into a comparative study of children's motivation under two sets of conditions. In the last chapter in this section Marianne Nikolov examines how different variables including learners' aptitude, language learning goals, motivation and classroom processes contribute to outcomes in large-scale studies on Hungarian learners of English and German.

The third section includes four chapters on literacy and skills development. In the first one Ion Drew investigates the challenges, advantages and effectiveness of adapting a special Australian literacy programme emphasising regular reading in Norwegian schools. The next two chapters used innovative research techniques to explore young learners' strategic thinking on reading and writing in the target language. Renata Šamo gives an account of a special study using think aloud protocols to investigate young

Croatian learners' reading strategies, whereas Eleni Griva, Helen Tsakiridou and Ioanna Nihoritou collected data on young Greek learners' strategies while writing in English to gain insights into their composing processes. A subskill, reading aloud, is examined in a laboratory study conducted by Vanda Marijanović, Nathalie Panissal and Michel Billières as they analyse young Croatian learners' pronunciation in French.

In the fourth section three chapters give an account of assessing young language learners. Ilona Huszti, Márta Fábián and Erzsébet Bárányné Komári tested young ethnic minority Hungarian learners in two languages they study: Ukrainian (the official language) and English (a foreign language). After analysing the first phase of their longitudinal study, they discuss how learners' performances on tests relate to what and how they are taught. Two chapters assess young learners' vocabulary. Andrea Orosz applied a validated test to examine Hungarian learners' vocabulary size and to compare results to achievement targets in the curriculum and in other studies. Magdalena Szpotowicz, on the other hand, gives an account of an experiment scrutinising the amount of words very young Polish learners remembered after one session.

The last part of the book includes two classroom studies: one focuses on classroom language in Chinese learners' English classes, the other one explores what children think about learning English. Jing Peng and Lily Zhang observed and tape-recorded classroom discourse in a large Chinese city and analyse the amount and quality of English language children are exposed to and use. Finally, young Hungarian learners' voices are heard in Krisztina Nagy's study. She asked children to do innovative tasks in pairs in order to explore why they think they learn English, and what they think helps and hinders their development in their new language.

Acknowledgements

First of all, I am indebted to the authors of the chapters. I thank them for their patience and attention to detail while working on previous versions of their chapters. I gratefully acknowledge the contribution of my friends and colleagues Jelena Mihaljević Djigunović, Marina Mattheoudakis, Gun Lundberg and Tanya Flanagan. They provided invaluable feedback on the chapters. Finally, this edited volume would not have been possible without the professional support of Professor David Singleton and the editors at Multilingual Matters, Marjukka Grover and Anna Roderick.

References

Edelenbos, P., Johnstone, R. and Kubanek, A. (2007) Languages for the children in Europe: Published research, good practice and main principles. On WWW at http://ec.europa.eu/education/policies/lang/doc/youngsum_en.pdf. Accessed 7.7.08.

Eurydice (2005) *Key Data on Teaching Languages at School in Europe. 2005 Edition.* Brussels: Eurydice.

García Mayo, M.P. and García Lecumberri, M.L. (eds) (2003) *Age and the Acquisition of English as a Foreign Language.* Clevedon: Multilingual Matters.

Graddol, D. (2006) *English Next.* London: British Council.

Harris, J. and Conway, M. (2002) *Modern Languages in Irish Primary Schools: An Evaluation of the National Pilot Project.* Dublin: Institiuid Taengeolaiochhta Eireann.

Harris, J., Forde, P., Archer, P., Fhearaile, S.N. and O'Gorman, M. (2006) *Irish in Primary Schools: Long-term National Trends in Achievement.* Dublin: Department of Education and Science.

Moon, J. and Nikolov, M. (eds) (2000) *Research into Teaching English to Young Learners.* Pécs: University Press Pécs.

Muñoz, C. (ed.) (2006) *Age and the Rate of Foreign Language Learning.* Clevedon: Multilingual Matters.

Nikolov, M. (2002) *Issues in English Language Education.* Bern: Peter Lang.

Nikolov, M. and Curtain, H. (eds) (2000) *An Early Start: Young Learners and Modern Languages in Europe and Beyond.* Strasbourg: Council of Europe.

Nikolov, M. and Mihaljević Djigunović, J. (2006) Recent research on age, second language acquisition, and early foreign language learning. *Annual Review of Applied Linguistics* 26, 234–260.

Nikolov, M., Mihaljević Djigunović, J., Mattheoudakis, M., Lundberg, G. and Flanagan, T. (eds) (2007) *Teaching Modern Languages to Young Learners: Teachers, Curricula and Materials.* Strasbourg: Council of Europe.

Chapter 1

A Third Language at Primary Level in Ireland: An Independent Evaluation of the Modern Languages in Primary Schools Initiative

JOHN HARRIS and DENISE O'LEARY

Introducing modern languages at primary level in Ireland involves challenges and possibilities which differ from those of some other countries. Irish, a minority language is the first official language. All but a small proportion of pupils speak English at home but begin to learn Irish as a second language as soon as they begin school. Learning a modern foreign language at primary level is, therefore, an entirely new experience of diversity for most Irish pupils. The *Modern Languages in Primary Schools Initiative* in Ireland began in 1998 with 270 schools and now has almost 400 (about 12% of primary schools). Pupils in the final two years in elementary school receive 1.5 hours of tuition within the normal school day in one of four languages: French, German, Spanish or Italian. Within the Initiative, there is also an emphasis on language diversity of a slightly different kind in that those European languages that traditionally were less commonly taught in Ireland (Spanish and Italian) are especially promoted. This chapter describes the experience of modern languages at primary level for pupils, parents and teachers. It draws on findings from Phases 1 (Harris & Conway, 2002) and Phase 2 (Harris & O'Leary, 2007) of an independent evaluation of the Project.

The Language Situation in Ireland

The early teaching of modern languages in Ireland takes place in a sociolinguistic context which differs in a number of respects from that obtaining in many other countries in Europe (Harris, 2007). Irish, an indigenous minority language, is also the first official language of the country. It has been taught to virtually all primary-school pupils since the foundation of

1

the state about 85 years ago. In the vast majority of cases, it is taught as a second language to pupils whose home language is English – as a single school subject in 'ordinary' mainstream schools. It is also taught in immersion ('all-Irish') schools in the main English-speaking area. While these immersion schools are still relatively small in number, they have grown significantly over the last 20 years. Irish is also taught, of course, in the relatively small Gaeltacht heartland areas, mainly along the western seaboard. The teaching of Irish in these different contexts is central to the larger national goal of revitalising Irish as a general means of communication.

Parents and the public generally are in favour of the teaching of Irish. Harris *et al.* (2006), for example, report that 67.4% of the parents of pupils in ordinary mainstream primary schools are 'favourable' or 'very favourable' to Irish being taught at this level. Only 14.5% feel that less time should be spent on the language.

But parents in Ireland are in general also anxious that their children would learn other modern European languages. As part of a national consultation process called 'Your Education System', a representative sample ($n = 1511$) of the population aged 15+ years was surveyed in order to establish views nationally on a number of education issues (Kellaghan *et al.*, 2004). Two key findings emerged in relation to foreign languages in primary school:

- 57.1% of respondents felt that 'too little emphasis' was placed on teaching foreign languages in primary schools (Kellaghan *et al.*, 2004: 6, 26).
- 78.7% considered the teaching of a continental language in primary school to be 'very important/important' in achieving the objectives of schooling (Kellaghan *et al.*, 2004: 35).

These percentages are notable given that statistics from 30 European countries show that Ireland is the only one where foreign-language learning at primary level is neither compulsory nor a core curriculum option (Eurydice, 2005: 24). The Irish Business and Employers Confederation (IBEC, 2004) identified a number of key priorities for the Irish education system, one of which was the development of a national coordinated system to make modern languages a compulsory subject in primary school. In addition, the Expert Group on Future Skills Needs (EGFSN) in its report *Languages and Enterprise* (EGFSN, 2005) called for the extension of the *Modern Languages in Primary Schools Initiative* to all primary schools nationwide and its full integration into the mainstream curriculum.

Yet another significant feature of the language situation in Ireland in recent years is the relatively sudden appearance of the languages of the 'New Irish' immigrant communities, such as Polish, Russian and Chinese. Until now, Ireland has not seen any immigration comparable to that experienced elsewhere in western Europe. The scale of this in-migration, largely as a result of the buoyant economy, is indicated by the fact that the population of non-nationals in Ireland grew from 7% to 10% between 2002 and 2006. By comparison, the non-national population of the UK grew by only two percentage points between 1960 and 1990 (Barrett & McCarthy, 2006).

The Modern Language Initiative and the Evaluation

In 1998, the national *Pilot Project on the Teaching of Modern Languages in Irish Primary Schools* was launched in response to growing public interest and debate. The Pilot Project (later renamed the 'Initiative') began with 270 schools and now has around 400. Pupils in the final two years of elementary school receive 1.5 hours of tuition within the normal school week in one of four languages: French, German, Spanish or Italian. The modern language teachers are either members of staff in the school or, more often, visiting (non-staff) teachers. The teachers are supported by a National Coordinator and a team of Project Leaders who conduct inservice training, source teaching materials and visit schools. Initially the Project was financed by the European Social Fund but later became part of the National Development Plan.

Clearly, early foreign-language learning in the Irish context has many features which distinguish it from enterprises in other countries. Some of these distinctive features derive from the particular sociolinguistic context in Ireland. Others derive from the fact that it is such a major innovation that it presents a whole range of educational and teacher-training issues. The present account of the early learning of modern foreign languages tries to map out the main features of the programme being implemented and to assess its impact on pupils' proficiency and attitudes, and on schools and education more generally. The account is based on an extensive independent evaluation of the Project which was funded by the Irish Government Department of Education and Science. The evaluation consisted of two phases. Phase 1 was carried out by Harris and Conway (2002) and Phase 2 by Harris and O Leary (2007).

Phase 1 involved a number of activities and instruments:

- Group and individual linguistic-communicative tests in all the languages were administered to pupils in 22 representative schools.
- Questionnaires were used to assess pupils' attitude-motivation as well as their experiences of learning a modern language.
- A survey of all modern language teachers involved in the Project.

Phase 2 is largely based on surveys of class teachers and principals. The former are regular class teachers who do *not* teach the modern language themselves but whose classes are being taught the language either by a visiting teacher or less often by another staff member in the same school. The views and experiences of regular class teachers are very important, since any significant expansion of the initiative would in the longer term have to be based on class teachers delivering the modern language programme.

Findings Relating to Early Foreign Language Learning in Ireland

Pupil success in learning the language

The evaluation shows that the vast majority of pupils have made real progress in developing (a) listening comprehension skills and (b) an initial competence in spoken communication. For example, in the case of the speaking test, the overall mean score achieved by pupils was 75.7 out of a possible 108. Girls performed better than boys.

No class or school could be said to be failing to make significant progress in learning the modern language and, within classes, only a minority of pupils in a small number of cases were not making worthwhile progress. Even where teachers felt that particular pupils were not coping well with the programme, the language tests we used still showed that these pupils were actually making significant progress. The Project has shown that the teaching of modern languages at primary level can be successfully extended to types of schools and pupils which previously had relatively limited access to them. Overall, 60% of the modern-language teachers said that, were it not for the Project, none of their pupils would have studied the language at primary level. It has made a particular difference to rural schools and disadvantaged schools. In general, pupils in disadvantaged schools have made as much progress in learning the modern languages as pupils in other schools.

Attitudes of pupils

Questionnaire data show that the majority of pupils have developed positive attitudes to learning the *target language itself* (mean = 3.8 on a scale of 1 to 5, where 1 is equivalent to a strong negative attitude and 5 a strong positive attitude); to *speakers of the target language* (mean = 3.5 on same scale as above); and *to the European country* in which the language is spoken (mean = 4.2 on same scale as above). Eighty-one percent of pupils agreed, slightly or strongly, that 'learning another language, besides English, can be very enjoyable'; 73% agreed that they 'really enjoy learning French'.

Most notably, the vast majority (84%) agreed with the statement 'I am glad that I began learning French in primary school rather than leaving it until later'. Only 7% disagree. (French in all these cases stands for whichever of the four languages pupils were studying.) The majority of pupils reported enjoying the modern language lesson, particularly the emphasis on games, songs and poems. They also like developing communicative competence in the language and cultural awareness activities.

Reaction of the modern language teachers

The vast majority (93%) of the modern-language teachers feel that they personally have benefited from participation. Similarly high percentages feel that the school itself (93%) and the pupils (98%) benefit from participation.

Teachers were very satisfied with the implementation of the Project, particularly the support and in-service training provided by Project Leaders. While substantial numbers of the modern language teachers began with no previous experience of teaching the language, their feelings of preparedness to teach improved substantially during the first year. Eighty-nine percent of teachers report a favourable parental reaction and only 2% report a neutral or unfavourable parental reaction.

Most frequently used and most popular classroom activities

One of the issues of particular interest is what kind of activities, techniques and teaching materials are used in primary modern language classes. First, we asked the teacher to read a detailed list of activities, techniques and materials and to indicate how frequently (e.g. once or more per class, once or more per month) each was *used*. Later we asked the teacher which of these same activities, techniques and materials their pupils *actually enjoyed*.

The five activities which are reported by the greatest proportion of teachers as being *enjoyed* by pupils are 'Wordgames', 'Raps/songs', 'Language awareness activities', 'Action games/sports' and 'Drama'. But these same five activities are only *used* by teachers moderately often. In a rank ordering of percentages, the five *most enjoyable* activities are only listed sixth, eighth, ninth, 11th and 16th out of a total of 18 in terms of frequency of use by teachers.

It is also notable that in the case of the *most frequently used* activities, relatively small percentages of teachers say that they *are enjoyed* by pupils. In fact, the most frequently used, 'Whole class repetition of sentences/ phrases', is actually ranked last of all in the list of 18 activities in terms of the percentage of teachers reporting it as being enjoyable for pupils (only 29% of teachers feel 'Whole class repetition of words or phrases' is enjoyed by pupils).

Achievement of Project aims

The overall assessment of Harris and Conway (2002) is that the Project has succeeded in installing a teaching programme which has a significant emphasis on communication, an experiential orientation to learning and a focus on pupil enjoyment of the learning process.

- Only 42% of teachers felt that the aim of 'using as much of the target language as possible as the normal language of the classroom' was successfully promoted. Thirty-seven percent reported that they conducted less than half the lesson through the modern language.
- There is scope for greater emphasis than at present however on (a) communicative/experiential activities and (b) learning activities which are enjoyable for pupils. As noted just above, some traditional approaches, such as whole class repetition, which children do not like, are still widely used.
- There is also a need for a greater emphasis on the development of cultural awareness.
- Thirty-seven percent of teachers failed to achieve the time allocation specified by Project Management (1.5 hours tuition each week). These teachers most often provided one hour of tuition instead. Staff members were much more likely (46%) to fail to provide the prescribed 1.5 hours than visiting teachers (20%). An overcrowded curriculum and timetabling problems were cited as the main reasons for this failure.
- A significant minority of pupils experience some degree of difficulty in understanding the lesson or teacher – general difficulty in understanding or learning the language, not understanding some words, the teacher going too fast, or specific difficulties with the language.

Phase 2: Principals and the Regular Class Teacher

The need to investigate the conditions and possibilities for extending the Project nationally provided the context for gathering information from Principals and Class teachers in Phase 2 of the evaluation. Principals and regular Class teachers are central to any plans to expand the Project nationally, and prior to this, little was known about their views. Findings from the two surveys are grouped under various thematic categories below and linked to findings from the earlier survey of modern-language teachers.

The shifting balance between staff and non-staff teachers

The profile of the modern-language teacher has changed dramatically over the time course of the Project. At the end of Year 1, 63% of modern-language *teachers* were staff members and 37% were non-staff (Harris & Conway, 2002: 28). At the end of Year 5, only 14.6% of Class teachers report that another staff member teaches the modern language to their class, 83.6% report that a *non-staff* (visiting) teacher does, while 1.8% report that both staff and non-staff teachers teach it. Even though the earlier data is at teacher level and the latter is at class level, the change in the proportion of staff to non-staff teachers is clear.

General reaction to modern languages

A high level of enthusiasm and approval for the teaching of modern languages in primary school exists among both Principals and Class teachers. Of Principals, 93.2% report a 'very positive/positive' reaction among staff to the teaching of modern languages. Less than 1% report a negative reaction. Of Class teachers, 89.6% hold 'very favourable/favourable' attitudes to the teaching of modern languages and 87.9% feel that it is 'very important/important' to start learning a modern language in primary. Of Class teachers, 77.5% also report a 'very positive/positive' reaction from parents. Only one Class teacher reported a negative reaction.

Programme impact on pupils

Virtually all Principals (99.4%) perceive benefits for pupils. When asked to list pupil benefits, four main categories of response emerged:

(1) Improved pupil self-esteem, attitude and enjoyment of the learning process (43.5%).
(2) Improved learning, awareness and use of different languages among pupils (36.3%).
(3) Preparation/Head Start for second level (23.9%).
(4) Increased cultural awareness (18.6%).

Class teachers also overwhelmingly (89.2%) see the impact on pupils as being 'very positive/positive'. Those who perceived a positive effect mention increased language (86.6%) and cultural (83.5%) awareness, preparation for second-level language learning (84.4%) and more positive attitudes to language learning in general (65.9%). Other benefits include increased awareness of language as a communication tool (54.8%), increased pupil-self-esteem/self-confidence (51%) and enhanced learning in other subjects (25.8%).

A majority of Class teachers (54.1%) see the programme as producing a positive change in pupils' attitudes to linguistic and cultural diversity (34.9% perceive no change while 11% were uncertain or did not respond). Class teachers who perceive change mention improved interest in, and awareness and appreciation of, other cultures and other languages among pupils.

Impact on pupils with difficulties in other subjects

Only 7.1% of Class teachers feel that the Project is hindering the progress of pupils with difficulties in other subjects. The majority (56.3%) perceive no particular effect on the progress of these pupils. Approximately a third of Class teachers feel that participation is actually enhancing the progress of such pupils.

Teachers (7.1%) who feel that the modern-language programme hinders pupils with difficulties mention that the Project is taking time away from the core subjects and that learning a modern language in addition to English and Irish is too much for these pupils.

Class teachers (34.1%) who feel that the programme enhances the progress of pupils with difficulties mention:

- Increased pupil self-esteem and self-confidence in their ability (35.7%);
- Pupil enjoyment of the language lesson and of the teaching methodologies in a nonthreatening learning environment (31.4%);
- The benefits of a fresh start in a new subject for these pupils (25.2%).

The fact that these data reflect the opinion of the regular Class teacher (who does not teach the modern language) may provide reassurance to teachers and parents in schools where a modern-language programme is being considered for the first time.

Positive and negative effects on the curriculum

Class teachers were also asked whether they perceived any positive or negative effects of the programme on other subjects and to explain the kind of effect observed. Of Class teachers, 74.5% perceive positive effects on other subjects; 24.4% perceive negative effects. Of these, only 8% perceive *solely* negative effects.

Geography (60.7%), Music (36.5%), Irish (31%) and Visual Arts (31%) are the subjects most often seen as being *positively* affected. Irish is also the subject, however, which is most often seen as being *negatively* affected (18.3%). Note that the proportion of all Class teachers who mention that the modern-language programme positively affects Irish (31%) is higher than the proportion who feel it is negatively affected (18.3%).

Class teachers who perceive negative effects on other subjects (24.4%) mention reduced time for all subjects especially English, Irish and Maths. Some also mention more negative attitudes to and increased disinterest in Irish compared to modern languages among pupils, and language confusion among weaker students.

Transfer of experience of learning Irish to modern languages

Numerous studies have shown the positive influence of the second language on the learning of a third language in institutional settings (e.g. Bild & Swain, 1989; Groseva, 1998; Valencia & Cenoz, 1992). In the present study, 49.4% of Class teachers feel that pupils' previous experience of learning Irish benefits their learning of the modern language. Virtually all Class teachers in Irish-medium schools (92.5%) report benefits of this nature. Benefits include:

- language awareness and skills transfer across languages (69.1%);
- pupils are more open to learning new languages (12.2%).

Time on modern languages

Providing the recommended 90 minutes tuition each week is proving difficult. As Table 1.1 (final column, rows three and four combined) below shows, just 52.6% of Class teachers report that classes are receiving the recommended time allocation. This represents a decline from the position in Year 1 when modern language teachers themselves reported that the proportion of classes receiving the recommended time was 63% (Harris & Conway, 2002: p. 35).

The type of teacher teaching the language makes a difference here. Just 31.1% of Class teachers whose classes are taught the language by another staff member report $1\frac{1}{2}$ hours tuition, compared to 56.7% of those whose classes are taught by a visiting teacher. Table 1.1 also shows considerable variation from school to school in the amount of time devoted to the language.

Primary/post-primary coordination

At the end of Year 1 just 18% of modern-language teachers felt that coordination between teaching at first and second level had been established. The Principals' survey provided us with the opportunity to revisit this issue at a later stage in the Project and to gather more detailed information from participating schools:

> Although 82.4% of schools report awareness of the Project among local second level schools, only 27.6% say that this awareness extends to knowledge of the kind of work being done at primary.

Table 1.1 Percentage of class teachers reporting different amounts of time being allocated to the modern language each week (broken down by the type of teacher teaching the language)

Time allocation	Modern-language teacher-type			
	Staff (n = 90)	Non-staff (n = 515)	Both staff and non-staff (n = 11)	Total (n = 616)
Less than 60 min per week	28.9	11.5	9.1	14.0
More than 60 min but less than 90 min per week	40.0	31.5	54.5	33.1
90 min per week	30.0	48.7	36.4	45.8
More than 90 min per week	1.1	8.0	0.0	6.8
Nonresponse	0.0	0.4	0.0	0.3
Total	100%	100%	100%	100%

Just 13.6% of schools report that provision is made at second level to accommodate pupils who have participated in the Project at primary level.

Numerous studies from other European nations have reported similar findings about the lack of curricular alignment and the limited contact between the two sectors in relation to modern languages (see, e.g. Brun & Panosetti, 1997; Driscoll *et al.*, 2004; Grenfell, 1993; Low *et al.*, 1995). An additional difficulty in the Irish context is the uncertainty regarding the future of the Project itself. Building up contact and curricular alignment with local second-level schools in relation to modern languages is difficult to sustain in this context.

Class teachers' linguistic skills and interest in teaching modern languages

The Class-teacher survey allowed us to obtain a range of information on how Class teachers view the prospect of teaching modern languages themselves, how well equipped they are in terms of existing language proficiency and their willingness and interest in undergoing training. Ninety-three percent of regular Class teachers report that they have learnt/ acquired at least one modern-foreign language; 84.7% had learnt/acquired French, while much smaller proportions had German (26.3%), Spanish (12.2%) or Italian (6.3%).

The highest level of academic qualification achieved in a modern-foreign language by the vast majority of teachers (68.2%) was the Leaving Certificate. Of these, 14.1% had studied a modern-foreign language at third level, mainly French. Class teachers were also asked for a self-assessment of their speaking ability in the modern-foreign languages learnt/acquired: 56.5% reported their highest level of speaking ability in a modern language as 'parts of conversations' or higher; 29.1% reported having 'a few simple sentences' in at least one modern-foreign language.

Class teachers were asked to select one of four statements which indicated their view on the prospect of teaching a modern language at primary level at some time in the future:

(a) I would not be interested in teaching modern languages at primary level at all. (36.5%)
(b) If a suitable modern language course were provided, I would be interested in taking it and going on to teach the modern language at primary level. (10.1%)
(c) I have the necessary modern language skills already and would be interested in teaching the language at primary level if the opportunity arose. (38.3%)

(d) I would be interested in teaching those aspects of a modern-language programme which require only minimal skills in the modern language itself (e.g. aspects of cultural awareness) if I received in-service training to do so. (13.5%)

Thus, 61.9% of Class teachers are interested in teaching the modern language or some aspect of the programme (options b, c and d above). Despite concerns about the overloaded curriculum, therefore, many fifth and sixth grade teachers (61.9%) not teaching the language at present would be prepared to do so (or to deliver aspects of the programme which are not language specific).

At the same time, the 36.5% of Class teachers who are not at all interested indicate the challenges which would be presented by any attempt to expand the programme to most or all schools. This figure is all the more significant because these are teachers who have seen a programme at first hand which is generally considered a success.

Expanding the Project: Views of teachers and Principals

Table 1.2 shows that Class teachers (39%) are more cautious about expanding the Project to 'all' schools than Principals (54.2%) or Modern-language teachers (50%). They compensate for this however, by opting in larger numbers for extending the Project to 'more' schools (49.7%).

It is important to bear in mind this high level of support for Project expansion among Principals and Class teachers when evaluating the significance of concerns about time pressures.

Table 1.2   Percentage of Modern-language teachers, Principals and Class teachers having various views on extending the Project

The Project should be...	Modern-language teachers (n = 301)	Principals (n = 323)	Class teachers (n = 616)
Extended to *more* schools	35	39.9	49.7
Extended to *all* schools	50	54.2	39.0
Confined to existing schools	10	2.8	2.1
Abandoned altogether[a]	—[b]	0.3	5.8
Missing[a]	5	2.8	3.4
Total	100%	100%	100%

[a]This answer option was not provided in the Modern-Language Teacher survey (Harris & Conway, 2002)
[b]Non-response/I do not know

Conclusion

The development of the *Modern Languages in Primary School Initiative* in Ireland is part of an 'enormous worldwide increase in early foreign language instruction' (Nikolov & Mihaljevic´ Djigunovic´ ,2006). Clearly, our research shows that, thus far, the Irish experiment has been successful in delivering a programme which pupils enjoy and which produces a worthwhile initial competence in the four languages. Principals, class teachers, modern language teachers and parents all acknowledge its positive impact. But, again as in many other countries, there are challenges and constraints in expanding early language learning nationally: such as the additional curricular pressure created by modern languages and the difficulties associated with the transition to post primary. Recent research showing a significant long-term decline in the standard of spoken Irish at primary level (Harris *et al.*, 2006) may also add to existing concerns among teachers and others about the possible impact on Irish. Despite all this, there can be little doubt that parents generally would like to see both Irish *and* modern European languages taught at primary level.

Perhaps the greatest challenge, however, will be how to expand the teaching of modern languages nationally and how to provide the training for those teachers whose existing linguistic competence is not adequate. Any effective strategy for a major expansion in the programme will need to consolidate support for the enterprise among teachers and parents, at the same time as the planning and implementation process itself goes ahead. To do this, it seems that opportunities will have to be created for many more schools and pupils to have at least some kind of engagement with modern languages at primary level. This can be best be achieved by

- extending the existing *Language Competence* programme used in the Pilot Project to include as many additional schools as are at present capable of delivering a programme of this kind and wish to do so;
- introducing a more limited sensitisation/language awareness modern language programme in other schools which are not equipped to teach a full programme yet but who would like to be involved at some level.

The goal of such increased contact would be to promote awareness, debate and consensus in relation to primary modern languages. This consensus, in turn, is essential to developing political support for the substantial deployment of public funds which would be required to implement a programme nationally.

A gradual expansion of the Pilot Project alone is not likely to be an adequate strategy if the long term goal is a programme in all primary schools. The experience of other countries is that implementing a modern language programme represents a major intervention in the educational system as a whole and requires comprehensive planning to respond to issues such as (a) increasing the availability of teachers with the requisite modern-language skills, and (b) coordinating language learning and teaching at first and second level.

An official commitment at this point to introduce a programme in all schools would provide a powerful focus for planning and infrastructural development, even if this commitment had to be tempered by an acknowledgement that the eventual attainment of a universal programme was still a considerable way off. Ideally, this commitment should be located within a broader plan for languages and language learning nationally. A national plan would reduce the likelihood of the kind of policy clashes and policy vacuums which have been associated with the introduction of primary modern language programmes in other countries.

References

Barrett, A. and McCarthy, Y. (2006) *Immigrants in a Booming Economy: Analysing Their Earnings and Welfare Dependence.* Discussion paper No. 2457. Bonn: Institute for the Study of Labour (IZA).

Bild, R. and Swain, M. (1989) Minority language students in a French immersion programme: Their French proficiency. *Journal of Multilingual and Multicultural Development* 10, 255–274.

Brun, A. and Panosetti, J. (1997) EILE/EILV: Enseignement d'initiation aux langues vivantes étrangères [Initial teaching of foreign languages]. In A. Bori, S. Quattrocchi, L. Torchio, A. Mackens, A. Brun, J. Panosetti, L. Low and R. Johnstone (eds) *Modern Languages at Primary School: Reflections on Monitoring and Evaluation.* ECP Report: Socrates Programme.

Driscoll, P., Jones, J. and Macrory, G. (2004) *The Provision of Foreign Language Learning for Pupils at Key Stage 2.* London: Her Majesty's Stationary Office.

Eurydice. The Information Network on Education in Europe (2005) *Key Data on Teaching Languages at School in Europe.* Brussels: Eurydice European Unit.

Expert Group on Future Skills Needs (EGFSN) (2005) *Languages and Enterprise: The Demand and Supply of Foreign Language Skills in the Enterprise Sector.* Dublin: Forfás.

Groseva, M. (1998) Dient das L2-System als ein Fremdsprachenlernmodell? [Does the L2 system serve as a foreign language learning model?]. In B. Hufeisen and B. Lindemann (eds) *Tertiärsprachen: Theorien, Modelle, Methoden.* Tübingen: Stauffenburg.

Grenfell, M. (1993) The Caen primary school foreign language project. *Occasional Paper 16.* Centre for Language in Education: University of Southampton.

Harris, J. (2007) Bilingual education and bilingualism in Ireland north and south. *International Journal of Bilingual Education and Bilingualism* (Special Issue) 10 (4), 359–368.

Harris, J. and Conway, M. (2002) *Modern Languages in Irish Primary Schools. An Evaluation of the National Pilot Project.* Dublin: Institiúid Teangeolaíochta Éireann (Linguistics Institute of Ireland).

Harris, J. and O'Leary, D. (2007) *Modern Languages in Irish Primary Schools. Views and Practices of Principals and Class Teachers*. Report submitted to the Department of Education and Science. Dublin: Department of Education and Science.

Harris, J., Forde, P., Archer, P., Nic Fhearaile, S. and O'Gorman, M. (2006) *Irish in Primary School: Long-term National Trends in Achievement*. Dublin: Department of Education and Science.

Irish Business and Employers' Confederation (IBEC)(2004) Education for life – the challenge of the third millennium. *Education Policy Document*. Dublin: Author.

Kellaghan, T., McGee, P., Millar, D. and Perkins, R. (2004) *Views of the Irish Public on Education: 2004 Survey*. Dublin: Educational Research Centre.

Low, L., Brown, S., Johnstone, R. and Pirrie, A. (1995) *Foreign Languages in Primary Schools: Evaluation of the Scottish Pilot Projects 1993–1995: Final Report*. Stirling: CILT.

Nikolov, M. and Mihaljević Djigunović J.M. (2006) Recent research on age, second-language acquisition, and early foreign language learning. *Annual Review of Applied Linguistics* 26, 234–260.

Valencia, J. and Cenoz, J. (1992) The role of bilingualism in foreign language acquisition: Learning English in the Basque Country. *Journal of Multilingual and Multicultural Development* 13, 433–449.

Chapter 2

Can Today's Early Language Learners in England Become Tomorrow's Plurilingual European Citizens?

JANET ENEVER

Introduction

A radical UK government initiative now provides for an entitlement of all children in England to learn a foreign language from age seven by the year 2010. Previous policy requirements were for the introduction of languages from the secondary phase of schooling at age 11+ only. It is proposed that this major shift in start age reflects the increasing trend of lower start ages throughout Europe and beyond, and may be viewed as a political recognition of the sociocultural value of being identified as 'in line with the rest of Europe'.

This chapter critically examines societal resistance to implementation and considers the likely impact of such resistance on motivation for learners, teachers and schools. The study draws on two sets of empirical data collected in one city, firstly during the pilot phase of the initiative and secondly during the early phases of the roll-out programme. The chapter argues that a substantial shift in societal perceptions is necessary if we are to ensure that motivation at primary level actually leads to real progress being made throughout the school system, by every child.

Across Europe societal contexts for second/foreign language learning vary substantially at both national and local levels for primary school children. This chapter aims to construct an argument relating the influence of the contemporary context to young children's motivation for learning foreign languages in England and considers how or why this might change in the future. Data is drawn from studies in one local authority in southern England to illustrate this thesis.

Political and Societal Background

During the late 1990s in the UK a shift in political perceptions of Europe became increasingly more evident. With the appointment of a new prime minister in 1997, strong support for a pro-European political perspective was well-reflected in a speech made by Tony Blair at Oxford University in which he signalled a belief in the value of early foreign language learning, by claiming: 'Everyone knows that with languages the earlier you start the easier they are' (Sharpe, 2001: 3).

Just four years later in England a policy commitment was launched, proposing that all children in key stage 2 (KS2) (7–11 years in the primary school) would have an entitlement to foreign language learning by 2010. The first step in this process was to be a two-year nationally-funded pilot phase in 19 local authorities in England.

Blair's claim came as something of a surprise to linguists, applied linguists and primary educators alike. According to Driscoll and Frost (1999), Singleton and Ryan (2004: 227) and Munoz (2006), to put it colloquially, the jury is still out on this one. As Munoz (2006: 6) elaborates, much of the data on early foreign language (FL) learning comes from naturalistic settings where the child learns in their own home, or from the reportedly immersion contexts in parts of Canada where children have been exposed to two languages across educational, social and public domains (Genesee, 1978/1979). Munoz suggests that the tendency has been for such evidence to be over-generalised to the very different context of the classroom, where children experience a substantially more limited exposure. Similarly, Singleton and Ryan's (2004: 116) extensive review of research in this area finds the evidence so far to be inconclusive and somewhat contradictory. At the anecdotal level of personal classroom observations conducted throughout Europe over a period of some 10 years, my impressionistic view is that much of value is achieved in some classrooms through an early start. However, the challenge of ensuring this can be replicated with a nation of seven-year-olds is much less certain.

Turning to other political perspectives, moves at European level appear also to have had an influence on the current policy initiative. The European Commission Action Plan 2004–2006 recommended that: 'member states should move towards ensuring that foreign language learning at primary school is effective' (Commission of the European Communities, 2003: 7). It should be noted here that power for educational legislation in Europe currently rests at the level of the individual nation state, hence only recommendations can be made by the centralised European state. Such centralised guidance on educational matters does appear to be on the increase however. For example, an intergovernmental forum convened by the Council of Europe's Language Policy Division in February 2007 reviewed current and future developments related to the impact of the Common

European Framework of Reference for Languages (CFER) with a view to identifying how to extend its impact (Martyniuk, 2007: 23). At the level of agenda setting, it could be proposed that the decision to introduce FLs at primary level in England may say more about the rules of the game being set by the centralised European state and about the current UK government's desire to be seen as in line with the rest of Europe, than about any wish to provide an inclusive FL learning opportunity for all children at primary level. This desire may well shift to becoming *a need* in the proximal future, as schooled language provision in Europe becomes an increasingly more public and comparative phenomenon. One recent example of how this trend may be precipitated is embodied in the decision of the European Commission (2005) to publish the Eurydice annual summary of data on languages provision in Europe; a publication which will, over time, further highlight such differences in provision that may arise across individual nation states.

In the light of the above perspectives, a review of very recent data indicating the downward start age shifts of mandatory FL policy decisions across the 27 member states of Europe (and the two further candidate countries of Turkey and Croatia) since 2000 serves to emphasise the points raised. Table 2.1 presents a remarkable shift in recent years. It appears that, since the year 2000, 19 countries have lowered the start age for the introduction of FLs to nine years or less (or are planning to shortly).

In the interpretation of Table 2.1 it should be noted that some particular national histories and individual variations exist which make direct comparison less clear (see numbered points). These points include the following: (1) the colonial histories of both Cyprus and Malta have left a strong legacy of English as either a first or second language throughout society; (2) the political history of Ireland has resulted in the designation of both English and Irish as national languages, taught from the start of schooling. Some primary schools have introduced further languages in a pilot phase since 1998; (3) at present three of Germany's 16 autonomous regions (Bundeslände) have introduced compulsory FL teaching from year 1, whilst the remaining 13 introduce FLs from either year 2 or year 3; (4) in Hungary the official start age for FLs was raised from 10 to 11 years in 1998, then lowered to 10 years again in 2003; (5) schools in Sweden may select to introduce English at any point between years 1 and 4, with a required syllabus to be completed by the end of year 5. Most schools now introduce English from years 1 or 2; (6) both Portugal and the Czech Republic have indicated plans to lower the official start age to six years from 2008. However, it should be noted that political priorities sometimes unexpectedly change. In reading this data it should also be noted that sources are the result of personal communications to the author from in-country experts. Accuracy is not always assured and the author welcomes any corrections/updates available. The recently available Eurydice

Table 2.1   Europe: Recent changes to compulsory start of age for foreign language learning (March 2007)

Compulsory start age						
5 years	*6 years*	*7 years*	*8 years*	*9 years*	*10 years*	*11 years*
	1974: Luxembourg 1974: Malta (1)	1994: Finland	1990: Slovakia	1994: Cyprus (1) 1994: Lithuania 1998: Romania	1994: Turkey 2003: Hungary (4)	1998: Ireland (2)
2002: France 2003: Netherlands	2003: Austria 2003: Estonia 2003: Sweden (5) 2003: Croatia 2004: Italy 2005: Spain 2006: Latvia 2008: Poland 2008: Czech Republic (6) 2008: Portugal (6)	2010: England	2002: Slovenia 2003: Belgium 2003: Bulgaria 2004: Greece 2004–2006: a number of German regions (3)	2004: Denmark		

source data for FLs in Europe (European Commission, 2005) relies on a data set from 2002, hence suffers also from the difficulties of ensuring both accuracy and current validity.

The escalation of the trend towards an earlier start, as illuminated by Table 2.1, now appears to have reached the point where there is a generally perceived wisdom that somewhere in the first three years of schooling children should be introduced to a second/foreign language in some way. The question of what drives such policy decisions is not the focus of this article (see Enever, 2007 for some further ideas on this). However, in the case of the British government decision it is perhaps pertinent here to draw a parallel with very similar suggestions made by Low (1999: 52) in reporting on the decisions to introduce primary FLs in Scotland from 1989. Here, he offers the opinion that 'political capital could (...) be made from an initiative which was considered likely to be very popular with parents'. We must be prompted to ask whether the new policy in England is *also* more about political capital than about cultural capital for our children's futures?

There are many perspectives to this complex, sociocultural and political question clearly. Perhaps as one final layering from the sociocultural perspective, I will refer here to the geographical separateness and the linguistic currency that England (and in some instances the wider British Isles) continues to trade on. As an island nation, historically, the protection from attack and the consequent sense of separateness created by a stretch of water between the British Isles and mainland Europe has been both valuable and at the same time divisive. Its continuing impact should not be underestimated. Despite the construction of a linking tunnel, the sense of physical separation does make a difference and is a factor to be considered. Similarly, in this somewhat less-than-ideal societal context for introducing primary FLs there is the question of the current position of the national language at a global level. Whilst English has continued to spread, the perceived need to learn other languages in England has declined amongst the population. Such patterns have been extremely visible in many classrooms of 14–16-year-olds across England in recent years, where these teenagers simply have not been interested in FL learning. This has recently resulted in the British government deciding to reduce the compulsory policy to a voluntary one from the age of 14 years (CILT, 2007: 70).

Research Contexts

It was within this context that research was undertaken at two phases of FL implementation. The first data set reported on here relates to a study conducted with co-researcher with Cathy Watts, comprising a two-year monitoring and evaluation of one of the 19 Pathfinder local authorities introducing FLs in the two-year pilot phase of policy implementation in

England. The second data set relates to data collected during the first year of a more extensive comparative, longitudinal European study which builds on this first study in some respects.

Pathfinder study context

A case study approach was adopted in the two-year monitoring process, using a qualitative methodology with the aim of documenting and analysing how individual schools met and coped with the challenges of substantial innovation. This research was carried out at the instigation of the local authority. The inevitably cautious political climate that existed during this initial pilot phase of implementation necessitated the local authority selection of the four study schools. Despite this lack of representative sample, the regular and informal access facilitated by the study schools did provide an opportunity to capture insights on the process of implementation which otherwise might have been lost over time. Substantial access was provided for the purposes of observing and commenting on the process of engagement as schools worked to identify appropriate models for the introduction and sustainability of FLs in the authority. Nonetheless, despite this substantial access, it should be noted that timetable constraints of some schools/classes during this two-year pilot phase resulted in irregular FL lessons, or lessons cancelled on some occasions. This limited opportunities for data collection and reduced the sample size at some points. Such difficulty can be viewed as a reflection of the challenges of managing an over-crowded primary curriculum and perhaps some caution or even resistance to prioritising FLs at this early, voluntary stage of implementation.

The further detail of the full study will not be elaborated on at this point. For this chapter, data is selected out from the study with the potential to illustrate questions around the attitudinal perceptions of these children.

Pathfinder Findings and Interpretation

Data was collected at four points across the two-year period from teachers, school principals, children, parents and from classroom observation. It was hoped that this range of sources would offer sufficient triangulation from which to report on the extent to which the pilot phase aims had been met. The additional evidence of gendered responses in our observations, interviews and questionnaires were an interesting additional finding which has since led to further investigation. Here follows a summary of responses and observations from data collection points one, two and four, since point three data offered no additional insights on this question.

Data point one occurred some three months into the pilot phase introduction. A total of 108 children were interviewed, varying in age from seven to 10 years [some schools had begun by introducing FLs from the first year of key stage 2 (age 7+), whilst others had begun in year 5 first (9+)].

At this point, children mainly indicated their strong support for the new language lessons, with comments such as:

Child 1: I like the songs 'cos they've got beat and rhythm.
Child 2: It's good that I'm learning French 'cos when I went to Disneyland I was a bit worried 'cos I didn't know how to speak French and I couldn't ask Mickey for his signature (autograph).
Child 3: If you learn to speak a different language sometimes it gives you a nice feeling inside.
Child 4: It's fun.

Confirming these positive viewpoints, teacher interviews overwhelmingly considered that this early start was likely to result in long-term increased confidence, better pronunciation and enthusiastic attitudes to continuing their FL learning. School principals and the researchers' observation records both further confirmed that at this stage almost all children appeared both positive and receptive to this new opportunity.

Data collection point two occurred at the end of the first year of the pilot phase, when all children had received approximately 10 months of FL lessons. At this point it was possible only to interview 55 from the original sample of 108 owing to schools' time constraints. Overall, the children's responses remained positive, with a few notable exceptions amongst the boys. Whilst girls had maintained a strongly positive attitude by the end of the first year, a larger number of the boys now declared themselves either uncertain or negative about the learning experience. In particular, there were four boys who stated that they did not like learning a FL and they did not enjoy anything in the lesson. These boys made comments such as:

'It's difficult trying to remember the words.'
'We have a lot of new words in our heads and it's hard to remember them all.'
'All the words sound the same to me. I didn't understand last week, so I just won't understand this week.'
'Learning to speak is boring.'

When asked if they would like to continue with learning a FL in the next school year 66% of the sample said 'yes' (13 boys and 19 girls), the remaining 34% were either neutral (7 boys, 7 girls) or negative (1 girl, 8 boys). Here then, a gender gap had begun to emerge.

Both teachers and school principals at this point confirmed some anecdotal indications of negative responses from some boys. In contrast, this was not evident in the classroom observations conducted by the researchers.

When observed, it appeared that boys participated as willingly and enthusiastically as girls. Whilst any interpretation of such contradictory evidence must, of necessity, be cautious, the positive classroom response of boys indicated their genuine engagement and enjoyment, yet their later somewhat less positive responses might suggest a reluctance to acknowledge this enjoyment or possible perceptions of the lack of 'cool' associated with such enjoyment by their wider peer group.

At this halfway point in the study a questionnaire to parents was distributed with a view to gaining a wider picture of how the outside-school impact of classroom FL learning might have manifested itself. On this occasion it was agreed that one school would not participate in this data collection as they had suffered too many staff losses to feel confident that the pilot was progressing sufficiently satisfactorily. A total of 45 questionnaires were returned (approximately a 50% return rate). From those returns, parents responded overwhelmingly positively (88%) on the introduction of primary FLs. Only four parents said they were unsure about it and two further parents responded negatively. Interestingly, just over 50% of respondents reported that they regularly helped their children at home with learning the language. This generally involved practising new words and dialogues together. Many parents commented enthusiastically on this new opportunity and volunteered to help their children in the future, often requesting guidance from the school on how best to offer suitable support.

Data from this questionnaire appears then to be somewhat at odds with views reported by the children themselves. The 50% return rate should be remembered here. It could be that the missing 50% included parents of those boys who felt less than positive about the new addition to the curriculum.

After 22 months of the project a final stage of collection was implemented with schools involved in the evaluation of the pilot phase. As indicated previously, data from collection point three will not be discussed here as no findings relevant to the attitudinal question were evident at this stage of analysis. At this final point the researchers conducted an anonymous questionnaire during class time with children, aiming to probe somewhat more deeply into their opinions and experience of FL learning over the two-year period than had previously been attempted (by this stage the sample was aged 9–11 years). Fifty-seven children were available this time to respond, all part of the original sample of 108 children (the slight increase in numbers is accounted for by fewer class absences on this occasion).

Questionnaire respondents were invited to rate their responses as positive, neutral or negative (neutral and negative responses are not included here, except in question 2 where they proved particularly significant). Care should also be taken in reading Table 2.2 to note the sample included a higher number of boys (32) than girls (25). The first question nonetheless

Table 2.2 Sumary of children's questionnaire responses in need of further investigation (Watts & Enever, 2005: 28)

n = 57 (girls = 25/boys = 32)	Girls	Boys
(1) Believed in the importance of speaking a foreign language	24	24
(2a) Positive feelings about learning the foreign language	21	7
(2b) Neutral feelings about learning the foreign language	4	14
(2c) Negative feelings about learning the foreign language	0	11
(3) Would like to continue learning the foreign language	19	15
(4) Rated self as a good/excellent language learner	23	12
(5) Happy to communicate in the target language	18	7
(6) Worried about communicating in the target language	0	9
(7) Would understand most/all of a conversation about the weather	6	9
(8) Would understand some of a conversation about the weather	19	18
(9) Does practise the target foreign language at home	19	9

indicates a fairly positive view amongst both girls and boys regarding the general importance of being able to speak a FL. Moving to the second question (2a,b,c), opinions between boys and girls on how positively they felt about learning a FL diverged sharply. Boys declared themselves almost 60% less positive than girls. In particular, no girl was entirely negative about the experience, whilst 11 boys were. The further detail of the summary indicates that boys responded less positively than girls throughout. Particularly interesting is the response where nine boys indicated that they felt worried about communicating in the target language (Q.6), yet a more equal number of boys and girls had confidence in being able to understand the FL if spoken to them (Q.7/8). Finally, boys practiced their FL at home substantially less than girls (Q.9). Could it be that already these boys had begun to feel anxious about the different pronunciation of the FL, yet recognised their own ability to grasp meaning fairly easily? Alternatively, this data may reflect a general pattern in England of boys being less likely to pay attention to completing homework than girls.

Given the unanticipated nature of this data, neither teachers nor school principals had been asked to comment specifically on gendered responses to FL learning. This area remains therefore in need of substantial further research before any valid conclusions are drawn. On a number of occasions during the researchers' school visits however, both teachers and school principals had commented anecdotally on the quite frequently observed negative response from some boys. Corroborating this, when the final Report was presented to the School Principals' Steering Committee (a body representing the 44 primary schools in the Pathfinder pilot phase) there was much agreement on this finding. Principals from many schools confirmed this tendency amongst the FL learners of their schools also. It seems possible that these findings may represent what Jones and Coffey (2006: 96) have termed more generally as 'social expectation and learnt ways of being'.

At the end of this two-year monitoring study the evidence suggests that there is some uncertainty relating to the potential of an early start to fully support the establishment of positive attitudes towards FL learning. A more nuanced, longitudinal study is likely to be helpful in providing a clearer understanding of the factors affecting this, whilst a comparative perspective from the wider Europe may help to understand how attitudinal responses might be nurtured differently in other cultural contexts.

Early language learning in Europe: Study context in England

The indicative findings of the Pathfinder research in relation to emergent attitudes to FL learning are sufficient to suggest a need for further research in this field. To support these findings more convincingly and with the aim of providing some initial baseline data from a larger study, I will report here on recent data gathered as part of the Early Language Learning in Europe study (ELLiE), a seven-country study tracking a cohort of FL learners longitudinally from an early start age of 6/7 years right through their primary years (co-researchers: Lindgren, E., Lopriore, L., Mihaljević Djigunović, J., Munoz, C., Szpotowicz, M. & Damhuis, R.). This study sets out to explore young children's early language learning experience in school drawing from a cohort of approximately 150 children in each country. The data presented here relates to a sample of 164 children aged eight years in England, gathered during the initial scoping year, 2006–2007). The school selection represents a socio-economic and geographical spread across six schools drawn from the same local authority as the earlier Pathfinder study, in southern England. The sampling basis for the socio-economic factor relates to local authority statistics regarding the number of free school dinners provided to each school (a standard measure used in England to categorise schools).

After just five months of learning either French or Spanish these 164 children aged seven to eight years have shown what can be described as a *fairly* positive start to their attitudinal development (see Table 2.3).

This somewhat larger data set than the previous one indicates a broadly similar response to that achieved after one year of the Pathfinder study. Here, some 64% of the sample (61 girls and 44 boys) declared themselves

Table 2.3 Question: How do you feel about learning a foreign language?

	Positive	*Neutral*	*Negative*	*Total*
Girls	61	17	3	81
Boys	44	28	11	83

Source: Early Foreign Language Learning in Europe (ELLiE) study (unpublished)

positive, with the remaining 36% either neutral (17 girls and 28 boys) or negative (3 girls and 11 boys). Previous figures were 66% and 34% respectively, for a question related to preferences for continuing with the FL in the next school year. A follow-up question asked if these children would like more frequent foreign language lessons (currently they receive one 30-minute focused language lesson, supported by five to 10 minute further inputs two to three times per week, integrated within the wider primary curriculum by the class teacher).

This data (Table 2.4) confirmed a more clearly uncertain viewpoint from amongst these children. Some 46% responded positively to this question (39 girls and 37 boys), whilst the slightly larger proportion of 54% were either neutral (34 girls and 24 boys) or negative (8 girls and 22 boys). The data relating to general responses reflects reported differences between how boys and girls feel about learning FLs, whereas their views on whether they would like more FL lessons are very similar.

Further data was also collected on other languages frequently spoken at home, in the expectation that this might identify those children who felt more 'comfortable' with languages and thus were more positive about their experiences of language learning at school. However, this factor represented less that 10% of the cohort and individual positive responses rarely correlated with exposure to other languages at home.

In summary, it can be said that data from the two studies appears not to reflect a pattern of overwhelming enthusiasm for FL learning and indicates some stronger evidence of this from boys, yet such data should be treated with caution. During data collection every effort was made to ensure that children reported their own views, with the researcher emphasising the

Table 2.4 Question: Would you like to have language lessons more often?

	Yes	*Neutral*	*No*	*Total*
Girls	39	34	8	81
Boys	37	24	22	83

Source: Early Foreign Language Learning in Europe (ELLiE) study (unpublished)

importance of this to the children. The researcher maintained identical procedures in each classroom, collecting all data personally. Nonetheless, given the young age of these children and their inexperience at responding to questionnaires, findings should not be regarded as convincingly robust.

In reviewing these findings and the degree of corroborative evidence from classroom observations, it is not easy to match the two with Jones and Coffey's (2006: 3) claim that 'young learners bring motivational capital to language learning'. They further propose that 'this has to be maintained throughout the entire primary phase and into the secondary phase' (Jones & Coffey, 2006: 3). The children of these two studies – and the boys in particular – appear to need help in building their motivational capital even at this early point.

The longitudinal and comparative nature of the ELLiE study will be important in providing many future opportunities to collect evidence of a more stable and nuanced quality, which should give a detailed indication of these children's emerging attitudinal responses through the years. Evidence to account for this could also offer further illumination of societal factors both inside and outside the classroom that may be contributing to shaping those responses. Some potential areas for further investigation will be briefly considered below.

Accounting for Attitudes

Accounting for the boys' attitudinal shift over the two-year period of their learning in the first study and for the stronger positive response of girls in the second, is a complex issue. One on which only tentative explanations might be put forward at this point.

Firstly, there is the evidence that boys generally perform less well in measurable literacy tasks at primary school, as indicated by both local and national scoring in the KS2 national tests. One explanation routinely offered for this is their slower progress to maturity, another is that the current primary school curriculum is a feminised one – more geared to the interests and potential of girls than of boys (Riddell, 1992). The longitudinal nature of the ELLiE study will provide a valuable opportunity to evaluate these findings in greater depth.

Related to the above point, there is the question of the precise role of the teacher and the learning context in influencing early positive attitudes. This factor was identified as important in an earlier study conducted by Nikolov of children aged between six and 14 years (Nikolov, 1999). It is anticipated that with the broader remit of the ELLiE study data will be collected from classroom observations and subsequent, more detailed interviews conducted with children which should shed further light on what may prove to be a key variable in this process, particularly in the early phases of learning.

Finally, there is the real concern of UK foreign language specialists related to boys' performance in FLs at secondary level (Stables & Wikeley, 1999). One oft-used argument for the introduction of an earlier start age to FL learning in England was the claim that it would be possible to engage and maintain boys interest as a result of this early start. If data such as that presented here should be replicated elsewhere over longer periods, arguably the programme for introduction may fall at the first hurdle.

The potential for societal change

Whilst educationalists are all too familiar with the complexities of introducing change and recognise the need for a period of some years before such a radical change can be sufficiently embedded and refined as to be able to offer a high quality learning experience for all, it may be that such time will not be available to nurture and feed the quality of this innovation in England. Given the very political nature of its introduction indicated in the opening section of this chapter and given a prior history in England of the political engineering which led to the cancellation of the 1960–1970s attempt to introduce primary FLs in schools (Burstall *et al.*, 1974), there may indeed be a limited future for this innovation unless urgent efforts are made to influence societal perceptions and hence boys' motivation.

The introduction of an inclusive policy with provision for all children to learn a FL is a demanding policy to implement at primary level. Children of seven years in England are unlikely to have much exposure to the FL outside the classroom (except possibly during holiday trips). In the main, their parents also are unlikely to encounter FLs in their daily lives. While this area of southern England does have some economic links, particularly with the northern coastline of France which can be regarded as its immediate neighbour, there remains little evidence of either French or Spanish in use locally in shops and businesses in the study area.

The underlying rationale for an *inclusive* policy is to ensure all sectors of the population should have equal opportunity. In practice, it may be that the result will be a wider sector of the population (than previously) take up the opportunity with enthusiasm, yet, that smaller, less enthusiastic proportion may operate against creating the necessary classroom context of engagement and willingness to participate, one in which peer pressure does not operate in opposition to the curriculum, and thus a context in which children are free to gain confidence *at their own rate*.

Reviewing the more negative responses of some boys from the first study may shed some light on the power of sociocultural influences. Additional comments on how they felt about FL learning made by two different groups of boys during small group interviews included the following:

Group 1:
'It's boring' (French).

'It's what the Froggies speak' (French) (this nickname relates to the popularity of frogs legs on French menus, a phenomenon not found in England generally).

Group 2:
Simply the sign of a Nazi salute was enough for the peer group to burst into giggles (from some children learning German in the first exploratory study).

Here, it became clear that some of these boys were much influenced by media images and the opinions of their elder siblings and parents. The further challenge of working with the local community to create a higher profile for the introduction of early FL learning can be cited as one possible way of beginning to change societal attitudes to such initiatives. Ways to achieve this are not currently at the forefront of the rollout process for local authorities. In addition, an increased use of undubbed cartoons and children's programmes as part of the mainstream TV programming might well have an impact, as has been highly successful in the Nordic countries and in the Netherlands.

Conclusion

This chapter set out to give the reader some insights into the early developing attitudes of young language learners in England and to account for them in the contemporary sociocultural and political context of England today. Findings presented suggest that we cannot claim such young children (and boys in particular) will necessarily view FL learning positively in England. To understand exactly how teachers and the wider society might nurture the emergence of positive attitudes further research of a longitudinal nature would be valuable. Creating the kind of societal change that may be necessary if children in England are to make progress towards becoming plurilingual European citizens appears to be a challenging task, at present.

References

Burstall, C., Jamieson, M., Cohen, S. and Hargreaves, M. (1974) *Primary French in the Balance*. Slough: NFER Publishing Co.

CILT (2007) *Languages 2007 Digest of Policy, Research and Statistics*. London: CILT, The National Centre for Languages.

Commission of the European Communities (2003) Communication from the Commission to the Council, the European Parliament, the European Economic and Social Committee and the Committee of the Regions: *Promoting Language Learning and Linguistic Diversity: An Action Plan 2004–2006*. COM (2003) 449 final. On WWW at http://ec.europa.eu/education/doc/official/keydoc/actlang/act_lang_en.pdf. Accessed 16.3.07.

Driscoll, P. and Frost, D. (eds) (1999) *The Teaching of Modern Foreign Languages in the Primary School*. London: Routledge.

Enever, J. (2007) Yet another early start language policy in Europe: Poland this time! *Current Issues in Language Planning* 8 (2), 208–221.

European Commission (2005) *Eurydice: Key Data on Teaching Languages at Schools in Europe – 2005 Edition*. Brussels: Commission of the European Communities.

Genesee, F. (1978/1979) Scholastic effects of French immersion: An overview after 10 years. *Interchange* 9, 20–29.

Jones, J. and Coffey, S. (2006) *Modern Foreign Languages 5–11*. London: David Fulton.

Low, L. (1999) Policy issues for primary MFL. In P. Driscoll and D. Frost (eds) *The Teaching of Modern Foreign Languages in the Primary School* (pp. 50–64). London: Routledge.

Martyniuk, W. (2007) Forum for progress. *EL Gazette* 328, 23.

Munoz, C. (ed.) (2006) *Age and the Rate of Foreign Language Learning*. Clevedon: Multilingual Matters.

Nikolov, M. (1999) Why do you learn English? Because the teacher is short: A study of Hungarian children's foreign language learning motivation. *Language Teaching Research* 3, 33–56.

Riddell, S. (1992) *Gender and the Politics of the Curriculum*. London: Routledge.

Sharpe, K. (2001) *Modern Foreign Languages in the Primary School*. London: Kogan Page.

Singleton, D. and Ryan, L. (2004) *Language Acquisition: The Age Factor*. Clevedon: Multilingual Matters.

Stables, A. and Wikeley, F. (1999) From bad to worse? Pupils' attitudes to modern foreign languages at ages 14 and 15. *Language Learning Journal* 20, 3–7.

Watts, C. and Enever, J. (2005) *Monitoring and Evaluation Report: BHCC Pathfinder Primary Modern Foreign Languages Project*. UK: B & H City Council.

Chapter 3

Young Learners of Croatian as a Second Language: Minority Language Speakers and Their Croatian Competence

ZRINKA JELASKA and LIDIJA CVIKIĆ

Introduction

The Croatian language is a South-Slavic language. It is estimated that it is spoken by 6 million people in total: 4.5 million Croatian inhabitants, over half a million of inhabitants in Bosnia and Herzegovina, and over 1 million speakers that live abroad as traditional minorities or immigrants. For some of them Croatian is a second language (L2). All Croatian speakers living outside Croatia (in neighbouring countries, other European countries and all over the world, particularly in the United States, Canada, South American countries, Australia, New Zealand) and BiH are bilingual speakers; many of them speak Croatian as L2, although it is their mother tongue.

According to the Census 2001 (http://www.dzs.hr) more than 96% of people living in Croatia consider Croatian as their mother tongue (L1). Since the number of non-native speakers of Croatian is relatively small, Croatia is considered to be a monolingual country. Less than 4% of Croatian inhabitants (155,190) are native speakers of other languages. The Census 2001 lists 23 such languages (Table 3.1).

Education in Croatia up to 18 Years for Minority Speakers

Despite the fact that Croatian is a non-native language to some primary school children in Croatia, for years it has been taught as a first language to all students. Because of this and various other reasons (social, cultural, political, etc.) certain types of bilingualism are typical of the communities of a particular first language: Italian, Hungarian, Roma, and so forth. Hence, within the borders of Croatia, various groups of bilingual speakers

Table 3.1 Native languages of Croatian L2 speakers in the Republic of Croatia

Mother tongue	Number	Percentage of speakers
Serbian	44.629	1.01
Italian	20.521	0.46
Albanian	14.621	0.33
Hungarian	12.650	0.29
Slovenian	11.872	0.27
Bosniak/Bosnian	9.197	0.21
Roma	7.860	0.18
Czech	7.178	0.16
Serbo-Croatian	4.961	0.11
Slovakian	3.993	0.09
Macedonian	3.534	0.08
German	3.013	0.07
Croato-Serbian	2.054	0.05
Rusyn	1.828	0.04
Rumanian	1.205	0.03
Russian	1.080	0.02
Ukrainian	1.027	0.02
Polish	536	0.01
Montenegrin	460	0.01
Turkish	347	0.01
Bulgarian	265	0.01
Hebrew	8	0.00
Vlach	7	0.00
other	2.824	0.06

Source: Census 2001

can be differentiated: from balanced bilinguals to speakers of Croatian with very limited proficiency (Cvikić *et al.*, 2004; Cvikić & Kuvač, 2003; Cvikić & Tomek, 2003; Kovačević & Jelaska, 2003; Kuvač & Cvikić, 2004). Minority speakers have a constitutional right to be educated in their first language and script (which is an issue for speakers who use Cyrillic script, for example, speakers of Macedonian, Bulgarian, Rusyn, Russian and Ukrainian, as well as Serbian and Montenegrin who use both Cyrillic and Latin scripts), from preschool to university level. There are seven minority and regional languages that use this privilege and educate their speakers in their native languages: Italian, Serbian, Hungarian, Czech, Slovak, Rusyn and Ukrainian, as well as three nonregional: German, Hebrew and Roma (VRH, 2004).

Types of education for minority speakers

Three types of education in language and script of minority speakers are complemented by other types of their L1 education, such as learning community languages, summer schools, winter schools, special educational programmes (preschool). All of them are part of a regular school system. Minority speakers choose one or the other model according to their preferences, legal and available possibilities. Only primary (age 7–14 years) and secondary (age 15–18 years) school models will be discussed in detail as the goal is to describe young learners. Most of the languages could be studied at the university level, but this is out of the scope of this chapter.

Type A: Monolingual L1 education (all subjects in L1 + Croatian course)

At Type A schools education is in the mother tongue (and script) of minority speakers. Students may be placed in a separate school or in separate classes within regular Croatian schools. This type of education is used by Serbian, Italian, Hungarian and Czech minorities. The Croatian language is taught as a subject. This type of education does not by itself lead to required communicative linguistic competence in Croatian if it is not complemented by communication outside class and school, which is lacking in some minority language communities. This is particularly the case with some young Hungarian speakers, as they live in small, closed communities of Hungarian L1 speakers. Since the Hungarian language is neither genetically nor structurally related to the Croatian language, Hungarian L1 speakers need more exposure to Croatian than it is required by the school curriculum in order to achieve sufficient competence in Croatian.

Type B: Bilingual education (instruction in L1 and L2)

At Type B schools education is bilingual; for example, classes in natural science are conducted in Croatian, while classes in social sciences and nationally important classes are conducted in the minority language. Students are typically placed within Croatian schools, but students attend separate classes. This type of education is used by Austrian, Czech, German and Hungarian minorities. If other factors are beneficial, this type of education may lead to balanced bilingual competence in both languages.

*Type C: Monolingual L2 education and L1 classes (instruction in
Croatian + L1 course)*

At Type C schools education is in Croatian, with additional five classes which cover language and literature of the minority language, as well as topics from history, geography, music and fine arts (language and culture). It is usually conducted as an additional programme, sometimes in the form of 'Saturday schools'. This type of education is used by the Czech, Slovak, Rusyn, Ukrainian, Serbian and Hungarian minorities. Although it is beneficial for Croatian communicative linguistic competence, mother tongue competence in this type of schooling depends on other factors, besides official education.

Summer schools and other courses

Summer schools in the minority language and culture are used by Rusyn-Ukrainian, Serbian, Montenegrin and Roma minorities. Learning of community languages is used by Italian minority. As this type of education is an additional L1 education, it does not influence competence in Croatian.

Types of education and numbers of minority speakers in 2004

There are more than 11,000 children and students involved in all types of regular minority language education in Croatia: kindergarten, primary school and high school. In 2004, 11,317 children and students were listed taught by 1117 minority language teachers. (There were not enough data on later years to be included in this chapter.) In Table 3.2 types of minority education, schools and programmes are presented. Numbers of children and students attending various programmes in 2004 are also listed. The table includes data on different groups of minority speakers.

Row 1 of Table 3.2 presents number of preschools, for example, kindergartens and number of children attending them. Rows 2, 3 and 4 present numbers of primary schools (compulsory for children from 7 to 14 years in Croatia) with three types of programme (A, B and C). Row 5 lists students attending Rusyn and Ukrainian language summer schools. Row 6 includes the number of high schools (are optional for children from 14 to 18 years) and students attending them. Some students are missing from Table 3.2, as the exact numbers were not given in the government report (VRH, 2004). Children attending Jewish kindergarten (25), Roma children who were part of a special preschool programme, students attending courses in Hebrew, Albanian and Italian, as well as Montenegrin, Serbian and Roma summer schools' students are not included in the table. As can be seen in Table 3.2, some young learners of Croatian who live in isolated minority language communities may face insufficient opportunities to reach necessary competences in Croatian as an L2 if they participate in educational programmes exclusively in their mother tongue with just five

Table 3.2   Education in minority languages in the Republic of Croatia (year 2004)

Minority	Italian	Czech	Slovak	Hungarian	Serbian	German and Austrian	Rusyn and Ukrainian	Total
Kindergartens	30	2	—	3	6	1	—	42
Number of children	624	145	—	98	410	26	—	1321
Primary A	17	4	—	1	19	—	—	41
Number of students	2,140	454	—	36	3100	—	—	5730
Primary B	—	—	—	4	—	1	—	5
Number of students	—	—	—	153	—	54	—	207
Primary C	—	7	4	17/42	27	—	3	58
Number of students	—	463	454	424	302	—	187	1810
Summer schools	—	—	—	—	—	—	—	—
	—	—	—	—	—	—	100	100
High schools	4	1	—	5	7	—	1	18
	786	37	—	130	1250	—	—	2203
Total students	3550	1099	454	805	5062	80	267	11,317
Total teachers	148	64	29	143	719	2	12	1117

classes of Croatian per week. An additional problem appears with some young learners who attend regular Croatian schools but their competence is not appropriate for their age when they enter primary schools. This has been noticed particularly in case of Roma speakers (Cvikić *et al.*, 2004; Cvikić & Kuvač, 2007). In 2004 there were reported 1700 Roma children attending regular Croatian primary schools.

Proficiency in Croatian

As psycholinguistic research on Croatian as a foreign and second language has been systematically conducted only for the last 10 years (Cvikić & Jelaska, 2005), few papers have been published on young learners learning Croatian as L2. Some of the findings are presented here.

Speakers of Serbian L1

Serbian is a language closely related to Croatian. As it shared part of cultural language history in 20th century with Croatian, contact influences enhanced their similarities. Almost all Croatian speakers were to some extent bilingual in Serbian, at the least possessing comprehension competence. If not with its speakers personally, they had contact with the language regularly through spoken and written media. For example, cartoons (e.g. Disney), magazines and journals for Croatian children were often published in the Serbian language and Latin script. TV news was read in different languages every day, Serbian was the language of many popular TV-series and films. However, due to the war (which started in 1991) and political changes, recently Croatian speakers – particularly young ones born shortly before and during the war or after it – have had no (or almost none) contact with Serbian, and far less with Slovenian or Macedonian. Therefore, many have no communicative linguistic competence in those languages other than what may result from their similarity. The fact that Croatian and Serbian are closely related languages is a facilitating factor for learning, but a hindering factor for research. The sociolinguistic status of the Serbian language in Croatia was not a facilitating factor for research.

Only one study (Jelaska & Hržica, 2002) was conducted concerning Croatian competence of bilingual speakers of Croatian who dominantly speak Serbian and live abroad. It compared written performance of Croatian-Serbian bilinguals and Croatian monolinguals. The task was a written translation of a text excerpted from a novel dictated by a four-year-old Serbian girl. The first group of informants was a group of 15-year-old Croatians born and raised in Vojvodina, a plurilingual part of Serbia. Although their mother tongue was Croatian, which they spoke as a family and religious language, Serbian was their dominant language. The second group of informants consisted of native speakers of Croatian, but kajka-vian dialect of Zabok, which shares one phonological feature with Serbian: it does not have the diphtong *ie* as the Croatian standard language. The results showed that bilingual and monolingual Croatian speakers could be easily identified by different results as well as strategies used, although some similarities were also found. Bilingual speakers did not acquire all Croatian phonological, morphological, syntactic, semantic and prag-matic features. In written translation all of them had interlanguage features, especially in words with the diphthong *ie*, which were very often either unrecognised, or replaced by nonexisting or nonstandard forms. Interestingly enough, bilingual speakers replaced some words that are similar, or even the same in Serbian and Croatian with nonexisting forms due to overgeneralisation. Hence, bilinguals had many interlanguage fea-tures and overgeneralisations, while Croatian monolinguals had wrong translations due to guessing and blank spaces as they did not understand Serbian words such as *plata* 'salary', *parčići* 'pieces', *šargarepa* 'carrot' (Croatian: *plaća, dijelovi, mrkva*), and so on. False pairs were, of course, a big problem for both groups. Bilinguals left more Serbian words and expressions without Croatian equivalents, especially the ones with morphological differences resulting in one or two phoneme differences, for example, Sr. *sekund, posmatrati, zečiji, bombona* instead of Cr. *sekunda, promatrati, zečji, bombon*. Large scale research needs to be conducted with Serbian L1 speakers from Croatia. It is hoped that the results will offer insights into the role of closely related languages in communicative competence and the best way of teaching and learning them.

Speakers of Italian L1

Italian is one of the widely learned languages. In Croatia it has been regularly learned as one of the four foreign languages, English, German and French being the other three. Now English prevails within Croatia, as it happens in many other European countries, and other languages are a popular choice as second foreign languages. But Italian is still very popu-lar on the Adriatic coast. The majority of 19,636 Italian speakers listed in the Census 2001 lives in Istria (14,284 in year 2001), and in the district of Rijeka (Primorsko-goranska distict – 3539). Italian speakers are mostly balanced bilinguals as adults.

Research on Italian L1 speakers

Two international projects involved Italian speakers in Croatia. One is the TEMPUS project *Communicative competence in plurilinguistic environ-ment*, conducted at the University of Zagreb, between 2001 and 2003 (financed mostly by the European Union). Among other things, it resulted in publishing a nicely illustrated multi-dialectal thematic dictionary for young learners (Jelaska & Kovačević, 2003), which also includes some language games and task-based activities prepared by Dobravac. Besides various Croatian dialects, Italian is included in the dictionary, as it is one of the languages of the Istrian town of Novigrad, where data was also collected. On the basis of questionnaires administrated to primary school students it was found that Italian L1 speakers have positive attitudes towards Italian and Croatian, high proficiency in both, and that Istria is a truly plurilingual environment (Cvikić, 2002; Kalogjera, 2003; Kalogjera & Palmović, 2002).

The University of Zagreb participated in the project organised by the Ludwig Boltzman Institute (Vienna, Austria) on monolingual and bilingual language development. Four languages were included in the research: Croatian, Italian, Czech and German. The proficiency in Croatian as L2 of Italian-Croatian bilingual speakers and German-Croatian bilingual speakers was compared. The first group of speakers includes speakers of Italian L1 who live in Croatia (Istria). Italian is their mother tongue, and Croatian is the language of their immediate environment as well as the official and state language. As a minority language, Italian has an official status in some parts of Istria. It is also the national and state language of neighbouring Italy. Sociolinguistically, its status in Croatia is very high, especially in Istria, due to political and cultural history, tourism, shopping excursions to neighbouring towns, and so on. The second group includes speakers of Croatian as L1 born in Austria or immigrated from Croatia or Bosnia and Herzegovina together with their parents. As Croatian of immigrant children is not highly valued in Austria, its sociolinguistic status is low. If they have a chance to attend classes in Croatian in the regular school, they are offered a few language classes per week in a mixed (nonhomogenous) group, organised by the Austrian school, or additional language and culture classes (something similar to model C in Croatia). Therefore, many Croatian children are not proficient speakers of Croatian as L1 (Jelaska, 2003), as German is their dominant language; only some are balanced bilinguals.

A study reported by Jelaska *et al.* (2003) showed that there are noticeable differences between bilingual speakers of Croatian in Croatia and Austria. Although the results of the speakers with the highest competence do not differ, the range of comprehension competence of German-Croatian speakers is much lower than that of Italian-Croatian speakers. This is illustrated in Table 3.3.

Table 3.3   Speakers of Italian (L1) in Croatia and Croatian (L1) in Austria

Understanding of Croatian sentences		
Italian L1	(Croatia)	82–97%
Croatian L1	(Austria)	37–95%

Speakers of Hungarian L1

Hungarian is a non-Indo-European language, which makes it different from many other minority languages in Croatia. The majority of 16,595 Hungarian speakers (listed in the Census 2001) live in a region of Baranja and near Osijek (9784), in the district of Vukovar and Srijem (2047) and in Bjelovarsko-bilogorska district (1188). Not all Hungarian speakers are balanced bilinguals even as adults (Cvikić & Tomek, 2003; Kuvač, 2002a, 2002b).

The research on the acquisition of Croatian as L2 by young speakers of Hungarian as L1 was reported in two studies (Cvikić & Kuvač, 2003; Kuvač & Cvikić, 2004). The participants in both studies are students of primary school (Grades 1–4) whose L1 is Hungarian and who attended school in their L1, with Croatian as a school subject. Although research participants were educated in their L1, they followed the same curriculum in their Croatian language classes as native speakers. The aim of both studies was to examine whether Hungarian L1 speakers have Croatian language competence at a level high enough to meet the curriculum requirements. On the basis of students' written school and home work Cvikić and Kuvač (2003) showed that there was a growing number of language errors produced by Hungarian L1 participants when writing in Croatian. The errors occured at all linguistic levels:

- Phonological level – usage of L1 graphemes, omission of diacritics, omission of phonemes.
- Morphological level – wrong case endings, errors in gender and number agreement, use of verb aspect.
- Syntactical level – word order, prepositions.
- Lexical errors.

The number and the variety of errors increased with grade (from 1st to 4th) due to the growing curriculum requirements. Students were expected to produce longer and more complex texts but not in accordance with their Croatian language competence. In order to investigate the Croatian language competence of Hungarian L1 students in more detail Kuvač and Cvikić (2004) used a specially designed non-standardised test that consisted of several subtests: a vocabulary comprehension and production subtest, a noun morphology subtest, a verb morphology subtest and a subtest on verbal aspect. For each subtest results of Croatian native speakers of similar age (1st and 2nd grade) were available.This study confirmed the findings of the previous one. The results showed that Hungarian L1 participants had a lower command of the Croatian language than the monolingual Croatian speakers of the same age. For example, for Hungarian L1 participants the average score on the vocabulary comprehension subtest was 74% and 27% on the vocabulary production subtest, whereas the monolingual Croatian speakers of the same age performed 100% on the comprehension test and 76% on the production subtest. Other features of the Croatian language (i.e. noun morphology and verb morphology) were acquired even less. Both studies showed that the Croatian language competence of Hungarian L1 lower primary speakers included in the study was not sufficient either to communicate in Croatian or to follow the Croatian language curriculum.

Speakers of Roma L1

The Roma minority in the Republic of Croatia speak two different languages/dialects, genetically related to Croatian in the sense that both belong to the Indo-European family of languages. One is Romani Chib, stemming from Indian languages. The other is Bayashi, based on the Romanian dialect, which is genetically much closer to Croatian. The majority of 9463 Roma speakers listed in the Census 2001 live in Medimurje (2887), the city of Zagreb (1946) and in Osijek and Baranja (977). According to the National programme for the Roma, a document issued by the government of the Republic of Croatia (www.vlada.hr/Download), it is estimated that the real number of the Roma in Croatia is between 30,000 and 40,000. In 2004 there were 1900 reported Roma children attending regular Croatian schools, and 200 of them in high schools, but it is estimated that one-third of all Roma children were never included in any form of education (www.vlada.hr/Download). Even though there is a certain percentage of Roma people that are fully integrated in the Croatian society, many of them are still not integrated. One of the most widely discussed issues regarding the education of Roma children in Croatia is an insufficient knowledge of the Croatian language. In order to investigate the level of Croatian competence of Roma children several studies were conducted (Cvikić *et al.*, 2004; Cvikić & Kuvač, 2007) and the research instrument was the mentioned test. Cvikić *et al.* (2004) investigated two groups of Roma speakers, Bayashi and Romani Chib and Croatian monolingual speakers. Table 3.4 shows the results on vocabulary production and comprehension for all groups.

Table 3.4 shows that for both groups of Roma participants the results on the vocabulary subtest were lower than the results of Croatian monolingual

Table 3.4 Vocabulary acquisition by Roma L1 and Croatian L1 children

	Comprehension	*Production*
Romani Chib	92%	54%
Bayashi	71%	42%
Croatian L1	100%	76%

speakers. Comparing the two groups of Roma speakers it is noticeable that the speakers of Romani Chib performed better than the speakers of Bayashi, especially on the vocabulary comprehension subtest. Figures 3.1 and 3.2 show the acquisition of Croatian grammatical features: masculine noun morphology (Figure 3.1) and verb morphology (Figure 3.2).

Since Croatian is a highly flective language with rich morphology, a high level of morphology acquisition is needed for both language comprehension and language production. The results of monolingual speakers as well as the findings from some other studies (e.g. Kuvač & Cvikić, 2003) show that the morphological system of the Croatian language is complex and demanding even for native speakers. Monolingual speakers of Croatian performed at the 80–100% level on verb morphology test (Figure 3.2) and

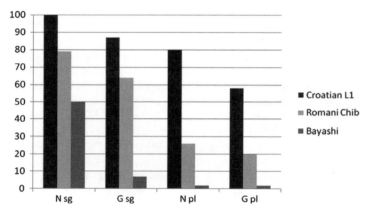

Figure 3.1   Declination of masculine nouns

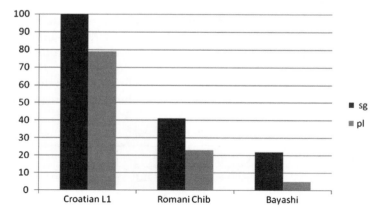

Figure 3.2   Verbal morphology

at the 60–100% level on the noun morphology test (Figure 3.1). The performance of both groups of Roma participants on both tests was much lower. Results of speakers of Romani Chib ranged from 20% to 80% (Figure 3.1) on the noun morphology test and between 23% and 41% on the verb morphology test (Figure 3.2). Results of speakers of Bayashi ranged from 2% to 50% on the noun morphology test (Figure 3.1) and from 5% and 22% on the verb morphology test. Research on other grammatical features (verbal aspect and prepositions) that was conducted only with speakers of Bayashi L1 (Cvikić & Kuvač, 2007) confirmed their low level of Croatian grammatical competence. Both studies suggest that Roma L1 speakers acquire only basic Croatian vocabulary at the comprehension level, while grammatical features of the Croatian language are not acquired at the level needed for language comprehension and production. It can be concluded that some Roma L1 children entering primary schools to get education in Croatian do not have Croatian language competence at a level needed for meeting curriculum requirements.

Groups of Croatian L2 Speakers According to Croatian Language Competence

Findings of all the conducted research on the acquisition of Croatian by minority speakers in Croatia show that several groups of Croatian L2 speakers could perhaps be differentiated. The first group comprises speakers whose acquisition of Croatian has not been investigated (e.g. Serbian, Czech, Albanian L1 speakers). However, insights from second language acquisition research, the socio-economic and political status of the language community and the speakers' attitudes towards the Croatian language suggest that this group will not be a homogenous one. Due to the similarities of L1 and L2 it can be predicted that Croatian will be better acquired by Serbian and Czech than Albanian speakers. On the other hand, due to socio-economic reasons it could be predicted that Croatian will be better acquired by Czech than Albanian L1 speakers. However, all these assumptions should be verified by research. The second group of speakers includes balanced bilinguals, as is the case with Italian L1 speakers in Istria. The third group of Croatian L2 speakers consists of speakers lacking Croatian language competence (Hungarian and Roma L1 speakers). There are several possible reasons for this. These speakers often live in small and rather closed communities. Many Hungarians live in villages with a majority of Hungarian population and members of the Roma minority often live in settlements isolated from the majority citizens. Only a small number of the children from both communities are included in preschool education. For these reasons children's exposure to the Croatian language before starting primary school is rather limited.

The Role of School in the Acquisition of Croatian

Children's language development is one among many goals and roles of primary school. Although this is the case with the first language, it might not always be a fact when it comes to learning Croatian as L2. The case of Hungarian and Roma L1 speakers shows that primary school might not have as strong an influence on their Croatian language competence as it should. The main reason might be found in an inappropriate curriculum. Both groups of children, Hungarian (educated in their L1) and Roma (educated in their L2), follow the same Croatian language course syllabus – a syllabus designed for native speakers of Croatian. Since that syllabus was more oriented to knowledge about Croatian than to knowledge of Croatian, Croatian L2 speakers lack the opportunity to develop their communicative competence in Croatian.

The non-existence of education in their L1 is an additional hindering factor for the Roma minority. The low level of competence in Croatian (the language of their education) that some Roma L1 speakers have influences their entire schooling and puts them in an unequal position with their peers, native speakers of Croatian.

Teacher education

Croatian language teachers are educated at two types of higher education institutions. Teacher training colleges offer studies for elementary school teachers (the four lower grades, 1–4). In the language classes, as well as in the university curriculum, the emphasis is put on linguistic content (grammar, lexicology, orthography, history of the standard language). Characteristics of acquiring and learning a second language, various types of bilingualism, language development at school and difficulties in L2 communication are not taught in the programme. Students of foreign languages encountered some of this content in their courses. Earlier this type of education lasted only two years and some teachers teaching today are such college graduates.

Faculties of philosophy belong to the second type of teacher education institutions. They educate teachers for four upper grades of elementary school teachers (5–8), four grades of high school (years 15–18) and university. As in the school curriculum for those grades, in the language courses the emphasis is on linguistic topics (Jelaska, 2002a, 2002b).

Topics on language acquisition, language development through school, comprehension difficulties, different types of bilingualism, theoretical and practical teaching of L2, especially Croatian as L2, were not part of the curriculum in Croatian teachers' education. There were no courses in the curriculum that would prepare the student to face teaching problems of learners of Croatian as L2. Only occasional courses on second language acquisition were offered to future teachers of Croatian at the University of Zagreb as optional courses. As a result, teachers lack skills and knowledge about L2 teaching and Croatian as a second language learning, as well as teaching in plurilingual environments. While supporting foreign language teaching and learning, Croatian teacher education does not support L2 learning appropriately.

Future Perspectives

The educational reform which started in 2004 on all levels of education gives a better perspective for learners of Croatian as L2. For the first eight grades of school there is a new programme of the Croatian language, which is more headed towards communicative linguistic competence, as well as HNOS (Hrvatski nacionalni obrazovni standard – Croatian National Educational Standard). Compulsory topics in the 5th grade of primary school are bilinguism, second language, minority and official languages, understanding the difference between monolingual and bilingual acquisition of Croatian, the difference between L1 and L2, and the role of minority language. Secondary school is undergoing national testing for school-leaving exam. This form of external testing influences the relationship between teachers and the outcomes in Croatian competences for L2 learners: four minority language groups expressed a wish to have test questions translated in their L1. The Bologna system of undergraduate, graduate and postgraduate studies at the university level gives students more chances for optional courses, and many are offered in new programmes. Promising examples are two interdisciplinary doctoral programmes: JEKON and Glotodidactics. The latter stresses Croatian as a foreign language in its title (Glotodidactics: modern foreign languages and Croatian as a foreign language). In some other doctoral programmes, there is also a growing number of students opting for research on second language acquisition with a focus on Croatian as L2.

References

Census 2001. On WWW at http://www.dzz.hr. Accessed 17.12.07.

Cvikić, L. (2002) Analiza upitnika za učenike osnovnih škola u jednojezičnoj i dvojezičnoj sredini [The analysis of the questionnaires filled in by pupils in monolingual and bilingual communities (Summary)]. In M. Kovačević and D. Pavličević-Franić (eds) *Komunikacijska kompetencija u višejezičnoj sredini I.: Prikazi, problemi, putokazi* [Communicative competence in multilingual contexts I: Overview, problems, directions] (pp. 105–120, 189–193). Zagreb: Sveučilište u Zagrebu i Naklada Slap.

Cvikić, L., Kuvač, J. and Dobravac, G. (2004) The acquisition of Croatian language for speakers of Roma language(s). Poster presented at *14th EUROSLA Conference,* San Sebastian, Spain.

Cvikić, L. and Jelaska, Z. (2005) Istraživanja hrvatskoga kao drugoga i stranoga jezika [Research into Croatian as a second and foreign language]. In L. Cvikić and Z. Jelaska (eds) *Hrvatski kao drugi i strani jezik* [Croatian as a second and foreign language] (pp. 127–134). Zagreb: Hrvatska sveučilišna naklada.

Cvikić, L. and Kuvač, J. (2003) Orši neljepo piše. Poteškoće djece, mađarskih govornika, u učenju hrvatskoga jezika [Orši writes un-nicely. Difficulties of Hungarian L1 children in learning Croatian]. In I. Vodopija (ed.) *Dijete i jezik* [Child and language] (pp. 55–66). Osijek: Sveučilište J. J. Stossmayera.

Cvikić. L. and Kuvač, J. (2007) Usvojenost hrvatskoga jezika u romske djece predškolske dobi [Acquisition of the Croatian language by Roma pre-school children]. In L. Cvikić (ed.) *Drugi jezik hrvatski* [Second language – Croatian] (pp. 86–96). Zagreb: Profil.

Cvikić. L. and Tomek, T. (2003) Hrvatski – prvi strani jezik? [Croatian – the first foreign language?]. In M. Kovačević and D. Pavličević-Franić (eds) *Komunikacijska kompetencija u višejezičnoj sredini II.: Teorijska razmatranja, primjena* [Communicative competence in multilingual contexts II: Theoretical considerations, applications] (pp. 126–135). Zagreb – Jastrebarsko: Sveučilište u Zagrebu i Naklada Slap.

Jelaska, Z. (2002a) Analiza programa nastave hrvatskoga jezika na filozofskim fakultetima [Analysis of Croatian language curricula at faculties of philosophy]. In M. Kovačević and D. Pavličević-Franić (eds) *Komunikacijska kompetencija u višejezičnoj sredini I.: Prikazi, problemi, putokazi* [Communicative competence in multilingual contexts I: Overview, problems, directions] (pp. 52–54, 140–142). Zagreb: Sveučilište u Zagrebu i Naklada Slap.

Jelaska, Z. (2002b) Analiza programa nastave hrvatskoga jezika na visokim pedagoškim školama [Analysis of Croatian language teacher education college curricula]. In M. Kovačević and D. Pavličević-Franić (eds) *Komunikacijska kompetencija u višejezičnoj sredini I.: Prikazi, problemi, putokazi* [Communicative competence in multilingual contexts I: Overview, problems, directions] (pp. 48–52, 137–140). Zagreb: Sveučilište u Zagrebu i Naklada Slap.

Jelaska, Z. (2003) Hrvatski jezik i višejezičnost [Croatian language and multilingualism]. In M. Kovačević and D. Pavličević-Franić (eds) *Komunikacijska kompetencija u višejezičnoj sredini II.: Teorijska razmatranja, primjena* [Communicative competence in multilingual contexts II: Theoretical considerations, applications] (pp. 106–125). Zagreb – Jastrebarsko: Sveučilište u Zagrebu i Naklada Slap.

Jelaska, Z. and Hržica, G. (2002) Poteškoće u učenju srodnih jezika: Prevođenje sa srpskoga i hrvatskoga [Difficulties in learning related languages: Translating from Serbian into Croatian]. *Jezik* 49 (3), 91–104.

Jelaska, Z. and Kovačević, M. (eds) (2003) *Zaviri: mali hrvatski zavičajni rječnik s igrama i zadatcima* [Take a peek: A small native Croatian dictionary with games and exercises]. Zagreb: Alfa.

Jelaska, Z. and Kovačević, M. (2003) Usvajanje hrvatskoga u jednojezičhome i dvojezičnome razvoju: Poredbena analiza na primjeru usvojenosti padeža [Acquisition of Croatian in monolingual and bilingual development: Comparative analysis of the case knowledge]. *3rd Croatian Slavic Conference*, Zadar, 15–19 October 2003.

Kalogjera, D. (2003) Notes about regional dialects in society and in language teaching. In M. Kovačević and D. Pavličević-Franić (eds) *Komunikacijska kompetencija u višejezičnoj sredini II.: Teorijska razmatranja, primjena* [Communicative competence in multilingual contexts II: Overview, problems, directions] (pp. 171–182). Zagreb – Jastrebarsko: Sveučilište u Zagrebu i Naklada Slap.

Kalogjera, D. and Palmović, M. (2002) Report on the visit to Novigrad. In M. Kovačević and D. Pavličević-Franić (eds) *Komunikacijska kompetencija u višejezičnoj sredini I.: Prikazi, problemi, putokazi* [Communicative competence in multilingual contexts I: Overview, problems, directions] (pp. 173–175). Zagreb: Sveučilište u Zagrebu i Naklada Slap.

Kovačević, M. and Jelaska, Z. (2003) Usvajanje hrvatskoga u jednojezičnome i dvojezičnome razvoju: Poredbena analiza na temelju usvojenosti padeža [Acquisition of Croatian in monolingual and bilingual development: Comparative analysis based on acquisition of cases]. Presentation at the *Treći hrvatski slavistički kongres* [Third Croatian Slavistics Congress], Zadar.

Kuvač, J. (2002a) Jezični jaz Baranje: odnos mađarskoga i hrvatskoga jezika [The Baranja language gap: Relationship between Hungarian and Croatian languages]. In M. Kovačević and D. Pavličević-Franić (eds) *Komunikacijska kompetencija u višejezičnoj sredini I.: Prikazi, problemi, putokazi* [Communicative competence in multilingual contexts I: Overview, problems, directions] (pp. 90–93). Zagreb: Sveučilište u Zagrebu i Naklada Slap.

Kuvač, J. (2002b) Utjecaj afektivnih čimbenika na usvajanje hrvatskoga kao stranoga ili drugoga jezika [Impact of affective factors on acquisition of Croatian as a foreign or second language]. In D. Stolac (ed.) *Primijenjena lingvistika- u Hrvatskoj–izazovi na početku XXI. stolje*ća [Applied linguistics in Croatia – challenges at the start of 21st century] (pp. 289–298). Zagreb – Rijeka: HDPL.

Kuvač, J. and Cvikić, L. (2003) Obilježja dječje gramatike na primjeru imenske morfologije [Features of children's grammar on example of noun morphology]. *Riječ*, 2 (9), 19–30.

Kuvač, J. and Cvikić, L. (2004) Hungarian kids and Croatian language. *Papers from 6th International Conference of Language Examination, Applied and Medicinal Linguistics* (pp. 140–148). Dunaújváros, Hungary.

National Program for the Roma. On WWW at http://www.vlada.hr/Download. Accessed 17.12.07.

Pavličević-Franić, D. and Kovačević, M. (eds) (2003) *Komunikacijska kompetencija u višejezičnoj sredini II.: Teorijska razmatranja, primjena* [Communicative competence in multilingual contexts II: Overview, problems, directions]. Zagreb–Jastrebarsko: Sveučilište u Zagrebu i Naklada Slap.

Vlada Republike Hrvatske (VRH) (2004) *Izvješće Republike Hrvatske o provođenju okvirne konvencije za zaštitu nacionalnih manjina* [Republic of Croatia report on implementation of national minorities protection convention framework]. On WWW at http://www.dijete.hr/adminmax/documents/IZVJESCE_NA_OKVIRNU_KONVENCIJU-2004.pdf. Accessed 17.12.07.

Chapter 4

Young Learners' Cognitive Skills and Their Role in Foreign Language Vocabulary Learning

THOMAÏ ALEXIOU

Introduction

This chapter presents the results of a three-year study into five- to nine-year-old Greek learners' cognitive abilities and their learning of English as a foreign language (EFL) vocabulary. Data were collected in different schools in the city of Thessaloniki, Greece and tests were administered on a one-to-one basis. As will be shown, significant relationships have been found between young children's aptitude and vocabulary development in English.

The impetus for research in the area of young learners' aptitude stems from the fact that there seems to have been no attempt to test aptitude in very young learners. Whereas the general consensus is that children are good at language learning, their aptitude is rarely discussed. This is surprising, as today teaching foreign languages to young learners is more a need than a fashion. As linguists are genuinely interested in discovering the nature of aptitude, attempts to explore and test this ability in young learners are now more than ever in order (Sparks & Ganschow, 2001).

Many children begin foreign language learning well before adolescence. In Greece it is common to begin around seven, but many learners begin even earlier than this. Very young learners are, according to common belief, good learners. It is not clear what the existing models of language learning can tell us about child foreign language learning, just as it is not clear what exactly young learners do to be so good – if indeed they are. Therefore, having an accurate idea of language learning aptitude in children is not a matter of purely academic interest. Unless it is clear how young learners learn, teaching can only be a hit and miss affair. At the moment we do not have a good model of how very young learners learn a foreign language (Milton & Alexiou, 2006b).

The background of the present study involves the investigation of the existence and nature of language learning aptitude in young learners. There are, of course, individual differences even in first language. Several psychologists have suggested that differences in cognitive abilities and cognitive development may account for the difficulties encountered by some young learners in early reading and writing. These differences in cognitive performance have been used in the study as a means of predicting performance in foreign language learning tasks in very young learners. However, this search for aptitude has shied away from the mere prediction aspect, which would not be as useful at such an early stage, and a more diagnostic purpose has been addressed. In this case, a relationship between cognitive abilities with foreign language acquisition may be established and then a learner's profile can be derived, indicating strengths, weaknesses and presumably learning styles.

Merely producing new norms with existing aptitude test formats was unlikely to be helpful. The whole point of an aptitude test is to differentiate between fast and slower learners, and even at a young age this is probably possible. This might be helpful if someone wanted to select learners for a specialist language school, for example, but is likely to be mistrusted, feared and criticised as deterministic. However, aptitude testing does not have to be crudely deterministic. It can allow talented individuals to make use of a special ability. Also, by offering the prospect of identifying learning strengths, it might allow all learners to benefit. Strengths can be identified and utilised, weaknesses can be identified and avoided or remedial action can help overcome them. There is a school of thought (Anderson, 2000) that suggests that these cognitive skills are trainable and may be plastic to some extent in very young learners, so remedial action may be a possibility.

A first requirement for that type of test was to examine the relationship between the types of general cognitive skills which develop in youngsters, and the learners' subsequent abilities in foreign language learning tasks. Not only would this reveal information about how these learners learn, and so lead to better directed materials and methodology, it would enable researchers to devise a more complete range of diagnostic tests. Currently, teachers have to rely on instinct and experience as to which approaches will suit their learners best, whereas aptitude tests may help them make far more objective judgements about their learners' linguistic profiles. There is some evidence that where teaching methods are correctly matched to learners' aptitude language learning is enhanced and where this matching does not occur learning is diminished (Wesche, 1981).

The importance of considering and controlling for variations in age of learners in language learning is explicitly discussed by Skehan (1989: 146–147) and Sparks and Ganschow (2001: 100) when they call for new norms in aptitude tests, including Carroll and Sapon's (1958a) elementary version of MLAT. Therefore, there is a need for empirical work in this area.

Language Aptitude in Young Learners

While considerable work has been done to pin down ways of testing aptitude, there is still much discussion about what really constitutes the nature of aptitude. Aptitude implies an individual difference in language learning and refers to the natural ability to acquire language at a fast and easy rate. Some commonly held notions around this concept are discussed below.

First, language learning aptitude is often conceptualised as a special skill which is separate from other skills. It is, apparently, different from intelligence or IQ or any other special skill. The particular contribution which Carroll and Sapon introduced to the field was that this special skill is comprised of several clearly identifiable subelements or subskills, which combine to create aptitude. While they considered their subelements of aptitude as cognitive abilities, they do not link these abilities with general cognitive abilities. Had they done so, this would imply crossover with other types of aptitude or ability. Even where researchers can demonstrate a close correlation between other abilities and language learning success, as in Pimsleur's (1968) work with IQ scores, language learning still appears to be viewed as a distinct and separate ability. At least part of this view must be based on the results of Carroll and Sapon's (1958a) results where MLAT and IQ scores are compared. Unlike other studies, they can find no significant correlation. Aptitude is also independent of other factors such as motivation, personality type, the opportunity to learn or the learning environment, which may also affect success in language learning (McDonough, 1981).

Second, as Carroll (1981: 85) points out, aptitude is innate. It is a 'gift', or what in English is often called an 'ear' for languages and is the ability to learn a foreign language at a fast and easy rate. Many teachers are uncomfortable with aptitude testing and feel that it is deterministic and condemns learners to fail even before they have had a chance to learn. Carroll however, takes a softer line and assumes that while all people can learn a language, not everyone is able to learn a language at the same speed. People who can learn quickly and easily have high aptitude, and people who cannot have low aptitude. The idea is that aptitude is relatively fixed and at least partly innate (Carroll, 1981: 86). However, Carroll did clarify later that other writers have suggested that it might have developed over a long period as a result of the individual's experience and activities (Carroll, 1981: 85).

Third, language learning aptitude is not language specific; it indicates a learner's capacity to do well in learning any language. It is a skill which is not influenced by the language background of the learner or the language which is being learned. Hence, a learner with high aptitude will do better at learning any language than a learner who has low aptitude, all other things being equal.

Recasting a model of aptitude with young learners in mind involves challenging elements of each of these three points. It poses questions whether language learning skill really is separate from other abilities and what these abilities really are, whether aptitude is something that is really fixed, and whether this special aptitude really does apply equally in all language learning situations (Milton & Alexiou, 2004).

Around the 1990s, with the adoption of a more communicative approach to teaching, foreign language aptitude has been reconsidered as a cognitive construct affected both by affective and language variables (Sparks & Ganschow, 2001). Moreover, it is now debatable whether language aptitude is an invariant characteristic 'and relatively hard to modify in any significant way' as Carroll (1981: 86) has suggested or whether it can be improved through instruction in language learning strategies (O'Malley & Chamot, 1990; Oxford, 1990). In any case, Lightbown and Spada (1993: 54) support that knowing the strengths and weaknesses of learners can help teachers 'ensure that their teaching activities are sufficiently varied to accommodate learners with different aptitude profiles'.

Since the linguistic abilities of young learners are not fully formed and are still developing, this aptitude is unlikely to be exactly the same language specific cognitive aptitudes which Carroll identifies. It seems more likely that aptitude in young children is related to far more basic and general cognitive abilities. It is not yet clear exactly what these skills are, or how many there are, but there is definitely a rising interest in researching this area.

The Study on Greek Learners' Aptitude

Developing a test battery for young learners

During 2001–2004 a series of young learner aptitude tests were conducted to identify qualities which will indicate or predict language learning success in very young learners, and which can then be tied back to a theory of language learning and language processing. In total, 220 learners were tested and the data are all taken from different schools in the city of Thessaloniki, Greece; some are public nursery schools, some private nursery schools and some private English Language schools.

For the present paper, data from 191, five- to nine-year-olds are discussed. The tests are done on a one-to-one basis. The whole test is run in Greek, because of the age of the learners these tend to be games rather than formal testing tasks. In designing these tests, existing tests of aptitude such as Carroll and Sapon's (1958a) MLAT have been taken into account and also cognitive tests drawn from the psychology literature and other less known work, for example, that of Esser and Kossling (1986) linking aptitude to general cognitive abilities.

Children's cognitive dexterities were tested twice per year, first in January where cognitive skills were examined and then in June along with an English vocabulary test (in a game form) to enable comparisons and correlations. Because the nature of language teaching at this age, which is not designed to stretch the most able learners and separate them from slow, medium or fast speed learners, moderate correlations were expected. It is suggested that anything around $r = 0.4$–0.5 level which Carroll obtained comparing MLAT with language progress test, would be satisfactory as is the sort of correlation that most tests produce over long stretches of language learning (Carroll & Sapon, 1958b).

Nature of aptitude in young learners

After a series of five tests, a CD ROM was devised that included the cognitive skills that appear to influence foreign language learning. These skills were presented in a game format for young learners to play and the tasks were getting progressively more difficult. In the sections below, all these tasks that formed the sixth experiment will be described and as they have yielded satisfactory correlations, the separate elements of cognitive ability that may be part of language learning aptitude in young learners are revealed. Some possible explanations on the reasons these abilities predict the way they do will also be attempted. In agreement with Skehan's (1989) suggestions, aptitude in young learners was expected to consist of a set of memory, analytic and phonetic skills.

Memory components that influence foreign language learning

Memory has not been regarded as a unitary entity. Several kinds of memories have been tested yet not all of them proved to be relevant to language learning. Memory is divided in three major stages: encoding, storage and recall, namely immediate and active retrieval of information stored (Glassman, 2001: 159). The tasks involved mostly recall and recognition forms of memory. What is more interesting is that 'recall and recognition are both examples of explicit memory and that the subject is unaware of having, is implicit' (Groome *et al.*, 1999: 125).

Based on the results obtained in a series of studies, certain memory types appear to facilitate language learning. These are as follows.

Short term immediate memory for pictures

This is the well known Kim's game. It is a rote learning game and the fact that scores on this exercise correlate significantly with language learning success indicates that learners with strong short term memory have an advantage over those with weaker memory especially, it might be thought, when it comes to learning new words in a foreign language (Milton & Alexiou, 2006a).

Associative short term memory (pictures-shapes)

In the paired associates different picture cards and a matched set of various shape-like figures are shown to the child. The figures are then mixed up and the child is asked to match them with the correct picture card. The aim is to measure the capacity to retain sign pairs as conclusions about the capacity to retain foreign language vocabulary can be drawn according to Esser and Kossling (1986).

Memory is an area of potential interest, especially its development in the early years; however, it proved that paired associative memory is the one factor that impacts more strongly language achievement. This is not a surprising result, bearing in mind Carroll's studies and the fact that language learning includes a certain relabelling of things, words, and so on (Aitchison, 1987).

Semantic integration

In this game the children are given a learning list of four shapes to memorise for 30 seconds (see Figure 4.1). The learning list is then taken away and replaced by a recognition list of six shapes. The children are asked:

- to recall the shapes from the learning list that are present;
- to identify the shapes which are new in the second list;
- to identify the shapes from the learning list that are missing from the recognition list.

This test is a semantic integration task (Esser & Kossling, 1986). The recoding ability which is measured here, according to recent literature serves to increase storage capacity and this has a benefit to language learners. It can be argued that this quality, the ability to recognise the presence or absence of significant information might be associated with the capacity to learn language features such as word endings.

The task of semantic integration is a clear example of recognition memory, which Carroll (1979: 19) regards as a special form of recall. This form

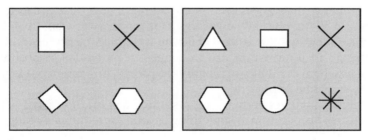

Figure 4.1   Learning and recognition tasks

of memory (recognition) appears to be relevant to young learners' language learning. Groome *et al.* (1999: 122) have maintained that recognition is even superior to recall, as it offers 'more feature overlap between input and output and recognition is seen as one of the sub process to recall'.

Analytic tasks that facilitate foreign language learning

There seem to be certain analytic skills that facilitate, affect or give an advantage to young foreign language learners. These are as follows.

Inductive learning ability (or artificial language, according to Esser & Kossling, 1986)

This test is presented as a game. There are colours that represent particular group. More specifically, at the beginning, it is explained to the child that it is important to remember that red represents all animals while blue represents all flowers. When the game is sufficiently explained, picture cards on the screen appear and the child has to drag the object (rose, tiger, etc.) to the appropriate colour. The test gets progressively more difficult as more colours and groups are demonstrated (i.e. yellow for food, green for drinks, purple for clothes, orange for means of transport). This is an analytic task of inductive learning ability where learners need to discover and apply new rules in the same way foreign grammatical rules work (Carroll, 1981; Esser & Kossling, 1986).

Inductive learning ability has proved to relate to language learning and possibly affects organising in the mind parts of speech and grammar inference rules as well as thematic concepts of words. As Cameron (2001) proposes, if simple categorisation is responsible for certain metalinguistic abilities then it would be reasonable to suggest that combined with inductive learning ability the results would probably be even more remarkable.

Visual perception (spot the difference)

This is a spot-the-difference game. Two similar pictures are shown to children and they are asked to find the differences between them. There are a number of differences such as the colour of objects, the placement of objects and in the objects themselves. It is an analytic visual perception task which identifies the testees' ability to recognise the presence, absence or a change in information. It can suggest a particular disposition for languages where the ability to identify the presence or absence of language features would be important.

Perceiving involves recognising a stimulus as in differences between two pictures. Recognition of something as familiar requires making use of memory (a cognitive process) that is not required, so it is a clear analytic task requiring acute sensory stimuli (Alexiou, 2005).

Reasoning ability (story sequencing)

In a story sequencing task, four jumbled pictures are shown and the child is asked to put the pictures in order to tell a story that makes sense (see Figure 4.2). The aim here is to measure reasoning ability with the aid of situational clues that resembles cloze tests or gap filling tasks in EFL. This is obviously an analytic task requiring both perceptual and conceptual skills. It requires an inductive reasoning ability, as there is no immediate rule but the child has to imagine logical rules to create the story and see the 'whole picture' from the parts. This is a task of analogical reasoning, as learners are tested on

> whether they can use relational reasoning to solve analogies (transfer appropriate knowledge from the familiar problem to the novel one). Related questions have been how early children are able to make relational mappings, and whether children can map relational similarities in the absence of surface similarities. (e.g. Gentner, 1989 cited in Goswami, 1998: 222–223)

Figure 4.2 Story sequencing task

Spatial ability (jigsaw puzzles)

This is a jigsaw puzzle in which certain pieces are missing and we can see them here. The children have to visualise these pieces and say which piece goes where in order to get the final picture (see Figure 4.3).

Even though this game tests a visual ability which may seem remote from language learning, it may require an ability in certain processing tasks which are essential to language use, such as analysis by synthesis. The better one is able to make sense of the limited information available,

Figure 4.3   Jigsaw puzzle task

the better he or she will be at language use, especially in foreign language where learners routinely have to make do with incomplete knowledge.

As Larsen-Freeman and Long (1991: 193) hypothesised, the perceptual challenge of the task is to be able to 'break up the visual field and keep part of it separate. This challenge was hypothesised to be analogous to a person learning a second language who has to isolate an element from the context in which it is presented'.

Results

Relationships between cognitive skills and vocabulary in English

As mentioned before, learners were tested not only on these tasks but their knowledge of vocabulary was also tested in English with the help of two vocabulary tests. Receptive vocabulary was tested when several objects would appear on the screen and the researcher asked the learner to point to the ones she was naming. Productive vocabulary was then tested with a different slide of objects and the learners naming as many as they could. The vocabulary included words that young learners were instructed through the academic year.

The relationships between children's scores on these cognitive tasks and on two tests of vocabulary (receptive and productive) were found

Table 4.1 Correlations between cognitive skills and language scores

Cognitive skills	Receptive vocabulary	Productive vocabulary	Language total
Short term memory	0.330[a]	0.381[a]	0.370[a]
Associative memory	0.530[a]	0.524[a]	0.548[a]
Semantic integration	0.413[a]	0.386[a]	0.416[a]
Visual perception	0.557[a]	0.557[a]	0.579[a]
Spatial ability	0.435[a]	0.368[a]	0.418[a]
Inductive ability	0.397[a]	0.351[a]	0.389[a]
Reasoning ability	0.447[a]	0.427[a]	0.455[a]
Cognitive total	0.649[a]	0.621[a]	0.660[a]

[a]Significant at 0.01 level

statistically significant; correlations ranged between 0.33 and 0.47. Table 4.1 shows the correlations between the cognitive skills tested and English language tests at the end of the term. As can be seen, very satisfactory correlations are yielded, higher than expected and the fact that the cognitive total scores offer a correlation as high as $r = 0.6$ further verifies that these cognitive qualities are closely related to aspects of language achievement.

Phonological aspects

There was also an attempt to test phonological skills, namely, phonetic repetition and distinction and recall between non-words. In the phonetic repetition task, the learner was asked to repeat a specific set of five nonwords. In the phonetic discrimination task, the learner was asked whether two non-words sounded exactly the same. In the phonetic recall task, the researcher pronounced a set of non-words and the learner was asked to recall if he/she had heard any of these non-words during the previous two parts. The aim in this series of tests is to measure the ability to accurately repeat, distinguish and recall phonetic sounds as this is vital in language learning and more specifically vocabulary learning.

Phonological aspects were tested only once for reasons of time and was rather a pilot study with small number of testing items for each subskill; however, they did give a significant correlation of 0.4. Cheung (1996) and Service and Kohonen (1995) in two studies had showed that phonological memory (pseudo word repetition) was important for learning foreign language vocabulary (cited in Sparks & Ganschow, 2001: 99), a fact that is confirmed in this study as well.

Although the study has not been replicated to support the validity and reliability of this type of test, it initially shows that Gathercole *et al.*'s (1992: 888) suggestion that there are developmental associations between short term phonological memory skills and vocabulary acquisition are not far from the truth. Their findings lead them to conclude that phonological memory (recall, to be more specific) contributes critically to the long term learning of new words. The studies here lend credence also to several other studies that link phonological memory achievements to children with language problems or poor linguistic ability (Adams & Gathercole, 1996; Gathercole & Baddeley, 1990; Raine *et al.*, 1992 all cited in Groome *et al.*, 1999: 102) or future language ability (Reynolds, 2002: 3). In addition, the results tie well with Skehan's (1989) findings where the capacity to remember material of unfamiliar phonemic structure and to be able to make meaningful analyses of material to be remembered appear to be distinct and important predictors of language learning success. Table 4.2 shows the correlations yielded in this pilot study. The results show reasonable and statistically significant correlations between phonological skills and vocabulary knowledge in a foreign language, which supports the idea that phonological ability is a contributor to aptitude. Table 4.2 shows the correlations that were found between phonetic skills and foreign language scores.

These findings might be particularly relevant to very young learners who will not have an orthographic system through which to mediate the second language. Recent observations (Milton & Hopkins, 2007; Milton & Riordan, 2006) support that while learners favour phonological vocabulary at the outset of learning, that is to say, they learn words by sound only, orthographic recognition vocabulary very quickly exceeds phonological vocabulary and a feature of just about all academically successful foreign language learners is that they have very large sight only vocabularies. This suggests that learners are predisposed in learning to acquire the sound form of words at the outset of learning and only later add knowledge of written forms.

Table 4.2 Correlations between phonetic skills and language scores

Phonetic skills	*Receptive vocabulary*	*Productive vocabulary*	*Language total*
Phonetic repetition	0.117	0.124	0.125
Phonetic discrimination	0.467[a]	0.383[a]	0.443[a]
Phonetic recall	0.359[a]	0.334[a]	0.360[a]
Phonetic total	0.442[a]	0.393[a]	0.434[a]

[a]Significant at 0.01 level

Discussion

The approach to aptitude relating to cognitive skills lends support to Stern's (1983 cited in Spolsky, 1989: 104) claim that language aptitude is 'not a single factor but a cluster of specific abilities'. These abilities appear to interact in logical ways and with certain kinds of exposure and methodology. With these in mind, several suggestions come to light.

Aptitude here has been seen as a set of cognitive abilities and a multi-component notion. As cognitive skills develop with age, aptitude appears to progress, therefore aptitude is not fixed at least at that early age. On the other hand, other studies suggest that not all cognitive skills develop with age in this way and this is particularly the case with at least one of the elements which we might expect to associate with language learning aptitude, that of memory. Gathercole *et al.* (1992) suggest that memory skills may actually decrease with age. As memory diminishes with time, analytic skills increase. The idea implied is that as the information and storage load increases with age so the abilities you need to cope with this increase also change. Good memory is not a good way of handling very large amounts of information. It must be organised; hence the growing importance of these analytic skills which provide the basis for effective organisation (Milton & Alexiou, 2006a).

It might be possible that aptitude becomes fixed after a certain period of time, where cognitive skills have reached their peak or at the point when children become cognitively mature. If this is the case, the issue of 'plasticity' becomes important. If aptitude is a flux of changes at least in the early stages of life, it is implied that certain weaknesses might be alleviated if appropriate instruction and training takes place. Singleton (2002) proposed that since cognitive abilities are measurable in children before they begin formal literacy, it becomes possible to anticipate which of them are likely to struggle before they fail. If, through aptitude testing, cognitive skills are revealed that facilitate aspects of second language learning, the possibilities of success rise. Teachers can then select appropriate materials and techniques that best fit the child's cognitive profile.

Not all children acquire language in the same way and the different approaches they follow in acquiring a language can offer clues to how language develops. In order to maximise learners' potential for success, therefore, aptitude can be considered as a language development indicator offering ideas of alternative language instruction to match and enhance learners' aptitude profiles.

Consequently, certain abilities or learning difficulties might be revealed in advance for appropriate instruction and remedial action. It would be interesting to see whether trainability on aptitude has any effect, as other researchers have suggested (Politzer & Weiss, 1969; Robinson, 2002; Skehan, 2002), at this age. Teachers can then alleviate weaknesses and play with the learners' strengths. Apparently, the concept of learners' trainability is evident in many studies (Chase & Ericsson, 1996; Humes-Bartlo, 1989; Lange & Pierce, 1992; Vecchi *et al.*, 2001).

If one considers the cognitive abilities found important in this study, it is clear that they relate to certain task types. Memory, semantic integration, visual perception skills are related to visual task types. Spatial and reasoning skills relate to kinaesthetic task types while phonetic skills fall into auditory task types. Therefore, an interesting path to follow would be to investigate the relationship between aptitude and learning styles in young learners.

Conclusion

Carroll first introduced the idea that aptitude has several elements, and that these elements are special linguistic cognitive skills. It seems that Esser and Kossling took this idea a step further by suggesting that aptitude should be viewed as a set of general cognitive skills that influence acquisition. The cognitive approach used in the study discussed in this paper is also largely affected by Skehan's perceptions on the three-component view of aptitude, namely memory, analytic and phonetic abilities.

A standardised test of cognitive skills that appear to facilitate foreign language learning would offer a valuable source for a child's learning profile at the very beginning of learning. The notion that one can train enhanced language learning ability in youth would be supported by both a whole series of case studies (e.g. Milton, 2001; Stevick, 1989) where really good language learners appear to be early and serial learners. This test designed in a game format can be a promising tool to provide information on learning styles and preferences as well as on particular strengths and weaknesses to be handled. Connected to this point, cognitive tests of aptitude can be a useful resource that will offer clues to the teachers when developing the curriculum and adopting teaching strategies that meet individual needs and are in agreement to learning styles. Learning styles in that sense should be viewed 'as aspects of language at which children excel rather than as styles for different types of children' (Shore, 1995: 2).

Questions for further study have also emerged. It would useful to examine how aptitude is related to learning styles, what other cognitive skills might facilitate language learning, and what sort of tasks should we include in our teaching and course books. These are interesting questions which, like much of the subject of aptitude and learning styles at young ages, require considerable further research before any firm conclusions can be drawn.

Acknowledgements

The author warmly acknowledges the help of Marina Matthaioudakis for her constant support and invaluable help. The author also acknowledges her gratitude to James Milton, for his continuous guidance as well as his constructive comments in this chapter.

References

Aitchison, J. (1987) *Words in Mind*. Oxford: Blackwell.

Alexiou, T. (2005) Cognitive development, aptitude and language learning in Greek young learners. Unpublished PhD thesis, Swansea.

Anderson, J.R. (2000) *Cognitive Psychology and Its Implications* (5th edn). New York: Worth.

Cameron, L. (2001) *Teaching Languages to Young Learners*. Cambridge: Cambridge University Press.

Carroll, J.B. (1979) Psychometric approaches to the study of language abilities. In C.J. Fillmore, D. Kempler and W.S-Y. Wang (eds) *Individual Differences in Language Ability and Language Behaviour*. New York: Academic Press.

Carroll, J.B. (1981) Twenty five years of research on foreign language learning aptitude. In K.C. Diller (ed.) *Individual Differences and Universals in Language Learning Aptitude* (pp. 83–118). Rowley: Newbury House.

Carroll, J.B. and Sapon, S.M. (1958) *Modern Language Aptitude Test, Form A*. New York: The Psychological Corporation.

Carroll, J.B. and Sapon, S.M. (1958b) *Modern Language Aptitude Test; Manual*. New York: The Psychological Corporation.

Chase, W.G. and Ericsson, A.K. (1996) Skilled memory. In M.J. Brosnan (ed.) *Cognitive Processes: Readings in Visual Cognition, Attention and Memory*. Kent: Greenwich University Press.

Cheung, H. (1996) Non-word span as a unique predictor of second-language vocabulary learning. *Developmental Psychology* 12, 867–873.

Esser, U. and Kossling, B. (1986) A general psychological approach to the diagnosis of foreign language aptitude. In V. Cook (ed.) *Experimental Approaches to Second Language Learning* (pp. 95–100). Oxford: Pergamon.

Gathercole, S.E., Willis, C.S., Emslie, H. and Baddeley A.D. (1992) Phonological memory and vocabulary development during the early school years: A longitudinal study. *Developmental Psychology* 28 (5), 887–898.

Glassman, W.E. (2001) *Approaches to Psychology* (3rd edn). Buckingham-Philadelphia: Open University Press.

Goswami, U. (1998) *Cognition in Children, Developmental Psychology, A Modular Course*. Sussex: Psychology Press.

Groome, D., Dewart, H., Esgate, A., Gurney, K., Kemp, R. and Towell, N. (1999) *An Introduction to Cognitive Psychology*. London: Psychology Press.

Humes-Bartlo, M. (1989) Variation in children's ability to learn second languages. In K. Hyltenstam and L.K. Obler (eds) *Bilingualism Across the Lifespan, Aspects of Acquisition, Maturity and Loss*. Cambridge: Cambridge University Press.

Lange, G. and Pierce, S.H. (1992) Memory-strategy learning and maintenance in preschool children. *Developmental Psychology* 28 (3), 453–462.

Larsen-Freeman, D. and Long, M.H. (1991) *An Introduction to Second Language Acquisition Research*. Essex: Longman.

Lightbown P. and Spada, N. (1993) *How Languages are Learned*. Oxford: Oxford University Press.

McDonough, S. (1981) *Psychology in Foreign Language Teaching*. London: Routledge.

Milton, J. (2001) The lessons of excellence: Sir Richard Burton and language learning. *The Linguist* 40 (5), 135–139.

Milton, J. and Alexiou, T. (2004) Reconsidering language learning aptitude with young learners in mind. In E. Kitis (ed.) *Working Papers in Linguistics (WPL)*. Thessaloniki: Aristotle University.

Milton, J. and Alexiou, T. (2006a) Language aptitude development in young learners. In C. Abello-Contesse, R. Chacón-Beltrán, M. Dolores López-Jiménez and M. Mar Torreblanca-López (eds) *The Age Factor in L2 Acquisition and Teaching* (pp. 177–192). Switzerland: Peter Lang Publishers.

Milton, J. and Alexiou, T. (2006b) What makes a young good language learner? Selection of papers for the 13th International Conference of Applied Linguistics. In A. Kavadia, M. Joannopoulou and A. Tsangalidis (eds) *New Directions in Applied Linguistics*. Thessaloniki: Aristotle University.

Milton, J. and Hopkins, N. (2007) Comparing phonological and orthographic vocabulary size. *Canadian Modern Language Review* 63 (1), 127–147.

Milton, J. and Riordan, O. (2006) Level and script effects in the phonological and orthographic vocabulary size of Arabic and Farsi speakers. In P. Davidson, C. Coombe, D. Lloyd and D. Palfreyman (eds) *Teaching and Learning Vocabulary in Another Language* (pp. 122–133). UAE: TESOL Arabia.

O'Malley, J.M. and Chamot, A.U. (1990) *Learning Strategies in Second Language Acquisition*. Cambridge: Cambridge University Press.

Oxford, R. (1990) Styles, strategies, and aptitude: Connections for language learning. In T. Parry and C. Stansfield (eds) *Language Aptitude Reconsidered* (pp. 67–125). New Jersey: Center For Applied Linguistics & Prentice Hall.

Pimsleur, P. (1968) Language aptitude testing. In A. Davies (ed.) *Language Aptitude Testing: A Psycholinguistic Approach*. Oxford: Oxord University Press.

Politzer, R.L. and Weiss, L. (1969) *An Experiment in Improving Achievement in Foreign Language Learning Through Learning of Selected Skills Associated with Language Aptitude*. Stanford: Stanford University (Eric Document Reproduction Service, ED 046 261).

Reynolds, B. (2002) Phonetic coding in language aptitude: Different roles for different languages. On WWW at http://owls.tuj.ac.jp/tesol/press/papers0014/renyolds.html. Accessed 31.1.02.

Robinson, P. (ed.) (2002) *Individual Differences and Instructed Language Learning*. Amsterdam: John Benjamins.

Service, E. and Kohonen, V. (1995) Is the relation between phonological memory and foreign language learning accounted for by vocabulary acquisition? *Applied Psycholinguistics* 16, 155–172.

Shore, C.M. (1995) *Individual Differences in Language Development*. London: SAGE Publications.

Singleton, C. (2002) Dyslexia: Cognitive factors and implications for literacy. In G. Reid and J. Wearmouth (eds) *Dyslexia and Literacy: Research and Practice*. London: John Wiley & Sons.

Skehan, P. (1989) *Individual Differences in Second-Language Learning*. London: Edward Arnold.

Skehan, P. (2002) Theorising and updating aptitude. In P. Robinson (ed.) *Individual Differences and Instructed Language Learning* (pp. 69–94). Amsterdam: John Benjamins.

Sparks, R. and Ganschow, L. (2001) Aptitude for learning a foreign language. *Annual Review of Applied Linguistics* 21, 90–111.

Spolsky, B. (1989) *Conditions for Second Language Learning*. Oxford: Oxford University Press.

Stevick, E. (1989) *Success with Foreign Languages: Seven Who Achieved it and What Worked for Them*. New York: Prentice Hall.

Vecchi, T., Phillips, L.H. and Cornoldi, C. (2001) Individual differences in visuo-spatial working memory. In M. Denis, R.H. Logie, C. Cornoldi, M. De Vega and J. Engelkamp (eds) *Imagery, Language and Visuo-Spatial Thinking* (pp. 29–51). Sussex: Psychology Press.

Wesche, M.B. (1981) Language aptitude measures in streaming, matching students with methods and diagnosis of learning problems. In K.C. Diller (ed.) *Individual Differences and Universals in Language Learning Aptitude* (pp. 119–155). Rowley: Newbury House.

Chapter 5

An Investigation into the Relationship of L2 Motivation and Cross-cultural Contact Among Elementary School Students[1]

KATA CSIZÉR and JUDIT KORMOS

Introduction

In this chapter we report the results of a nationwide representative survey conducted with 1777 Hungarian primary-school children aged between 13 and 14 studying English and German. We investigated the differences in the motivational and intercultural contact measures as well as their relationship with motivated behaviour. Our results indicate that students of English have more positive attitudes towards the native speakers of the language they study than learners of German, and children who study English have higher level of linguistic self-confidence, invest more energy into language learning and receive more support from their environment than students of German. Learners in general, however, showed low expectancy of success in acquiring an L2, and they did not report investing substantial effort into language learning. The findings also reveal that learners of English experience more frequent direct written contact and contact through media products than learners of German. Integrativeness, linguistic self-confidence and perceived importance of intercultural contact were found to be closely related to how much effort students are willing to invest into foreign language learning. For children with low levels of motivation, however, it was primarily contact experience and in the case of English, instrumentality that influenced motivational intensity.

It is widely assumed in language pedagogy and second language acquisition research that language-related attitudes and motivated behaviour play a highly important role in second and foreign language (L2) learning. Since the question what drives language learning behaviour has great pedagogical relevance, it is no wonder that studies on the relationship of language attitude, motivation and L2 competence are abundant (for a review see Dörnyei, 2001, 2005). For a long time, motivation researchers sought to establish a model of language learning motivation that is relevant and applicable to every situation and for every type of learner (e.g. Dörnyei & Ottó, 1998; Gardner, 1985, 2001; Noels, 2001). In the past few years, however, a number of studies (e.g. Kormos & Csizér, 2008; Lamb, 2004; Yashima, 2000) have pointed out that different motivational characteristics might be meaningful for students of various ages and in different geographical settings. Moreover, depending on the learning situation and learners' age, motivational variables might interact in different ways. It is not only geographical, instructional and age characteristics that will produce different models of language learning motivation, but most likely the language being studied also influences the constellation of motivational variables especially if intercultural contact is also taken into consideration.

Intercultural contact is an important issue in second language acquisition for several reasons. First of all, one of the main aims of learning second and foreign languages is to be able to communicate with members of other cultures who do not speak one's mother tongue. In addition, interaction with speakers of other languages creates opportunities for developing L2 learners' language competence [see e.g. Swain's (1985) output hypothesis]. The learners' experience of these encounters can influence both their disposition towards the target language and their attitude to L2 speakers and the L2 culture. Intercultural contact can also be assumed to affect L2 learners' motivated behaviour, that is, the energy and effort they are willing to put into L2 learning. Therefore, as Dörnyei and Csizér (2005: 2) pointed out, 'intercultural contact is both a means and an end in L2 studies'.

General characteristics of the language learning motivation of Hungarian elementary school children have been extensively studied in Hungary in the past 15 years. From Dörnyei *et al.*'s (2006) summary of the series of quantitative studies they conducted, it becomes apparent that English is the most popular foreign language among Hungarian teenagers, and German still maintains its second position as a regionally important language. The findings of their study also reveal that integrativeness, that is, students' wish to become similar to native speakers, was the most important factor contributing to learners' motivated behaviour. Instrumentality and attitudes to native speakers indirectly influenced the effort students were willing to invest into language learning through the mediation of integrativeness. Nikolov's (1999) study concluded that elementary school children are mainly motivated by factors associated with the classroom situation (i.e. positive attitudes towards the learning context and the teacher as well as intrinsically motivating activities, tasks and materials).

Based on our interview study with highly motivated learners of English and German (Kormos & Csizér, 2007), we hypothesised that for students who are willing to put more energy into language learning, intercultural contact experiences might play a different role than for learners with lower levels of motivational intensity. In our study we investigated one of the largest groups of Hungarian language learners: primary school students who studied the two most popular foreign languages in Hungary: English and German (Halász & Lannert, 2004). In our representative questionnaire survey conducted with children aged between 13 and 14, we addressed the following questions that have not yet been studied in a Hungarian context:

(1) What are the differences in the motivational and intercultural contact measures between learners of English and German?
(2) How do the correlations among the motivational and contact variables vary for students of English and German with different levels of motivational intensity?

The comparison of learners of English and German is expected to yield pedagogically relevant results not only in Hungary but also for the Central-European region where despite its decreasing significance, German is still a regionally important language (Clyne, 1998) and English is gaining an increasingly important role as a lingua franca (James, 2000).

Method

Participants

The participants of the survey were 1777 students of English and German, with 58% studying English and 38% German. Four percent of students, all of whose first foreign language was German, studied both languages at the time of the data collection. Participants were all between the ages of 13 and 14 and attended the final, eighth grade of the primary school system and studied within a homogenous curricular and organisational framework (i.e. the national primary school system). The sampling followed a stratified approach, and we selected students evenly from each main region and type of settlement in Hungary.

Instrument

The questionnaire was specifically designed for the purpose of this survey and consisted of 71 items, out of which 45 were used in this study. Apart from eight open-ended questions at the end of the questionnaire inquiring about students' foreign language learning background, all items used a five-point rating scale. The items for this questionnaire came from two sources.

First, some questions were drawn from the questionnaire used in the survey reported in Dörnyei *et al.* (2006). Other questions were designed based on the results of Kormos and Csizér's (2007) interview study, which investigated the contact experiences of the same age group using a qualitative approach. The first version of the questionnaire was piloted with three students from the target group using the think-aloud technique. The questionnaire was then revised and administered to 100 students prior to the main study as a pilot. Based on the statistical analyses of this pilot-run, the questionnaire was finalised.

The main variable groups in the questionnaire were as follows, with the total number of items given in parentheses.

Items concerning the target languages (German and English)

- *Integrative motivation*, that is, the attitudes students display towards the L2 and its speakers and their cultures (3 items).
- *Instrumental motivation*, that is, to what extent students attach pragmatic values to the learning of the language (6 items).

Items concerning the direct and indirect aspect of cross-cultural contact

- *Direct spoken contact* both in the target language country and in Hungary (5 items).
- *Direct written contact*, snail mail and e-mails as well as chatting (3 items).
- *Indirect contact*, that is, seeing foreigners but not talking to them and receiving information on them from others (4 items).
- *Media usage* (e.g. watching L2 TV programmes, films, reading magazines) (5 items).

Items measuring other motivational variables

- *Linguistic self-confidence* in L2 learning and use (3 items).
- *Language learning milieu*, that is, the extent of the parents' support (1 item) and the friends' attitudes toward L2 learning (1 item).
- *Perceived importance of contact*, why students find it important to be involved in cross-cultural contact situations (8 items).
- *Motivated learning behaviour*, that is, how much effort learners invest into L2 learning, how persistent they see themselves as language learners, and the enjoyment students derive from L2 learning (7 items).

Data collection

Data collection for this study followed the established routes of earlier similar studies conducted in Hungary by the authors. We first approached the selected schools by an official letter from Eötvös University, Budapest (which hosted the project), providing information about the purpose of the survey and details of the actual administration of the questionnaires. Once permission was granted by the principal of the school, we contacted the class teachers of the selected classes individually, asking for their cooperation. The questionnaires were filled in during class time, with a representative of the university always present to provide the introduction and oversee the procedure. Answering the questions took the students approximately 20 minutes on average.

Data analysis

All the questionnaires were computer-coded and the SPSS (Statistical Package for Social Sciences) 13.0 was used for analysing the data. The answers to the questionnaires were first submitted to factor analysis and multidimensional scaling. Next descriptive statistics were computed for investigating the significant differences between various learner groups. In order to differentiate between students with higher and lower levels of motivation, cluster analysis was employed. First, hierarchical clustering was carried out on a smaller subsample of the students – in our case a 5% random subsample was selected for this purpose. Based on this first step, the number of clusters and their positions (i.e. the initial cluster centres) were defined and subsequently nonhierarchical clustering was run on the whole sample by inputting the cluster centres received previously. The procedure of nonhierarchical clustering was iterated until stable cluster centres were received. We also used correlational analyses to investigate to what extent specific variables contribute to the variance in the dependent variable of motivated behaviour.

Results and Discussion

The comparative analysis of the motivational and contact scales

In order to identify broader dimensions underlying the attitudinal/ motivational variables measured by the questionnaire, we submitted the items to factor analysis (conducting separate analyses for both languages) using the principle component method. Based on the results, we can conclude that students' motivational profile can be described by a four-factor solution, which includes integrative motivation, instrumental motivation, linguistic self-confidence and milieu as latent dimensions. As for intercultural contact, five dimensions were identified: direct spoken and written contact, indirect contact, foreign media usage and the perceived importance of contact. Items concerning the different aspects of students' learning behaviour formed one dimension, which was named motivated learning behaviour and served as the criterion measure of the study. Next, the results of the factor analysis were transformed into multi-item scales, and the Cronbach Alpha internal consistency reliability coefficients were computed (Table 5.1). The mean reliability coefficient of the scales was 0.71, which was acceptable for such short scales.

In terms of the language-related scales, that is, integrative motivation and instrumental motivation, it is not surprising that learners of the given

Table 5.1 Cronbach alpha internal reliability coefficients and descriptive information about the scales comparing students of English and German

| | *Cr. αᵃ* | *Learners of English (n = 1025)* | | *Learners of German (n = 660)* | | |
		Mean	*St. dev.*	*Mean*	*St. dev.*	*t-value*
Motivational scales						
Integrative motivation: English	0.76	3.50	0.91	3.31	0.90	4.16***
Integrative motivation: German	0.79	2.56	0.93	3.12	0.88	−12.34***
t-Value		28.44***		32.29***		
Instrumental motivation: English	0.71	4.39	0.54	4.23	0.62	0.567***
Instrumental motivation: German	0.79	3.56	0.81	3.98	0.59	−12.30***
t-Value		4.90***		9.70***		
Milieu	0.63	4.36	0.70	4.28	0.73	0.236*
Self-confidence	0.64	3.22	0.81	3.06	0.70	0.397***
Contact scales						
Direct spoken contact	0.77	1.95	0.79	1.92	0.72	0.92
Direct written contact	0.72	1.65	0.86	1.45	0.69	0.499***
Indirect contact	0.63	2.84	0.79	2.76	0.82	1.88
Foreign media contact	0.69	2.47	0.80	2.26	0.72	0.543***
Perceived importance of contact	0.53	3.24	0.86	3.15	0.87	1.94
Criterion measure						
Motivated learning behavior	0.74	3.08	0.97	2.90	0.96	0.361***

*p < 0.05; **p < 0.01; ***p < 0.001
ᵃCr. α = Cronbach Alpha internal consistency reliability coefficient

language scored higher on both scales than students who do not learn the foreign language. It has been documented in earlier Hungarian studies (Dörnyei *et al.*, 2006) that the mere fact that students are engaged in the study of an L2 enhances their attitudes towards the particular language. In this respect, our study confirms that the instruction of a given foreign language has a positive effect on students' motivational orientation. The fact that the scale measuring instrumental motivation received higher endorsement from students than integrative motivation indicates that Hungarian students, even at a relatively young age, are well aware of the possible pragmatic benefits the knowledge of a foreign language might offer in the European context, although the predictive value of instrumentality on learning behaviour could not be verified (Csizér & Kormos, 2008). We can also observe that our participants show lower levels of willingness to identify themselves with target language speakers and their cultures than in a study of a similar learner population in 2004 (Dörnyei *et al.*, 2006). This finding indicates the tendency documented in a number of other studies in various parts of the world (Lamb, 2004; Yashima, 2000) that the English language has become dissociated from its native speakers and acts as a lingua franca, which is used in communication across different cultures.

If we compare attitude scales for German and English, we can see that learners of German scored higher on the English-related scales than on the scales measuring the language they are learning, that is, German. In other words, despite the fact that students study German, they have more positive attitudes towards English than German, whereas learners of English score considerably lower on German-related scales than on English-related ones. The positive attitudes towards English as a global language at the expense of German, regionally a highly important language in Hungary, reinforce our previous results about the leading role English plays in Hungary (Dörnyei *et al.*, 2006). These results are also reiterated by students' scores concerning the environmental support they receive (milieu), linguistic self-confidence and motivated learning behaviour. On each of these scales learners of English outperform students of German: learners of English are willing to put more effort into language learning, are more self-confident about their use of the foreign language and receive more encouragement from their environment. This can be due to a number of factors. First of all, because many cultural products such as the internet, pop music, computer games are in English, this young generation is considerably more interested in studying English than in German. In addition, due to the shortage of elementary school teachers in English, children are often not granted a choice of languages to study. Therefore, it can happen that even though they would like to learn English, children are placed in a German class.

We can also observe that the investigated sample of students has relatively unfavourable motivational characteristics in terms of motivated behaviour and linguistic self-confidence, that is, they put modest effort into learning foreign languages and have a moderate level of expectation of success in learning foreign languages. These figures are especially low if we compare them to the motivational characteristics of Hungarian grammar school and university students (Kormos & Csizér, 2008). Our data in this regard probably reflect the generally low quality of foreign language instruction in Hungarian primary schools (see Nikolov, 2001a, 2001b).

Concerning the contact variables of the study, we see that both learners of English and German score higher on the perceived importance of contact scale (mean values of 3.24 and 3.15) than on any other contact-related scales, although the mean values indicate that students attach moderate importance to the role of intercultural contact in language learning. The results of the scales measuring different types of indirect contact all show mean values lower than average (expressed by value 3 in the mid-point of the scale). Based on our results, we might conclude that it seems that students rarely experience direct contact, as the mean values of both direct spoken and written contact are lower than 2, which is not unexpected in a foreign language environment. In other words, although students acknowledge that intercultural contact has some importance for success in language learning, the actual contact experiences involving the foreign language they study at school are rare in the primarily monolingual Hungarian society. Moreover, our data suggest that the Internet and other media-related indirect contact possibly experienced in a foreign language are not frequent among the investigated group of teenagers, although even this relatively low exposure to intercultural contact situations might affect students' motivated learning behaviour (for actual results see below).

As regards differences between students of English and German in terms of intercultural contact, we can conclude that out of the five scales, two show significantly different results for the two groups of learners: students of English have a higher level of direct written contact and media contact than participants who study German. Our results reveal a somewhat different picture from previous Hungarian studies (see Dörnyei *et al.*, 2006; Kormos & Csizér, 2007). In a previous qualitative study involving 40 successful and highly motivated learners of English and German (Kormos & Csizér, 2007), we claimed that tourism does not create many contact opportunities for the majority of students in this country; it is rather family resources and relations as well as school visits that play an important role in helping students experience intercultural contact. It seems, however, that if assessed on a national level neither family nor school resources provide enough opportunities for students to accumulate contact experiences to a large extent. In conclusion, when the direct and indirect levels of contact are measured on a national sample in Hungary involving a relatively young population, the results indicate that despite the rare experience of intercultural contacts, students attach considerable importance to these contact opportunities.

The relationship between the motivational and contact scales and the criterion measure within groups of learners with various levels of motivation

In our research we were also interested in the question how the different motivational and contact variables are related to motivated behaviour for groups with different levels of motivation. Table 5.2 presents correlations between the obtained scales and the criterion measure for three groups of students of English and German with various levels of motivation. These motivational groups were computed by submitting the motivational scales (integrativeness, instrumentality, self-confidence and milieu) to cluster analysis. As a result of the cluster analysis, we were able to define three distinct groups of learners for both English and German. The first group contains students with the lowest level of motivation,

Table 5.2 Correlations between the motivational/contact scales and motivated learning behaviour for English and German computed for learners with high, medium and low levels of motivation

	The level of L2 motivation					
	English			German		
	High (n = 340)	Medium (n = 466)	Low (n = 219)	High (n = 238)	Medium (n = 301)	Low (n = 120)
Integrativeness	0.15**	0.12**	0.21**	0.22**	0.05	0.25**
Instrumentality	0.08	0.07	0.14*	0.11	0.08	−0.08
Self-confidence	0.30**	0.21**	0.24**	0.22**	0.30**	0.30**
Milieu	0.20**	0.08	0.09	0.21**	0.06	0.17
Perceived importance of contact	0.18**	0.20**	0.38**	0.26**	0.24**	0.59**
Direct spoken contact	0.18**	0.17**	0.23**	0.11	0.21**	0.35**
Direct written contact	0.20**	0.18**	0.24**	0.21**	0.20**	0.32**
Indirect contact	0.24**	0.12**	0.19**	0.11	0.20**	0.39**
Foreign media usage	0.32**	0.17**	0.31**	0.27**	0.25**	0.25**
Multiple correlations (R)	0.49	0.38	0.48	0.43	0.43	0.66

*Correlation is significant at the 0.05 level
**Correlation is significant at the 0.01 level

self-confidence and environmental support. Students with a medium level of motivation were put into Group 2, while those students who were highly motivated and received a higher than average environmental support formed Group 3.

In terms of the motivational dimensions, self-confidence shows the most substantial positive correlations with motivated learning behaviour, and its role seems to be stable across all three groups for both languages. As for the contact scales, foreign media usage plays a central role. An interesting result is that whereas the correlational coefficients remain in a very similar range for the German-related groups (0.25–0.27), for learners of English, the strength of relationship fluctuates as it is more important for learners with high as well as low motivation, and the connection is weaker for learners with a medium level of motivation. This finding might indicate the disharmonious dispositions of students with a 'medium' level of motivation towards the English language and the limitations of their self-concepts as learners of foreign language. In other words, these learners might have positive attitudes to the L2 community and culture but might place little emphasis of the incentives of L2 proficiency or might be aware of the benefits of speaking a foreign language, but display negative attitude to the L2 and its speakers (see also Csizér & Dörnyei, 2005 as well as Dörnyei *et al.*, 2006). Perceived importance of contact also shows strong association with motivated behaviour, and its role seems to be more substantial for learners with lower levels of motivation. With the exception of foreign language media use, for all the other contact measures, we can observe a similar tendency, namely that with the decrease of the level of motivational intensity, the relationship between contact and motivated behaviour becomes stronger. This indicates that for students who have unfavourable motivational characteristics overall, the actual frequency of contact is related to how much effort they are willing to invest in studying either English or German. These students might be aware of their motivational limitations, or more pessimistically, school environment and/or teachers' discouragement might have created their demotivated state. This, however, is not reflected in their attitudes to intercultural contact, in other words, they are not demotivated because they do not see the intercultural importance of the given language. This issue is the most apparent for learners of German with the lowest level of motivation, as for them the multiple correlation coefficient (0.66), which expresses to what extent all the variables listed in the table predict motivated behaviour, is only marginally higher than the correlation between the perceived importance of contact and motivated learning behaviour (0.59). These figures indicate that students' perception of the importance of intercultural contact explains nearly as much variance as the multiple correlation coefficients for all scales and the criterion measure. Another interesting finding of our study is that the relationship between motivated behaviour and the environmental support students receive from their milieu is only significant for the group with the highest level of motivation.

Conclusion and Implications

In this chapter we reported the results of a nation-wide representative survey conducted with Hungarian primary school children studying English and German in which we investigated the differences in the motivational and intercultural contact measures as well as determinants of motivated behaviour between learners of English and German. Our results indicate that students of English have more positive attitudes towards the native speakers of the language they study than learners of German, and children who study English have a higher level of linguistic self-confidence, invest more energy into language learning and receive more support from their environment than children studying German. We have to note, however, that students in general showed low expectancy of success in acquiring an L2, and they did not report investing substantial effort into language learning. This might be due to the fact that even though students are aware of the instrumental benefits of speaking a foreign language, they still regard English and German as one of the compulsory school subjects. Since their level of competence is generally low at this age despite five to six years of instruction (Nikolov, 2001a, 2001b), they are not confident that they will ever be able to acquire a useable knowledge of the language.

Our findings also reveal that learners of English experience more frequent direct written contact and contact through media products than students of German, but the participants in general only rarely engage in direct intercultural encounters, and indirect contact is also infrequent. Participants were found to attach an average level of importance to the role of contact in language learning. Despite the fact that this result does not fully correspond to students' actual contact experiences, it shows that students are aware of the importance intercultural contact plays in the language learning process, which might help teachers to engage students in more contact situations within the school environment.

Our study also revealed that although integrativeness, linguistic self-confidence and perceived importance of intercultural contact are closely related to how much effort students are willing to invest in foreign language learning, for students with low levels of motivation it is primarily contact experience and in the case of English, instrumentality that influences motivational intensity. The findings also indicate that even though students' environment actively supports language learning, it only has an effect on motivated behaviour for students who are highly motivated.

Several pedagogical conclusions emerge from our study. First of all, given the motivational profiles of children studying German, it is highly important that every child and/or parent in every school should be given a chance to choose which language they study. Second, since Hungarian primary school students seem to be well aware of the instrumental benefits of learning foreign languages, have positive attitudes to native speakers and receive strong support from their environment, it is logical that the reason why students still do not invest sufficient energy into language learning is to be sought in the school environment. Students can only be expected to display sufficient level of motivation if they receive high quality instruction. The third implication of our study refers to increasing the motivational intensity of demotivated students. Whereas intercultural contact seems to play an important role in influencing the motivated behaviour for all the participants, it has the highest level of importance for students who have an unfavourable motivational profile. It seems that contact experiences might help these students to invest more energy into language learning. This finding indicates that teachers can play an important role in providing positive contact instances for students, for example, film clubs in schools might be organised, foreign visitors might be invited and intercultural e-mail or chat projects might be set up. These meaningful and hopefully successful contact experiences might enhance students' willingness to engage in more contact situations on their own. Even if a school cannot provide opportunities for these intercultural contact experiences, teachers can also raise students' awareness of the importance of intercultural contact in language learning, which might make students seek out situations for contact for themselves.

Acknowledgement

The research reported in this chapter was supported by the Research Funds of the Hungarian Academy of Sciences (OTKA T047111).

Note

1. An extended version of this chapter was accepted for publication in *Journal of Multilingual and Multicultural Development* with the title The relationship of intercultural contact and language learning motivation among Hungarian students of English and German.

References

Clyne, M. (1998) *The German Language in a Changing Europe*. Cambridge: Cambridge University Press.
Csizér, K. and Dörnyei, Z. (2005) Language learners' motivational profiles and their motivated learning behaviour. *Language Learning* 55, 623–669.
Csizér, K. and Kormos, J. (2008) The relationship of intercultural contact and language learning motivation among Hungarian students of English and German. *Journal of Multilingual and Multicultural Development* 29 (1), 30–48.
Dörnyei, Z. (2001) *Teaching and Researching Motivation*. London: Longman.
Dörnyei, Z. (2005) *The Psychology of the Language Learner: Individual Differences in Second Language Acquisition*. Mahwah, NJ: Lawrence Erlbaum.

Dörnyei, Z. and Csizér, K. (2005) The effects of intercultural contact and tourism on language attitudes and language learning motivation. *Journal of Language and Social Psychology* 24, 1–31.

Dörnyei, Z., Csizér, K. and Németh, N. (2006) *Motivational Dynamics, Language Attitudes and Language Globalisation: A Hungarian Perspective*. Clevedon: Multilingual Matters.

Dörnyei, Z. and Ottó, I. (1998) Motivation in action: A process model of L2 motivation. *Working Papers in Applied Linguistics (Thames Valley University, London)* 47, 173–210.

Gardner, R.C. (1985) *Social Psychology and Second Language Learning: The Role of Attitudes and Motivation*. London: Edward Arnold.

Gardner, R.C. (2001) Integrative motivation and second language acquisition. In Z. Dörnyei and R. Schmidt (eds) *Motivation and Second Language Acquisition* (pp. 1–19). (Technical Report #23). Honolulu, HI: University of Hawai'i, Second Language Teaching and Curriculum Center.

Halász, G. and Lannert, J. (eds) (2004) *Report on the Hungarian Education 2003*. Budapest: Országos Közoktatási Intézet.

James, A. (2000) English as a European lingua franca. Current realities and existing dichotomies. In J. Cenoz and U. Jessner (eds) *English in Europe. The Acquisition of a Third Language*. Clevedon: Multilingual Matters.

Kormos, J. and Csizér, K. (2007) An interview study of inter-ethnic contact and its role in language learning in a foreign language environment. *System* 35, 241–258.

Kormos, J. and Csizér, K. (2008) Age-related differences in the motivation of learning English as a foreign language: Attitudes, selves and motivated learning behaviour. *Language Learning* 58 (2), 327–355.

Lamb, M. (2004) Integrative motivation in a globalizing world. *System* 32, 3–19.

Nikolov, M. (1999) "Why do you learn English?" "Because the teacher is short." A study of Hungarian children's foreign language motivation. *Language Teaching Research* 3, 33–56.

Nikolov, M. (2001a) A study of unsuccessful language learners. In Z. Dörnyei and R. Schmidt (eds) *Motivation and Second Language Acquisition* (Technical Report #23) (pp. 149–169). Honolulu, HI: The University of Hawai'i, Second Language and Curriculum Center.

Nikolov, M. (2001b) Quality language teaching [in Hungarian]. *Iskolakultúra* August, 3–12.

Noels, K. (2001) New orientations in language learning motivation: Towards a model of intrinsic extrinsic, and integrative orientations and motivations. In Z. Dörnyei and R. Schmidt (eds) *Motivation and Second Language Acquisition* (Technical Report #23) (pp. 43–68). Honolulu, HI: The University of Hawai'i, Second Language and Curriculum Center.

Swain, M. (1985) Communicative competence: Some roles of comprehensible input and comprehensible output in its development. In S. Gass and C. Madden (eds) *Input in Second Language Acquisition* (pp. 235–253). Rowley, MA: Newbury House.

Yashima, T. (2000) Orientations and motivations in foreign language learning: A study of Japanese college students. *JACET Bulletin* 31, 121–133.

Chapter 6

Impact of Learning Conditions on Young FL Learners' Motivation

JELENA MIHALJEVIĆ DJIGUNOVIĆ

Introduction

This chapter looks into young foreign language (FL) learners' motivation under two different sets of learning conditions. Our aim was to see if young learners' attitudes and motivation for learning English as a foreign language (EFL) would be significantly different when the teaching setting is highly favourable and when it is not favourable.

Most research on age-related differences in attitudes and motivation, although not totally uncontradictory, seem to suggest that, in general, younger learners have more positive attitudes than older learners and that interest wanes with time (e.g. Burstall, 1975; Chambers, 2000; MacIntyre *et al.*, 2002; Nikolov, 1999). Findings of the Croatian longitudinal project, however, show that, under favourable learning conditions, positive attitudes and high motivation can be maintained over extended periods of time (Mihaljević Djigunović, 1998). Some studies, on the other hand, have found no significant age-related differences in the extent to which young learners of differing age liked FL learning (Lasagabaster, 2003; Williams *et al.*, 2002). Some other studies (e.g. Julkunen & Borzova, 1996) found mixed results.

A number of researchers investigated fluctuations in attitudes and motivation of young learners with different starting ages. It is difficult to make firm conclusions here either. Muñoz (2000) and Muñoz and Tragant (2001), for example, found no significant differences in motivation between learners starting at ages eight and 11. On the other hand, on the basis of her research Cenoz (2004) found that those young learners that started learning a FL earlier had higher motivation, with larger differences existing between those that started at four years and later starters than between those that started at eight or 11 years. Tragant (2006: 239) suggests that the general pattern that emerges implies a decline in positive attitudes around the age of 10–11.

Another factor that has been taken into consideration in studies of young learners' attitudes and motivation in FL learning is intensity, that is the number of hours of instruction. Tragant (2006: 262), however, concludes that the young learners' biological age has a higher effect on their motivational orientations than the hours of instruction.

Apart from a few studies that included the hours of instruction as a variable, there has been almost no research investigating the impact of learning conditions on young FL learners' attitudes and motivation. Learning conditions, as defined in this context, would include intensity of teaching, the teacher's qualifications and training, quality of teaching and the size of the group. Quality of teaching is a particularly important but the least investigated of the listed learning conditions.

Croatian FL Education Context

Formal FL teaching has a very long tradition in Croatia and dates back to the 19th century, when French and German were part of the secondary education curriculum, in addition to Latin. During the first half of the 20th century a growing number of learners opted for English as a second FL (Russian being the compulsory first FL) to be learned at school. From the 1950s until a few years ago the FL was introduced in grade four of primary school (at the age of 10). Most schools offered four FLs and the usual choice included English, French, German and Russian. In areas bordering on Italy, Italian was offered either instead of one of or in addition to the four listed languages. Interested learners were given a chance to take up a second FL in secondary school (age 14+).

Being a quite well-known tourist resort and orienting itself towards tourism as the most important source of national income, Croatia paid a lot of attention to teaching FLs. The first attempts at private education as an alternative to state schools were linked with FL learning. Two large semi-private FL schools opened during the 1950s and started offering FL courses for young children. One of these schools came to specialise in teaching kindergarten children. As these schools invested more money in educating their teachers than the educational authorities invested in state education, a growing body of FL teachers using the latest approaches to teaching was slowly appearing on the scene. Thanks to the teachers who moved from this semi-private to the official state education system, new ideas were spread to state schools as well. This kept the quality of FL teaching at a decent level over years.

In the 1970s interest into studying early learning of FLs developed. Several small-scale research studies were done on early learning of English and German and results were published internationally (e.g. Vilke, 1976a, 1976b, 1979). These studies were the starting point of an experimental longitudinal research project, supported by education and science authorities, that was initiated in 1991 and lasted for 10 years. It resulted in several publications (Vilke & Vrhovac, 1993, 1995; Vrhovac, 2001; Vrhovac *et al.*, 1999) on the research results as well as syllabi and teaching materials. The project was recognised internationally as well. Its main conclusions, based on research findings, were the following: the optimal starting age for FL learning in the Croatian context is the first grade of primary school; such early FL learning can be successful provided it is carried out under favourable conditions which imply intensive teaching at the very beginning, groups that do not exceed 15 learners and teachers that have been trained to teach young learners.

With the increasing awareness of the need for good competence in FLs in private and professional life, the demand for lowering the starting age grew stronger and, finally, in 2003 the FL was introduced as a compulsory part of the primary curriculum from the first grade (age 6–7 years). However, none of the conditions that the 1991–2001 research project proved to be necessary for successful early learning were secured. Thus, young beginners now learn the FL in large groups, with only two class periods per week and in most cases their teachers have not been trained to work with young children.

The Study

Aim

By comparing attitudes and motivation of two groups of young learners learning EFL under different learning conditions, we wanted to get an insight into the relationship between learning conditions and these two affective learner factors. Such an insight could make possible the drawing up of guidelines for defining FL educational policy.

Sample

Two samples are referred to in this comparative study. The first sample included eight groups of Croatian young learners ($n = 100$), drawn from four primary schools in Zagreb, who were learning EFL under highly favourable learning conditions. They were included in the Croatian national experimental project of early learning of FLs that was carried out between 1991 and 2001. They had five class periods of English per week (one period per day, each period lasting 45 minutes) in Grades 1 and 2, four periods in Grades 3 and 4, and three periods per week from Grade 5 until the end of their eight-year primary education. The teaching they were exposed to, relied on story-telling, content-learning and TPR. Their teachers were specialist EFL teachers with a university degree and additional training in teaching young learners. They attended first grade classes that were regularly split into two for English lessons so that in no case did group size exceed 15 learners per group.

The second sample comprised a total of 138 first graders from four regular first grade classes in four different towns in Croatia. These participants were learning English as one of their school subjects under 'regular conditions', not as part of any project. 'Regular conditions' imply that first graders have two class periods of English per week, the classes are not split into groups but could include up to 32 pupils, and the teacher of English might not have had much training in teaching young learners. In the case of the young learners in our study, the groups included 25 learners on average. In this study we focused on intensity of teaching and group size as measures of learning conditions.

Instrument

The same semistructured oral interview (Mihaljević Djigunović, 1993, 1995) was used with both samples. The questions were intended to elicit young learners' attitudes to English as a school subject, to native speakers of English, learners' motivational orientation, perception of and attitudes to classroom activities, self assessment of English competence and perception of parental attitudes. The original interview comprised 21 questions but some questions were not relevant for the 2006 sample (e.g. *Would you like to continue learning English next year?*).

Procedure

The interview was conducted on an individual basis and in a separate room. The interviewers underwent a brief training before going to schools to do the interviews. They reported no problems with either the pupils or the schools. The interviews lasted seven minutes on average. During the interview, in order not to confuse the pupil, the interviewer did not take notes but jotted down the answers only after the pupil left the room. According to the interviewers, all the pupils reacted well to the interview.

Interviews with the first sample were carried out in November and December of 1991 and with the second sample in November and December of 2006.

Results and discussion

In the presentation of our findings below we will be grouping participants' answers according to the attitude target.

Attitudes to the English language as a school subject

Although English was mentioned as their favourite school subject with the same frequency by both samples (see Figure 6.1), the attitudes to English were, in fact, different in the two samples. Those participants that did not mention English as their favourite subject were asked an additional question: *What about English?* In the 1991 study, almost all participants

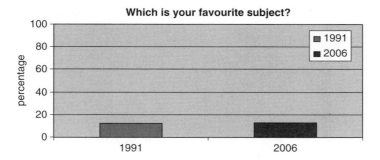

Figure 6.1 Frequency of English as a favourite school subject

said that they loved English but did not think of it because it did not look like a school subject to them but, instead, just like nicely and pleasantly spent time. None of the corresponding pupils in the 2006 study offered such an explanation but stuck to their original choice.

Learning English in a large group and with fewer hours per week seems to be less likely to create the same perception of English as a school subject as in the case when the learning conditions are more favourable. One of the main conclusions of the 1991 study (Vilke & Vrhovac, 1995), in fact, was that intensity of teaching and small groups were conducive to positive attitudes of young FL learners. In our view, it is particularly important that good conditions of learning be secured at the very start of FL learning: the first contact with the FL may be decisive for the young learner's attitudes and motivation for the rest of their life.

In the interview we also wanted to find out how young learners perceived what was going on in their English classes. Their answers were categorised according to whether the activities they mentioned referred to teaching (e.g. learning how to count in English, learning new words), to playing (e.g. singing and dancing, playing games) or to both (Figure 6.2).

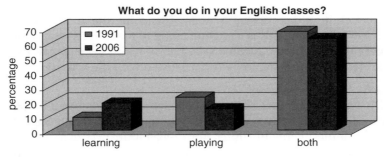

Figure 6.2 Perception of classroom activities

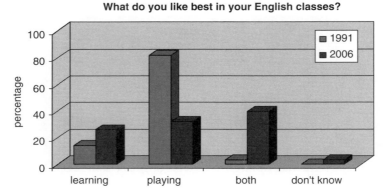

Figure 6.3 Frequency of activities participants enjoyed most during English classes

In both samples young learners reported that they learned, played and did both. The percentage of answers that referred to learning, however, was higher in the 2006 study, and the opposite is true for activities perceived as playing. This is not surprising as in the 1991 study children were taught by teachers specially trained to teach young learners, and one hour of English per day five days a week allowed them to include many more and varied activities.

Young learners' preferences for a particular type of classroom activities were looked into next. Participants were asked about what they liked best in their English classes. Results are shown in Figure 6.3.

As can be seen from the figure, the 1991 study participants significantly more frequently preferred playing activities than the 2006 participants. This could have two possible explanations. Thanks to the better conditions, they may have been exposed to more age-appropriate ways of teaching, which would imply activities with game elements, or playing activities were carried out more appropriately by the teacher. Unfortunately, we do not have enough data on the quality of teaching the 2006 study participants were exposed to. It is also interesting to note that a new category of answers appeared in the 2006 sample. The 'don't know' response by young learners may indicate that they did not like any of the activities.

Attitudes to native speakers

Two aspects were looked into. We first wanted to know if first graders were aware of who native speakers of English are. The differences between the two samples were quite interesting (see Figure 6.4).

The 1991 study participants were more aware of who native speakers of English are than the 2006 study participants. Many more in the latter

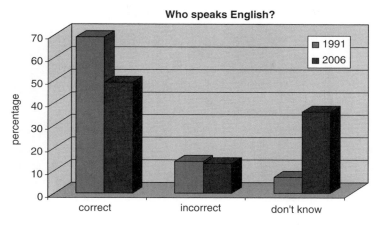

Figure 6.4 First-graders' awareness of native speakers of English

sample reported not knowing. On the one hand, participants learning English under favourable conditions had more exposure to formal teaching and had a better chance of learning about native speakers too; on the other, in 2006 first graders had less formal but more informal exposure to English. The informal exposure, especially through electronic media, however, might have been confusing for young learners as it mostly implies being in touch with English as an international language.

By asking participants about what native speakers of English are like, we wanted to gain insight into what characteristics of native speakers of English young learners found prominent. The replies obtained were classified according to whether they implied character features (e.g. good, kind), physical characteristics (e.g. good-looking, tall) or cultural characteristics (e.g. like to drink tea).

Comparing the results of the two samples presented in Figure 6.5, we can see that a higher percentage of the 2006 sample reported not knowing what native speakers of English are like. Although frequency of answers in the other categories follows the same pattern in the two samples, the percentages are consistently higher for participants learning English under favourable conditions. It seems that in order to form an opinion about native speakers young learners need a lot of input and the input needs to be clear enough.

Motivational orientations

Here we first looked into whether young learners thought that it was good to know English (Figure 6.6).

A vast majority of young learners in both samples reported that it was good to know English. This is not surprising considering the overall

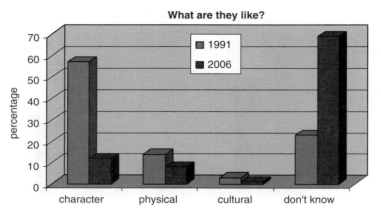

Figure 6.5 Perception of native speakers of English

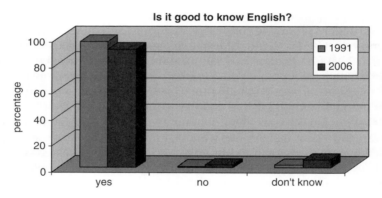

Figure 6.6 Value of knowing English

perception among Croats about English being the most important language for international communication. None of those learning English under favourable conditions said that is was not good. Slightly more participants in the 2006 sample than in the 1991 one reported they did not know whether it was good to know English, but in both cases the numbers are very low.

The next question in the interview elicited the reasons (Figure 6.7). Participants' replies were grouped into seven categories. As is shown in Figure 6.7, participants learning English in large groups and with only two class periods per week more frequently did not know why it was good to

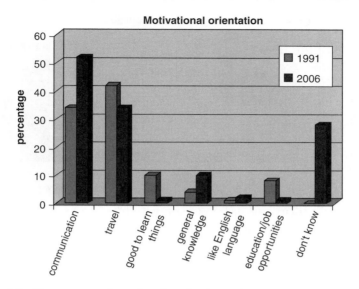

Figure 6.7   Frequency of motivational orientations

know English. Most of these young learners claimed that knowledge of English is part of one's general knowledge. This, of course, is not surprising as competence in English in the Croatian context, like in many others, is now considered a must in both private and professional life. Young learners' replies probably reflected their parents' views on the role of English.

It is interesting to note that the frequency of communication as a motivational orientation increased between 1991 and 2006, while orientation towards travel decreased. In our opinion, this reflects the higher accessibility and importance of Internet facilities and electronic communication at present. Earlier, travel symbolised the real opportunity to use English and that was what motivated young learners: it was either travelling abroad or simply spending summer holidays on the Adriatic, where one could meet foreigners and talk to them in English.

Perception of parental attitudes

As Gardner (1985) stresses, parents exert an important influence on children's FL learning and they may do it in both active and passive ways: they can, for example, actively encourage their child to learn the FL and help with homework, and so forth; but they may also influence the child's attitudes to FL learning implicitly through the way they comment or react to things or people connected with the FL. Our participants' perceptions of their parents' attitudes to their learning English in school are presented in Figure 6.8.

As expected, most participants in both samples reported positive parental attitudes to their learning English. The 2006 participants, however,

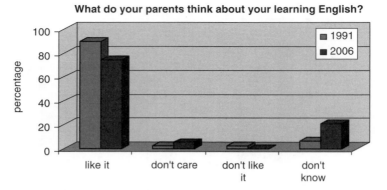

Figure 6.8   Participants' perception of parents' attitudes to their learning of English

more frequently said that they did not know what their parents thought or that their parents did not care about it. Fewer young learners in 2006 than in 1991 replied that their parents liked their learning English. We believe that this reflects some of the 2006 parents' view of English as just another school subject their children have to deal with. In contrast, in the framework of the 1991 study, English was treated – to say the least – as a special school subject that was taught in such a way that initial success was secured for all children (on importance of initial success in early FL learning, see Mihaljević Djigunović, 1993).

Self-perception of English competence

We elicited information on how young learners perceived their competence in English by asking them about their knowledge of English before they started school and to assess their present competence in English. Two questions were put to them concerning their preschool knowledge of English: whether they had known any English before starting school and where they had learned it. Results are presented in Figures 6.9 and 6.10.

In both samples more than half of participants knew some English before enrolling in first grade of primary school. The percentage is slightly higher in the 2006 sample, which probably reflects the growing trend in the Croatian society to start as early as possible.

It is interesting to note in Figure 6.10 that the pattern of frequency of reported sources of exposure to English is the same for the two samples: closest members of family, embodying the home, feature as the most frequent tutors, followed by the kindergarten and EFL courses in language schools. In contrast to EFL courses, the other two sources mentioned are more frequent in the 1991 sample. As the 1991 study children were selected to participate in the experiment on the basis of their parents' wish and

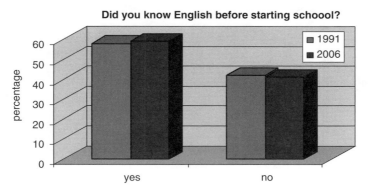

Figure 6.9 Knowing English before school

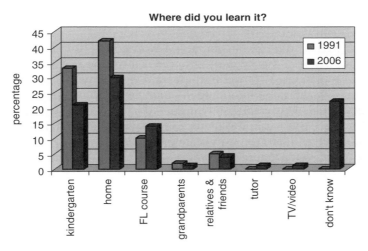

Figure 6.10 Sources of exposure to English

consent, it appears logical to conclude that the consenting parents were those who – because they thought English was important – had agreed to pay for English classes already in the kindergarten, and who knew English and tried to teach them some English themselves. The fact that more than 20% of young learners in the 2006 sample said they did not know where they had learned English, perhaps, shows that English did not play a big role in their life, it was just one of the school subjects, both to them and to their parents.

Participants in both samples were also asked to assess their own competence in English. They were supposed to do so by saying which grade

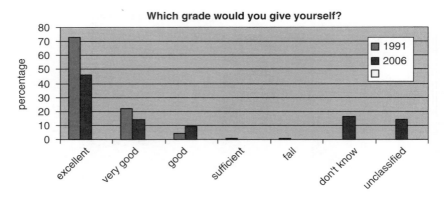

Figure 6.11   Participants' self-assessment of English competence

they would assign themselves for English. Figure 6. 11 shows their self-assessments.

The Croatian grading system recognises five marks, four (excellent, very good, good and sufficient) of which are passes and one is a fail. As can be seen in Figure 6.11, the 1991 sample young learners perceived their competence much more favourably than the 2006 study learners. Another interesting thing to note is that a number of young learners from the latter sample were not able to assess their competence in English. These participants either said they did not know what mark to assign themselves, or offered imprecise answers (e.g. 'my English is not too bad', 'I'm making progress', etc.).

In our opinion, participants from the earlier study, having had 60% more classes of English at the time of the interview than participants in the latter sample, in fact really had a higher competence and, what is more important in this context, had more confidence and a better self-concept as English language learners. The feeling of success in the earliest stages of FL learning has already been acknowledged in research on young learners (Rijavec, 1993).

Attitudes to early start of EFL learning

We were interested in what our participants thought was the optimal age to start learning English. Their replies are presented in Figure 6.12.

Participants' replies could be classified into four groups. The majority of the 1991 study young learners believed their own age, that is first grade of primary school, was the best time to begin learning English, with one-quarter of the sample saying that starting even earlier was optimal. These participants seemed to have a clear picture about when it was best to start and none said they did not know. The pattern of answers in the second sample is a little different. Most participants said they did not know when

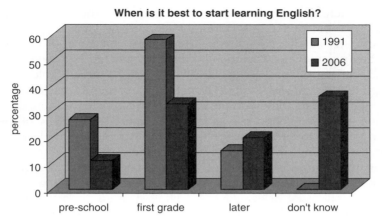

Figure 6.12 Participants' views on optimal age to start learning English

it is best to start learning English. Most of those who had an idea about the optimal age to start also claimed it was the first grade of primary school. It is interesting to note that almost 20% of participants thought a later start was a better idea. The percentage of these young learners in this sample was higher than that of those who believed the preschool age was the right starting time.

It is, of course, possible that young learners are just voicing their parents' attitudes to an early start. Early learning of FLs is perceived as very desirable in Croatia and there has been quite a tradition in early FL learning. Up to 2003, when the FL was introduced as a compulsory part of the primary curriculum, many parents would send their children to private FL schools, or would invest in their children's FL education by providing private tutoring for them. Many state primary schools also offered an FL as an optional subject, providing it either free of charge or at a nominal price. On the other hand, we believe that considerably higher percentages of young learners in the 1991 study opting for their own or even an earlier age as the optimal time to start may also be evidence of the more enjoyable experience they had in their English classes, which took place under highly favourable conditions.

Conclusions and Implications for Further Study

The comparative study of Croatian young beginners of EFL, which used the same instrument for eliciting data on their attitudes and motivation for learning English, suggests a number of differences that may be attributed to the conditions of learning. In contrast to young learners who learned this foreign language under very favourable conditions (appropriately trained teacher, intensive classes, small groups), learners who were exposed to formal learning under less favourable conditions viewed English as a favourite school subject less frequently and enjoyed age-appropriate class activities (playing) less. Their nonlinguistic knowledge, especially that connected with native speakers of English and their cultures, was lower. They seemed to be getting less support from their parents and were less aware of that support. Also, they thought less of their competence in English and showed lower self-confidence as language learners. For many of them it would be better to start learning English later than the first grade as, apparently, learning English in the first grade is not easy.

Despite the conclusions made above, even beginners who learn English under unfavourable conditions believed it was good to know English. They, too, saw a lot of benefit in knowing such an important means of international communication. It seems to us that the status and role of English in the Croatian social, cultural and educational context compensated for the effects of unfavourable conditions in which it was taught.

Future research that would look more directly into how learning conditions influence young learners' motivation could show whether our conclusions are valid. Probably the most revealing insights would be achieved by including classroom observation as an essential part of the research framework.

A longitudinal follow-up study would be warranted to see how the interaction of the social role of English and the conditions of learning affects linguistic and nonlinguistic achievements. It would be interesting to find out if, with years of study, the importance of English would succumb to the conditions of learning.

Following attitudes and motivation for learning other FLs such as French, German or Italian in the same context might throw light on the impact of the social role of the language being learned on achievements under the same conditions of learning. Comparative studies might offer information on the minimum required conditions beyond which early learning of foreign languages not only does not benefit young learners but may be detrimental to successful further language learning as well as their affective learner characteristics.

References

Burstall, C. (1975) Primary French in the balance. *Foreign Language Annals* 10 (3), 245–252.

Cenoz, J. (2004) Teaching English as a third language: The effect of attitudes and motivation. In C. Hoffman and S. Ytsme (eds) *Trilingualism in Family, School and Community* (pp. 202–218). Clevedon: Multilingual Matters.

Chambers, G. (2000) Motivation and the learners of modern languages. In S. Green (ed.) *New Perspectives on Teaching and Learning Modern Languages* (pp. 46–76). Clevedon: Multilingual Matters.

Gardner, R.C. (1985) *Social Psychology and Second Language Learning: The Role of Attitudes and Motivation*. London: Edward Arnold.
Julkunen, K. and Borzova, H. (1996) *English Language Learning Motivation in Joensuu and Petrozavodsk*. Joensuu: University of Joensuu.
Lasagabaster, D. (2003) Attitudes towards English in the Basque Autonomous Community. *World Englishes* 22 (4), 585–597.
MacIntyre, P.D., Baker, S.C., Clément, R. and Donovan, L.A. (2002) Sex and age effects on willingness to communicate, anxiety, perceived competence, and L2 motivation among junior high school French immersion students. *Language Learning* 52 (3), 537–564.
Mihaljević Djigunović, J. (1993) Investigation of attitudes and motivation in early foreign language learning. In M. Vilke and Y. Vrhovac (eds) *Children and Foreign Languages* (pp. 45–71). Zagreb: Faculty of Philosophy, University of Zagreb.
Mihaljević Djigunović, J. (1995) Attitudes of young foreign language learners: A follow-up study. In M. Vilke and Y. Vrhovac (eds) *Children and Foreign Languages* II (pp. 16–33). Zagreb: Faculty of Philosophy, University of Zagreb.
Mihaljević Djigunović, J. (1998) *Uloga afektivnih faktora u učenju stranoga jezika* [Role of affective factors in foreign language learning]. Zagreb: Filozofski fakultet Sveučilišta u Zagrebu.
Muñoz, C. (2000) Bilingualism and trilingualism in school students in Catalonia. In J. Cenoz and U. Jessner (eds) *English in Europe: The Acquisition of a Third Language* (pp. 157–178). Clevedon: Multilingual Matters.
Muñoz, C. and Tragant, E. (2001) Attitudes and motivation towards foreign language learning. In S.H. Foster-Cohen and A. Nizegorodcew (eds) *Eurosla Yearbook 2000* (pp. 211–224). Amsterdam: John Benjamins.
Nikolov, M. (1999) 'Why do you learn English?' 'Because my teacher is short.' A study of Hungarian children's foreign language learning motivation. *Language Teaching Research* 3 (1), 33–56.
Rijavec, M. (1993) Fitting syllabus and method to the young learner. In M. Vilke and Y. Vrhovac (eds) *Children and Foreign Languages* (pp. 147–152). Zagreb: Faculty of Philosophy, University of Zagreb.
Tragant, E. (2006) Language learning motivation and age. In C. Muñoz (ed.) *Age and the Rate of Foreign Language Learning* (pp. 238–268). Clevedon: Multilingual Matters Ltd.
Vilke, M. (1976a) The age factor in the acquisition of foreign languages. *Rassegna Italiana di Linguistica Applicata* 2 (3), 179–190.
Vilke, M. (1976b) Implications of the age factor on the proces of an L2. *SRAZ*, 87–104.
Vilke, M. (1979) English as a Foreign Language at the age of eight. *SRAZ*, 24, 297–335.
Vilke, M. and Vrhovac, Y. (eds) (1993) *Children and Foreign Languages I*. Zagreb: Faculty of Philosophy, University of Zagreb.
Vilke, M. and Vrhovac, Y. (eds) (1995) *Children and Foreign Languages II*. Zagreb: Faculty of Philosophy, University of Zagreb.
Vrhovac, Y. (ed.) (2001) *Children and Foreign Languages III*. Zagreb: Faculty of Philosophy, University of Zagreb.
Vrhovac, Y., Kruhan, M., Medved Krajnović, M, Mihaljević Djigunović, J., Narančić Kovač, S., Sironić-Bonefačić, N. and Vilke, M. (eds) (1999) *Strani jezik u osnovnoj školi* [Foreign Language in Primary School]. Zagreb: Naprijed.
Williams, M., Burden, R. and Lanvers, U. (2002) 'French is the language of love and stuff': Student perceptions of issues related to motivation in learning a foreign language. *British Educational Research Journal* 28 (4), 504–528.

Chapter 7

Early Modern Foreign Language Programmes and Outcomes: Factors Contributing to Hungarian Learners' Proficiency

MARIANNE NIKOLOV

Introduction

In this chapter, data collected in large-scale studies in the early 2000s is drawn on. These surveys inquire into Hungarian students' language achievements in English and German in public education, their aptitude, language learning goals, motivation and classroom processes. Besides these factors data were also collected on the number of years and weekly classes in which participants study the target languages, as well as on their socio-economic status. The aim is to examine how and to what extent these factors contribute to language learning outcomes in a socio-educational context where both English and German are foreign languages, attitudes are very positive towards language study, but few citizens claim to be able to use a foreign language. A more specific focus is to explore the actual benefits of early foreign language learning by analysing data of two specific age groups: years 6 and 10 (ages 12 and 16).

Background to Foreign Language Education in Hungary

In Hungary Russian used to be mandatory for all learners for over four decades. This was an early language programme, as all students started at the age of nine in Grade 4, but the majority of the population failed to achieve useful competencies by the time they graduated from secondary or tertiary education despite the fact that continuity was assured. After the change of regime in 1989, language choice was limited only by a sudden shortage of teachers, a difficulty overcome in the 1990s when Russian teachers were retrained in more popular languages, most importantly English and German.

Hungarians' attitudes towards foreign language study have been extremely favourable. During the early 1990s German was the most desired language because of close links with Germany and Austria, whereas by now English as a lingua franca has become the most popular foreign language (Dörnyei *et al.*, 2006). In sharp contrast with positive language learning attitudes few Hungarians speak foreign languages, though the trend is favourable: the number of Hungarians claiming to be able to use a foreign language has tripled in a decade: in the most recent Eurobarometer survey 29% of Hungarians claim to be able to converse in a foreign language (*Europeans and Languages*, 2005).

The Study

Focus of present study and research questions

In recent years large-scale studies have enquired into foreign language education in state schools. Some of them explored students' language learning orientations and motivation (e.g. Dörnyei *et al.*, 2006; Nikolov, 2003), aptitude (e.g. Kiss & Nikolov, 2005) and some studies triangulated data on cognitive, affective variables and performances on language proficiency tests (Nikolov & Ottó, 2006). In a large nationwide project (Study 1) in 2000 and 2002 Hungarian students' foreign language skills were assessed in English and German to monitor the levels and efficiency of foreign language education (Csapó & Nikolov, 2002; Nikolov & Csapó, 2002). A second (Study 2), similarly large-scale project was implemented in 2003 (Nikolov & Józsa, 2003, 2006). In a smaller-scale inquiry (Study 3) Grade 6 learners of English were involved (Kiss & Nikolov, 2005), whereas in Study 4 (Nikolov & Ottó, 2006) an innovative programme was examined: year 9 students in a year of intensive language learning project.

This chapter looks into how cognitive, socio-economic, affective and classroom factors contribute to young Hungarian language learners' proficiency in English and German. First, learners' performances in English and German proficiency tests will be examined, and how learners' aptitude, socio-economic status (SES), attitudes and motivation contribute to outcomes. Then, interaction between years of study and weekly hours will be explored together with other classroom variables, like frequencies of certain tasks and how learners relate to them. The aim is to examine relationships between these variables and students' achievements in English and German, the two target languages learnt by the overwhelming majority of learners.

Participants

In Study 1 in the years of 2000 and 2002 representative samples of years 6, 8, 10 and 12 learners were involved ($n = 41,015$; see Csapó & Nikolov, 2002; Nikolov, 2003; Nikolov & Csapó, 2002 for details).

In Study 2 in the year of 2003 participants were representative samples of years 6 and 10 learners (n = 20,804; see Nikolov & Józsa, 2003, 2006).

Study 3 was also conducted in 2003 and it involved 6th graders in 10 schools (n = 412) in two small towns in the east of Hungary (Kiss & Nikolov, 2005).

Participants in Study 4, implemented in the 2004/2005 academic year, were 1851 9th graders in 'year of intensive language learning' two phases: before starting their intensive courses and after their second term (Nikolov & Ottó, 2006).

Data collection instruments and procedures

First, data collection instruments are introduced. In order to assess participants' language proficiency (L2) tests were administered in English and German. In order to examine participants' cognitive contribution, three types of data were collected: test results on an inductive reasoning test, data on school achievements in grade point averages (GPA), and two validated aptitude measures were also used. The affective contribution, classroom and background data were elicited with the help of questionnaires.

Data were collected with the following instruments: In all four projects three language skills (listening comprehension, reading comprehension and writing) were assessed by paper and pencil proficiency tests in learners' regular classroom settings at the end of the school year (except for Study 1 and 2 where a subsample took an oral test, and in Study 4 participants were tested both at the beginning and at the end). The English and German tests were based on the prescribed achievement targets of the national core curriculum. They were identical in their construct, structure, type of texts and tasks and length (number of items) for the two target languages; the texts were longer and more complex and varied as the number of years increased (all test booklets for years 6 and 10 are available on the internet in Nikolov & Józsa, 2003). The construct was the same, whereas the task and text types were parallel in all studies. The task types were familiar to the vast majority of the participants, as they were similar to published course materials used in schools (for detailed descriptions of measuring instruments in English see Nikolov & Józsa, 2006).

All tasks focused on meaning (and not form), the reading texts were authentic, whereas scripted materials were used in listening tasks, as listening comprehension was expected to be the least developed skill according to classroom previous observation studies and questionnaire data (Nikolov, 1999, 2003). In Grade 6 writing tasks integrated reading with writing, thus, tasks required learners to choose words based on their meanings and copy them into a gapped invitation to a party and to fill in a form based on a short text with personal data. In year 10 students wrote a guided letter on a dream holiday along six content points. Booklets were produced in two versions: the sequence of the tasks was different, but the actual tasks were identical. The reliability (Cronbach alpha) of these tests varied between 0.90 and 0.93 for both English and German reading tasks and writing tasks in year 6, whereas between 0.72 and 0.85 for listening comprehension. Inter-rater reliabilities for the assessment of writing tasks in year 10 ranged between 0.91 and 0.95.

Besides language tests, questionnaires were administered to all students on their family background (SES was measured by parents' level of education, the most widely used indicator in Hungarian educational research), end of term school mark in English or German, number of weekly classes and years of study.

For the assessment of the cognitive contribution learners' GPA data were collected. A validated inductive reasoning test was used in Study 1: its three subtests (verbal analogies, number series and number analogies) tap into verbal and numeric contents of inductive processes (Cronbach alpha = 0.94; Csapó, 1997, 1998). Two aptitude tests validated for Hungarian learners were in Studies 3 and 4: a special aptitude test designed, piloted and validated for young learners was used in Study 3 (Kiss & Nikolov, 2005) and MENYÉT (Ottó, 1996), the Hungarian version of MLAT designed and validated for adults (Ottó & Nikolov, 2003) was applied in Study 4.

Learners' attitudes, motivation and language learning goals were examined with the help of questionnaires. Data were also collected on typical classroom tasks where learners needed to indicate on a 1–5 scale how frequent they were and to what extent they liked them (Nikolov, 2003).

The paper and pencil tests and questionnaires were administered locally with the help of external assessors in students' own classrooms at the end of school years. All students were coded; and data were assessed centrally by teams of trained assessors.

Students' performances on standardised proficiency tests in English and German

Findings of the nationally representative large-scale projects need to be summarised before analysing the contribution of various factors. For the sake of simplicity, only data for Grades 6 and 10 will be analysed from Study 1 and 2. Some main findings stand out.

First, in Study 1 and 2, involving nationally representative samples, levels were consistently and significantly higher in English than in German in years 6 and 10, despite the fact that the proficiency tests were the same in the two languages (see Figures 7.1 and 7.2). Second, large differences characterise participants' levels of proficiency: some students performed on a very low level, while others achieved top scores. Huge differences were found between groups, indicating a strong streaming tradition typical in Hungarian schools. Significant differences were found across types

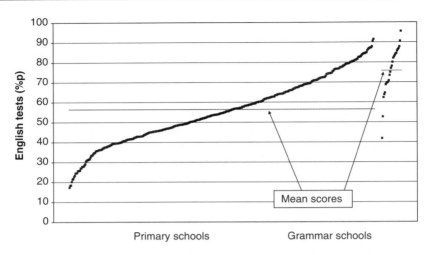

Figure 7.1 Distribution of year 6 English learners' groups in primary schools and grammar schools (Nikolov & Józsa, 2006: 201)

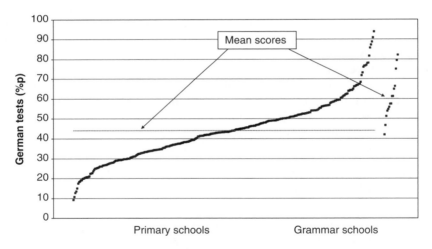

Figure 7.2 Distribution of year 6 German learners' groups in primary schools and grammar schools (Nikolov & Józsa, 2006: 201)

of schools students attend. For example, students in year 6 (age 12) attend two types of institutions: the majority study in their sixth year at eight-year primary schools, whereas some of their peers attend eight-year grammar schools where they are in their second year. Achievements in the tests are significantly different in the groups attending these two types of institutions. The mean score in English tests in primary schools is 56.3%, whereas learners in secondary schools achieved a mean score of 75.7%. In German tests the achievements are 44.0% and 60.0% respectively. Standard deviations are large, indicating a wide range of performances (Nikolov & Józsa, 2006: 201).

As these results indicate, learners of the two target languages performed on significantly different levels, and learners of English outperformed their peers in both groups. Outcomes are in line with previous research on general school achievements (Csapó, 1998, 2002) and with findings of the two previous nation-wide studies (Csapó, 2001; Csapó & Nikolov, 2002): students in grammar schools tend to outperform learners in other schools.

The significant differences between results in the two foreign languages need an explanation, as both English and German are foreign languages, and none of them is related to the Hungarian language, therefore no linguistic argument would explain this finding.

An analysis of data from nationally representative samples in year 2000 (Csapó, 2001; Csapó & Nikolov, 2002) provides insights into the contribution of different factors. Data were collected on a number of background variables including grade point average (GPA: general school achievements); language grade (achievement in foreign language classes); attitudes towards language learning (to what extent students like to study English or German); intended level of education (showing students' academic ambition); language learning plans (how important students think English or German is in their future, from giving it up as soon as possible to majoring in the language at university); parents' level of education (SES); language self-concept (students' estimate on how they would score on an English or German proficiency test); and inductive reasoning.

As can be seen in Table 7.1, figures show minor but statistically significant differences between students of English and German. More favourable data characterise learners of English: their families enjoy higher social status; their inductive reasoning skills are slightly better than those of their peers studying German. Also, they earn better grades in all subjects and English, enjoy learning English more, and their self-assessment is also higher. As the questionnaires and the inductive reasoning test were identical for the two age groups, data of years 6 and 10 can be compared directly. The patters are similar: all means characterising learners of English are significantly higher than those of German. Similar results were found in 2002 (Csapó & Nikolov, 2002).

Cognitive contribution

In Study 1 (Table 7.1) inductive reasoning skills and GPA were tapped into. In Study 3 and 4, language learning aptitude was measured with two

Table 7.1 Comparison of year 6 and 10 students studying English and German in 2000

	Year 6			Year 10		
	English	*German*	*diff. sign*	*English*	*German*	*diff. sign*
Grade point average (GPA)	3.94	3.86	$p < 0.001$	3.70	3.63	$p < 0.005$
Language mark	3.86	3.71	$p < 0.001$	3.85	3.68	$p < 0.001$
Attitude toward language learning	3.74	3.59	$p < 0.001$	3.82	3.59	$p < 0.001$
The intended level of education	4.73	4.49	$p < 0.001$	5.30	5.04	$p < 0.001$
Language learning plans	3.37	3.09	$p < 0.001$	3.28	3.03	$p < 0.001$
Parents' education	6.08	5.52	$p < 0.001$	6.09	5.72	$p < 0.001$
Language self-concept	65.04	61.83	$p < 0.001$	63.92	60.36	$p < 0.001$
Inductive reasoning	35.44	34.46	$p < 0.05$	59.88	58.00	$p < 0.001$

Source: Csapó and Nikolov (2002)

different tests. In Study 3 a convenience sample of 419 learners of English in year 6 (Kiss & Nikolov, 2005) filled in a new validated test. Although learners of German did not participate, the findings are relevant for our discussions. Language learning aptitude explained 22% of the variance in English language performance, whereas motivation (an index was applied on a number of motivational items) also had a significant contribution (8%). Besides these two variables, grades in English (17%), and the length of exposure (8.5%) explained a total of 55.5% of the variance. Correlations on the level of individual learners showed a strong relationship between aptitude and English scores (0.627).

In Study 4 ($n = 1851$, age 15) students were involved in a special intensive year of language learning programme (Nikolov & Ottó, 2006). Students were assessed at the beginning and at the end of the academic year and they filled in MENYÉT, a validated Hungarian aptitude test (Ottó, 1996). At the end of the intensive year the correlations between students' performances on the aptitude and proficiency measures ranged between 0.39 and 0.52. The best predictor of achievements, however, was students' level at the beginning of the year. In the case of learners of English, over 60% of variance in achievements at the end of the year was explained by the level at the beginning of the year. Higher correlations were found for English than for German.

The role of students' socio-economic status (SES)

It is known from large-scale studies enquiring into the relationships between Hungarian students' GPA and their socioeconomic status (Andor, 2000; Csapó, 1998, 2002; Nikolov & Józsa, 2003) that students' progress at school is related not only to what they are exposed to in their classes, but also to their socio-economic status (SES), indicated by parents' level of education. Table 7.2 shows the distribution of students according to their mothers' and fathers' level of education in Study 2, as well as their mean scores and standard deviations. Parents' educational levels range from eight years in primary schools, to vocational trade schools, secondary schools, college and university degrees. The figures show that the ratio of learners with more educated parents is higher for English than for German. In other words, the higher the learners' SES, the more probable it is that they study English, and vice versa: more of the less educated parents' children study German than English both in years 6 and 10. The ratio of children learning English whose parents graduated from university is the double of those learning German. The ratio of English learners with parents in the three more educated groups is higher in both years, whereas the ratio of German learners with parents in the least educated groups is higher. Therefore, more learners of English come from more favourable family backgrounds, and more learners of German may get less support from home.

The relationships between students' achievements on the proficiency tests and their school achievements indicated by their end of term grades

Table 7.2 Distribution of participants according to their parents' level of education (SES) with their mean scores (%) and standard deviation

	Mother				*Father*			
Level of education	*Year 6*		*Year 10*		*Year 6*		*Year 10*	
	E	*G*	*E*	*G*	*E*	*G*	*E*	*G*
Eight-year primary	15.3	24.8	11.8	16.6	10.3	16.4	8.0	9.3
Skilled worker	24.4	28.9	22.8	30.9	40.2	48.1	38.6	49.3
School-leaving exam	33.9	30.0	36.8	34.8	26.9	21.5	29.1	26.3
College	17.5	11.9	19.8	13.6	11.2	7.6	12.5	8.4
University	8.8	4.4	8.7	4.1	11.4	6.4	11.7	6.6
Mean score	2.80	2.42	2.91	2.58	2.73	2.39	2.81	2.54
SD	1.16	1.12	1.14	1.05	1.15	1.05	1.13	1.00

E: English; G: German
Source: Nikolov and Józsa (2006: 219)

Table 7.3 Students' mean scores on proficiency tests (%) and their school grades (on 1–5 scale) according to their mothers' level of education (SES) in year 6

Mean scores		Eight-year primary	Skilled worker	School-leaving exam	College University	
English	Proficiency tests	40.6	50.5	61.4	68.7	75.7
	School grade	3.0	3.5	3.9	4.2	4.4
German	Proficiency tests	33.8	43.1	49.6	56.3	63.2
	School grade	2.8	3.3	3.8	4.2	4.2

Source: Nikolov and Józsa (2006: 219)

on a 1–5 scale are shown in Table 7.3 according to parents' educational categories for year 6.

The relationships are systematic: the higher the educational level of the parent, the higher the figures are for both languages, for achievements on the proficiency tests and school grades in both years. There are large differences between mean scores achieved by the two extreme groups: children of parents with university degrees achieved almost twice the mean of learners of parents with eight-year primary school education: learners of English whose parents graduated from university achieved a mean score of 75.7, whereas the offspring of the least educated group scored 40.6%, whereas learners of German scored 63.2 and 33.8, respectively. Data also show that school grades in German tend to be lower than in English even within the same educational categories. Very similar results were found for year 10 students. These trends must be related to attitudinal, motivational, and methodology issues.

Time variables and outcomes: Do early starters outsmart later ones?

In Study 2 the relationship between variables related to time can be examined: how the length of language study in years and the frequency of weekly language classes influence outcomes based on questionnaire data (Nikolov & Józsa, 2006). Correlations show weak relationships between years of language study and students' performances in years 6 and 10 in both languages and across the three skills. As a devoted advocate of an early start, stronger relationships would have been expected. Despite the fact that year 4 is the compulsory year of foreign language study, over 50% of learners start learning a foreign language in lower primary years (Vágó, 2005). This means that learners in year 6 have learnt English or German for six, five, four or three years, whereas the situation in year 10 is more complex, as the longest period of language study is 10, the shortest may be two years only (if students started the target language in year 9 after having learnt another language in primary school). The low correlations indicate very slow progress for many students, and the earlier they study English or German, the better they will be over the years is a weak rule.

In Study 4 involving year 9 students in a special year of intensive language learning project even lower correlations were found for the same relationship: 0.22 for English and 0.15 for German (Nikolov & Ottó, 2006). These findings seem to challenge the efficiency of early programmes. Also, a stronger relationship would have been expected between years of study and scores in listening comprehension, as the early years should boost young learners' receptive skills.

To gain better insights into these results, we can look at the distribution of year 6 students in percentages according to the length of their language study in years. They are similar for the two languages: 45% of learners studying English and German learnt the target language for three years, the compulsory length of time. Eight percent of the learners had fewer years of exposure than mandatory, whereas 47% of the 12-year-olds learnt English or German for more years than expected, with little variation in the groups studying for four or more years. It is interesting to note that 4% of the students learning English and 2% of German learners started their language experience in kindergarten years. These figures show that schools launch foreign language programmes one to three years before the compulsory start (year 4). The reason is simple: all schools are sponsored per capita, therefore the more students (parents) they manage to attract the more financial support they get. As early foreign language programmes are highly appreciated by parents when they decide where their child will attend school, they offer modern foreign languages early. In addition to this general tendency, German is supported with extra funds as an ethnic minority language; therefore, more extra money is allocated to the teaching of German (Imre, 1999).

If we analyse participants' achievements in percentages (with standard deviations) in year 6 according to the number of years they have studied English and German (Table 7.4), we realise that the numbers increase in each row between three and six years. Learners who started learning English or German in year 4 tend to achieve somewhat lower scores than their peers with four, then five and six years of language study. This latter group contains students who started in Grade 1 at age six. Interestingly, learners who started in kindergarten (more than seven years of study) do not show any advantage (except for reading in German), meaning that young learners do not seem to benefit from exposure to English or German before primary school. On the contrary: learners in the group with six years of study achieved somewhat better scores. The column with two years or fewer is thought provoking, as the scores are higher than for

Table 7.4　Year 6 students' performances on language tests in relation to years of language study (%)

Language	Skill	Years of language study					
		≤2	3	4	5	6	7≤
English	Reading	49 (25)	45 (20)	56 (22)	58 (22)	60 (22)	58 (23)
	Writing	58 (28)	57 (23)	68 (23)	70 (23)	70 (23)	68 (25)
	Listening	56 (24)	55 (19)	64 (20)	63 (22)	68 (20)	66 (21)
	Three skills	54 (24)	52 (18)	62 (19)	64 (20)	66 (19)	64 (21)
German	Reading	36 (19)	36 (18)	42 (19)	44 (21)	50 (19)	52 (22)
	Writing	46 (28)	45 (25)	51 (26)	52 (26)	58 (23)	53 (26)
	Listening	45 (25)	41 (19)	44 (19)	49 (23)	53 (21)	53 (22)
	Three skills	42 (21)	41(17)	45 (18)	48 (20)	54 (18)	52 (20)

Source: Nikolov and Józsa (2006: 210)

learners in the three-year column. Most probably these students study English or German as a second foreign language. It is known from statistics on schools that although only one foreign language is mandatory in primary school, some students study two. These students have been found to outperform their peers, as they transfer study skills successfully and they tend to have better cognitive skills (grade point averages) (Bors *et al.*, 1999).

Overall, performances vary systematically with the year of study, but the relationships are weak and similar trends characterise year 10 students. These findings are not surprising, as research has shown that young learners' development is slow.

Besides years of study, frequency of weekly classes is also worth examining. The results show a clear trend: the more frequent the weekly exposure, the higher the mean scores in both languages, although overlaps across groups are large. On the whole, a systematic but weak relationship characterises the relationships between how many years students study the target language, whereas the number of classes a week seems to be better predictor of performances in English and German in years 6 and 10.

Language learning goals and outcomes

Studies on language learning motivation have revealed an important relationship between goal setting and success in language study, as it may determine how students persist in the effort to become more proficient over years (Dörnyei, 2001). In Study 1 and 2 learners were asked to indicate their long-term goals. They were offered six options reflecting typical instrumental motives Hungarian students tend to identify with: five options indicate positive documented achievements along a prestige scale, whereas one is negatively worded. In the Hungarian context the school-leaving examination is available to everyone but is not seen as a major indicator of language proficiency, though a recent school-leaving examination reform is supposed to change the situation (Fekete *et al.*, 1999). On the other hand, intermediate and advanced level external exams are highly valued by society and schools, students, parents and the job market. Degrees in the target language reflect not only a pragmatic value (e.g. student may find better job opportunities) but also intrinsic motivation (i.e. they enjoy the actual study of the language): a four- or five-year university degree in English and German is considered as a top achievement in language study, whereas a three- or four-year college degree is somewhat less prestigious.

The figures in Table 7.5 show the distributions of students in percentages according to what plans they identified with. Different patterns emerge for the two target languages: learners of English tend to strive higher, as the ratio of students aiming for external proficiency exams is larger. In year 6, 62% of English learners and 51% of German learners set such an exam (intermediate or advanced) as a goal for themselves, whereas the ratios for year 10 students are 66% and 52%, respectively. Younger learners tend to be more optimistic, as more of them identified with the advanced degree than the older learners. In other words, in year 10 students seem to see options more realistically. As for the ratio of students aiming for a school-leaving exam, more learners of German chose this

Table 7.5 Students' distributions according to their plans to continue language study (%)

	Year 6		Year 10	
Plans with language study	*English*	*German*	*English*	*German*
Give it up as soon as possible	10	16	10	18
Take school-leaving examination	18	25	19	26
Take proficiency exam at intermediate level	34	34	47	42
Take proficiency exam at advanced level	28	17	19	10
Get a college degree	4	4	2	2
Get a university degree	6	4	2	2

Source: Nikolov and Józsa (2006: 220)

option and these ratios are very similar in the two age groups. The highest level of devotion to language study is represented by students aiming to get a college or university degree in English and German. The percentages indicate younger learners' higher level of optimism, and learners of English seem to be slightly more ambitious. An equal level of interest is reflected in year 10 for both languages.

Looking at the negative end of the scale of goals, the ratio of students wishing to give up language study as soon as possible is worryingly high in both years and a significantly less favourable picture emerges for German than for English. In years 6 and 10, one out of 10 learners of English set no meaningful goals for themselves, whereas 16% of year 6 and 18% of year 10 students want to quit German programmes as soon as possible. This is a very high ratio indicating low level of self-esteem in foreign language study and a threat to the aim of learning foreign languages set for state education in national and European language policy documents. To become a plurilingual individual is definitely an unrealistic goal for these students.

The higher ratio of German learners in this negative category is controversial: most probably many of these students want to give up German not only because they do not experience success, but as they would have liked to study English, therefore, they lack motivation. This seems to be a recent but increasing problem in Hungarian schools: as language teachers are tenured in their posts and many language teachers were retrained to teach English and German in the 1990s, schools are cornered. The overwhelming enthusiasm towards English (Dörnyei *et al.*, 2006) forces them to introduce criteria along which they select students they place in English groups, whereas the others are 'placed' in German groups. The criteria they apply include students' grade point average and/or test results on cognitive skills, reflecting their learning abilities and motivation. This vicious circle may be responsible for lower levels of achievement and higher ratios of frustrated learners of German. Learners of German are less able, less motivated, and their socioeconomic status is less favourable than those of learners of English (Csapó & Nikolov, 2002). Very similar findings characterise participants in Study 1 (Nikolov, 2003: 65–67), but in Study 2 the ratio of students wanting to give up language learning is higher in both languages and the ratio of students aiming for a higher education degree is about half of ratios in Study 1 showing a slight shift in the extreme categories: more students want to give up language study and fewer want to major in languages in tertiary education. Less interest in language degrees is understandable, as speaking a foreign language has recently become a tool and a must in studying other content areas in tertiary education and for finding good job opportunities. The most proficient users of foreign languages take up other challenges (e.g. business, law, computer, medical studies) and this is a

Table 7.6 Students' performances according to their plans to study English or German (%)

Plans with language study	Year 6		Year 10	
	English	German	English	German
Give it up as soon as possible	37 (16)	31 (14)	26 (11)	24 (11)
Take school-leaving examination	46 (17)	38 (16)	34 (12)	30 (12)
Take proficiency exam at intermediate level	58 (18)	48 (16)	52 (18)	45 (19)
Take proficiency exam at advanced level	71 (17)	59 (17)	67 (19)	64 (21)
Get a college degree	64 (18)	51 (19)	58 (19)	52 (21)
Get a university degree	65 (19)	56 (19)	66 (23)	61 (26)
F*	446	256	530	398

* *F* scores of variance analysis significant at $p < 0.001$
Source: Nikolov and Józsa (2006: 217)

favourable trend. Nowadays, a degree in English or German is less prestigious than it used to be.

A comparison of students' language learning goals and their performances (Table 7.6 shows distributions of achievements in percentages with standard deviations in brackets) shows systematic patterns: the higher learners set their goals, the more successful they are in both languages, whereas the lowest achievers want to give up language learning as soon as possible.

Also, large *F* values need to be pointed out: they indicate huge differences across groups in both languages in both years and they are higher for English than for German. They document a strong streaming tradition in Hungarian schools, especially characteristic of foreign language study (Nikolov & Józsa, 2006: 217).

Affective factors and classroom processes

Study 1 inquired into participants' language learning attitudes and motivation, as well as into their attitudes towards classroom activities. Results of learners' language learning goals in Study 1 and 2 revealed that both English and German learners showed strong instrumental motives in the form of prestigious external proficiency exams or less ambitious school-leaving exams. As has been shown, the majority was optimistic about their language learning and had high hopes, but targets for German were consistently more moderate and the level of optimism decreased in the older age-groups (Nikolov & Józsa, 2006). When asked about their attitudes towards learning English and German, most students reported that their parents were enthusiastic for them to learn English or German. They agreed that knowing a foreign language would be useful, they liked both English and German and claimed to be interested in the speakers of both languages. Yet, again, all data for learners of English were consistently more advantageous than those for learners studying German. When asked about their classroom experiences, a high ratio of students did not find language classes challenging enough, many failed to come up to expectations and reported anxiety in class – once again, as expected, a more problematic picture emerged for learners of German (Nikolov, 2003).

As is known from motivation research, favourable attitudes and motivations at the language level (Dörnyei, 2001) function only as necessary preconditions; classroom processes may shape learners' motivations differently and influence outcomes more profoundly. Learners in Study 1 filled in a questionnaire on classroom processes. They were asked to rate on a 1–5 scale to what extent they liked classroom activities and how often they used them in their foreign language classes (Nikolov, 2003). In learners' views, traditional form-focused activities typical of the audio-lingual and grammar-translation methods characterise their classes in both languages. The most frequent way of meaning making is translation, reading out texts, answering teachers' questions in a lockstep fashion, grammar exercises, and tests are among the most frequent tasks, as Table 7.7 illustrates for the youngest age group (figures in left columns indicate frequencies, in the right columns popularity). Playful activities, conversations, role plays, pair and group work are the least frequent in both English and German classes; stories, visual prompts, listening tasks and pair work are slightly more frequent in English classes.

The least popular classroom tasks include everything related to testing; whereas videos, listening tasks, games, pair and group work, tasks involving some creativity and physical movement feature the highest on learners' lists of appreciated activities. Interestingly, some mechanical tasks (copying, dictation, reading out) are more popular in German, but it is unclear whether this is the case because less able learners tend to perform more successfully in such cognitively less demanding activities. All other activities are slightly more liked by learners of English. Whether this means that these tasks tend to be more successfully implemented in English classes, or learners feel they benefit from them more is unclear.

In conclusion, questionnaire data have confirmed what was known prior to our study from observations (Nikolov, 1999): many of the foreign language classes emphasise traditional cognitively demanding, decontextualised activities. These most probably provide better learning opportunities for more able learners.

Table 7.7 Frequency and popularity of classroom activities in English and German classes in year 6 (Likert scale 1–5)

Classroom activity	*English*		*German*	
(1) Answering questions	3.83	3.17	3.72	3.13
(2) Talking about pictures	2.79	3.29	2.48	3.10
(3) Acting out dialogue or role-play	2.54	3.38	2.55	3.32
(4) Reciting memorised text	3.17	2.95	3.17	2.94
(5) Talking freely	2.42	3.65	2.37	3.55
(6) Copying from board or book	3.31	3.14	3.38	3.32
(7) Writing a dictation	2.44	2.50	2.57	2.59
(8) Solving grammar exercises	3.71	3.06	3.84	3.05
(9) Understanding grammar explanations	3.57	3.15	3.54	3.10
(10) Writing compositions	1.97	2.51	2.02	2.45
(11) Writing vocabulary tests	3.43	2.85	3.37	2.70
(12) Writing sentences with words	3.39	3.26	3.52	3.26
(13) Listening to tape recorder	3.48	4.27	2.51	4.02
(14) Doing listening comprehension tasks	3.51	3.39	3.14	3.24
(15) Watching video	1.37	4.17	1.25	4.06
(16) Translating heard texts	3.25	3.11	3.00	2.94
(17) Translating read texts	4.12	3.42	4.11	3.31
(18) Reading out texts	4.09	3.60	4.07	3.64
(19) Reading texts to understand message	3.81	3.39	3.83	3.30
(20) Reading stories or articles	2.70	3.38	2.29	3.17
(21) Working in pairs	2.73	3.88	2.41	3.82
(22) Working in teams	2.57	3.77	2.51	3.76
(23) Working alone	3.85	3.19	3.86	3.10
(24) Playing language games	2.65	3.93	2.52	3.77
(25) Writing tets	3.58	2.66	3.62	2.60

Source: Nikolov (2003)

Summary and Conclusions

The aim of this chapter was to examine how various factors contribute to Hungarian students' performances on proficiency tests in English and German in early start programmes. Students learning English tend to outperform their peers learning German; their SES, attitudes and motivation, as well as their GPA and cognitive abilities are slightly better. The relationships between length of study in years and outcomes are weak, whereas between language proficiency and frequency of language lessons are stronger. Large differences characterise groups in general, and groups in different types of institutions showing that schools stream learners according to their abilities and their parents' wishes. These findings reflect how the trend of English becoming a lingua franca has influenced the prestige of two school subjects: English and German as foreign languages. An analysis of classroom activities indicates that the methods teachers apply are eclectic, borrowing from the grammar-translation method spiced with drills. These methods are not conducive to young learners' language development and may negatively impact on their attitudes and motivation (Bors *et al.*, 2001; Nikolov, 2002). These classroom-related factors may indeed be responsible for very slow development over years and learners' loss of motivation over time.

Acknowledgement

I gratefully acknowledge the support I received while working on this study from the Research Group on the Development of Competencies, Hungarian Academy of Sciences (MTA-SZTE Képességkutató Csoport).

References

Andor, M. (2000) A nyelvtudás szociális háttere [Social background to language knowledge]. *Educatio* 9 (4), 717–728.

Bors, L., Lugossy, R. and Nikolov, M. (2001) Az angol nyelv oktatásának átfogó értékelése pécsi általános iskolákban [An overall evaluation of the teaching of English in Pécs schools]. *Iskolakultúra* 11 (4), 73–88.

Bors L., Nikolov M., Pércsich R. and Szabó, G. (1999) A pécsi nyolcadik osztályosok idegen nyelvi tudásának értékelése [Assessment of year 8 students' proficiency in English in Pécs schools]. *Magyar Pedagógia* 99 (3), 289–306.

Council of Europe (2001) *Common European Framework of Reference for Languages: Learning, Teaching, Assessment.* Cambridge: Cambridge University Press.

Csapó. B. (1997) The development of inductive reasoning: Cross-sectional assessments in an educational context. *International Journal of Behavioral Development* 20 (4), 609–626.

Csapó, B. (ed.) (1998) *Az iskolai tudás* [School knowledge]. Budapest: Osiris.

Csapó, B. (2001) A nyelvtanulást és a nyelvtudást befolyásoló tényezök [Variables influencing proficency and langauge learning]. *Iskolakultúra* 11 (8), 25–35.

Csapó, B. (ed.) (2002) *Az iskolai műveltség* [School literacy]. Budapest: Osiris.

Csapó, B. and Nikolov, M. (2002) The relationship between students' foreign language achievement and general thinking skills. Paper presented at the American Educational Research Association Annual Meeting, April, New Orleans, USA.

Dörnyei, Z. (2001) *Teaching and Researching Motivation.* London: Longman.

Dörnyei, Z, Csizér, K. and Németh, N. (2006) *Motivation, Language Attitudes and Globalisation: A Hungarian Perspective.* Clevedon: Multilingual Matters.

Europeans and Languages (2005) On WWW at http://europa.eu.int/comm/public_opinion/archives/ebs/ebs_237.en.pdf. Accessed 7.7.08.

Fekete, H., Major, É. and Nikolov, M. (eds) (1999) *English Language Education in Hungary: A Baseline Study*. Budapest: British Council.

Imre, A. (1999) Az idegennyelv-oktatás kiterjedésének hatása a nemzetiségi-nyelv-oktatásra [The impact of the spread of foreign language teaching on the teaching of ethnic languages]. In I. Vágó (ed.) *Tartalmi változások a közoktatásban a 90-es években* [Changes in the content of state education in the 1990s] (pp. 175–202). Budapest: OKIKK Okker Kiadó.

Kiss, Cs. and Nikolov, M. (2005) Preparing, piloting and validating an instrument to measure young learners' aptitude. *Language Learning* 55 (1), 99–150.

National Core Curriculum [Nemzeti alaptanterv]. (2003) Budapest: Oktatási Minisztérium.

Nikolov, M. (1999) Classroom observation project. In H. Fekete, É. Major and M. Nikolov (eds) *English Language Education in Hungary: A Baseline Study* (pp. 221–246). Budapest: British Council.

Nikolov, M. (2002) What do teachers of young learners claim and do? An empirical study of their claims and practices. Paper presented at the Dijete i Jezik Danas/ Child and Language Today. *2nd International Conference*, November, Osijek, Croatia.

Nikolov, M. (2003) Angolul és németül tanuló diákok nyelvtanulási attitűdje és motivációja. [Attitudes and motivation of learners of English and German]. *Iskolakultúra* 13 (8), 61–73.

Nikolov, M. and Csapó, B. (2002) Twelve-year-olds' attitudes towards classroom activities and their performances on tests of English and German as a foreign language. Paper presented at the American Association of Applied Linguistics Annual Conference, April, Salt Lake City, USA.

Nikolov, M. and Józsa, K. (2003) *Idegen nyelvi készségek fejlettsége angol és német nyelvből a 6. és 10. évfolyamon a 2002/2003-as tanévben* [Developmental levels of year 6 and 10 learners' in English and German in the 2002/2003 academic year]. On WWW at http://www.om.hu/letolt/okev/doc/orszmer2003/idegen_nyelv_beliv.pdf. Accessed 7.7.06.

Nikolov, M. and Józsa, K. (2006) Relationships between language achievements in English and German and classroom-related variables. In M. Nikolov and J. Horváth (eds) *UPRT 2006: Empirical Studies in English Applied Linguistics* (pp. 197–224). Pécs: Lingua Franca Csoport, PTE.

Nikolov, M. and Ottó, I. (2006) A nyelvi előkészítő évfolyam [The year of intensive language learning]. *Iskolakultúra* 16 (5), 49–67.

Ottó, I. (1996) Language aptitude testing: Unveiling the mystery. *Novelty* 3 (3), 6–20.

Ottó, I. and Nikolov, M. (2003) Magyar felsöktatási intézmények elsöéves hallgatóinak nyelvérzéke [The aptitude of Hungarian first-year university students]. *Iskolakultúra* XIII (6-7), 34–44.

Vágó, I. (2005) Kilencedik évfolyamos diákok idegennyelv-tanulási útjai [Language learning paths of year 9 students]. Unpublished manuscript. Budapest: Országos Közoktatási Intézet Kutatási Központ.

Chapter 8

Using the Early Years Literacy Programme in Primary EFL Norwegian Classrooms

ION DREW

Introduction

This chapter investigates the challenges, advantages and effectiveness of using the Early Years Literacy Programme (EYLP), which was originally designed for English L1 teaching in Australia, in third and fourth grade EFL classrooms in a Norwegian primary school. The approach emphasises regular reading suited to each pupil's level of ability. Classrooms are organised on the principle of homogeneous groups of pupils rotating between different learning centres. The experimental school is compared with two control schools using different teaching approaches. The data is based on classroom observations, teacher interviews and pupil assessment.

Only tentative conclusions may be reached thus far since the study is in its preliminary stages. The EYLP approach has been popular among the pupils using it, has stimulated their reading interest, and has catered well for pupils of different abilities. During the study period, the pupils in the experimental school developed their language skills, especially their oral skills, at a higher rate than those in the control schools. However, it has been demanding for teachers to practise the approach, which requires a high degree of commitment and expertise. Monitoring the pupils' language development and attitudes to reading over a longer period of time would be beneficial.

Nylund Primary School in Stavanger became a pioneer school in Norway in 2003 when it introduced the Australian Early Years Literacy Programme (EYLP) into its mother tongue teaching, attracting a great deal of interest from other schools both regionally and nationally because of significant improvements in its pupils' literacy levels. In 2005, the school decided to implement the same programme in its EFL teaching from Grades 3 to 7. In so doing, it became one of the few schools in Norway to try out this approach in English classes. The aims of this chapter are to investigate how effectively the approach has functioned in third and fourth grade EFL classrooms at the school during the initial stages of its implementation, comparing it with two control schools. The three main research questions were:

(1) How do the different schools approach early primary EFL teaching?
(2) What are the challenges and advantages of using the EYLP pro-gramme in early primary EFL teaching?
(3) How effective is the programme in promoting pupils' English lan-guage skills?

Interest in early first language reading and writing has increased in recent years, especially as a result of research into children's 'emergent literacy' in the preschool period and its significance for later literacy devel-opment (Lancy, 1994; Teale & Sulzby, 1986). Although reading and writing have not traditionally been given as much attention in early foreign lan-guage teaching as oral skills, research has shown that very young children also have a potential to develop second language literacy in a supportive learning environment (e.g. Cambourne, 1986; Cambourne & Turbill, 1987; Seda & Abramson, 1990). A number of studies, for example Elley and Mangubhai (1983) and Hafiz and Tudor (1989), have shown the benefits of extensive reading programmes on primary L2 learners' language skills, thus supporting Krashen's (1984) emphasis on extensive reading as an important source of language input.

EFL in Norway

English is the first foreign language in Norway and is compulsory from Grades 1 to 10. The onset age was lowered from Grade 4 (age 9) to Grade 1 (age 6) in 1997. Norway has national curriculum guidelines which are revised roughly every 10 years. The two most recent national curriculum guidelines, *L97* and *K2006*, have both emphasised literacy in the primary EFL classroom to a much greater extent than their predeces-sors. The most recent national curriculum, implemented in 2006 (*K2006*), describes reading and writing in English as *basic subject skills* at all levels. Some of the literacy-related competence aims after grade 4 are for pupils to be able to:

- understand and use common English words and phrases connected to day-to-day life, recreation and interests, both orally and in writing;
- use some common grammatical structures, words, simple sentence structures and spelling patterns;
- use some stock expressions that are common in familiar situations, both orally and in writing;
- read and understand the main points in texts about familiar topics;

- write short messages and simple sentences that describe, narrate and ask;
- use digital tools to find information and create texts.

Because of Norway's strong historical and cultural ties to the UK and United States, the English language enjoys high status in the country, and exposure to the language, especially through TV, film and radio, is widespread. The level of English language skills among Norwegians is generally considered to be high. For example, Norwegian tenth graders scored highest in oral and written production, and second highest in listening and reading comprehension, in a recent comparative study in eight European countries (Bonnet, 2004).

In spite of these promising results, there is considerable room for improving the quality of English education in Norwegian schools. The recent reforms of national curricula in English have not been followed up with reforms in Norwegian teacher education. English has always been an optional subject for students taking a bachelor of Education, which is the only recognised qualification for primary school teachers. In recent years, fewer and fewer student teachers have chosen English as one of their optional subjects. As a consequence there is a dramatic shortage of qualified English teachers in primary schools. Seven out of ten English teachers in Grades 1 to 4, and every second teacher in Grades 5 to 7 have no formal education in the subject (Lagerström, 2000).

Moreover, a recent survey among primary EFL teachers indicated that reading and writing seemed to be practised to a far lesser extent at the primary level than intended by the curriculum (Drew, 2004). It was suggested that the potential to develop these skills at an early age was largely being unexploited. Furthermore, scholars such as Lehmann (1999) and Hellekjær (2005) have expressed concern that many Norwegian students of higher education, in spite of a generally high level of oral proficiency, struggle with basic reading and writing skills in English. Apparently the English that many of them learn during their compulsory and upper secondary school education is inadequate for the literacy demands in English placed on them in Higher Education. It would therefore be interesting to see if an earlier emphasis on literacy in EFL teaching, as in the EYLP approach at Nylund School, will have positive effects on pupils' later literacy and language growth in English.

The EYLP Programme

The EYLP programme was originally developed by the state of Victoria in Australia following a three-year project involving 27 trial schools and 25 reference schools, and was instrumental in enhancing pupils' literacy levels in the schools in which it was tried out (Crévola & Hill, 1988). It is a whole-school literacy-promoting approach that aims to reduce the level of variation between classes within a school. The effectiveness of the approach is based on three premises (Hill & Crévola, 2006):

- high expectations of pupil achievement;
- engaged learning time;
- focused teaching that exploits the individual pupil's 'zone of proximal development' (Vygotsky, 1978).

Other important characteristics of the approach are substantial amounts of regular reading, teachers with expert knowledge, monitoring and assessment of pupils, and parental participation. The Wings series of books from Australia, comprising 290 titles over 26 levels, provides the core reading. These are well-illustrated graded books with relatively little text on each page, especially at the lower levels. The association between pictures and text is extremely important for helping pupils to understand and internalise language. The books are designed to introduce high frequency words in a systematic way, thus enhancing pupils' reading fluency through automatic word recognition and lexical access, namely the automatic retrieval from memory of 'the word's meanings and its phonological representation' (Stanovich, 1992: 4). The principle is for pupils to read most or all of the titles at a given level, sometimes 25, before progressing to the next level. In addition to the Wings series, pupils are encouraged to read other books extensively. 'Reading records', carried out regularly by the teacher, provide a detailed and systematic record of each pupil's reading strengths and weaknesses (Clay, 1993).

Two important principles underlie the classroom organisation of the EYLP approach. The first is that pupils are divided into homogeneous ability groups. The second is the organisation of the classroom into a number of learning centres, or 'stations'. One of these is always led by the teacher, whereas in the others pupils work autonomously on pre-prepared tasks in their groups. The principle is that each learning centre will have basic tasks that all pupils should manage, whereas faster learners will be able to do extra tasks at a higher level. Pupils rotate in groups from learning centre to learning centre, spending approximately 10 to 15 minutes at each. The teacher centre is normally devoted to monitoring the pupils' reading.

Participants and Methods

Three classes totalling 57 pupils participated from Nylund School. Control School 1 (C1) was represented with two classes totalling 35 pupils and Control School 2 (C2) with one class of 23 pupils. Both the control schools are situated in areas with higher socio-economic status than Nylund School. The study started in the spring of 2006 when the pupils were approaching the end of the third grade. At the time they had one lesson of English a week, and had had about 50 hours of English in total during the first three grades. When using the learning centre model in the third grade, the Nylund School pupils combined English with maths in a double lesson. In the fourth grade contact time in English increased to two lessons a week. Nylund School did not use the EYLP model every week in its English lessons, thus allowing for a certain degree of flexibility in its approach to English language teaching.

Data was collected through teacher interviews, observation of lessons and tests. Observation was used to gain insight into classroom organisation and materials, the organisation and focus of lessons, the role of the teacher and the way pupils worked with and reacted to activities. Semi-structured interviews were conducted with two teachers from Nylund School, and one teacher from each of the control schools. The teachers were asked questions about materials used in their teaching, classroom organisation, time spent on different language skills, typical classroom activities, the use of computers in English teaching, to what extent they read aloud to pupils and successful and less successful aspects of the English teaching. Finally, Cambridge Young Learners Starters tests were used to assess the pupils at the end of the spring term 2006 and the end of the autumn term 2007. Each test was divided into three components: listening (20 min), reading and writing (20 min), and oral (5 min). The listening test had a maximum score of 20 points, the reading and writing test 25 points, and the oral test a maximum score of 9 points. Twelve pupils from Nylund School and four pupils from the control schools for whom English is a third language, in addition to one native speaker from Nylund School and three native speakers of English from the control schools, have been removed from the test results since their performances were not considered to be representative of the main group of pupils, who have Norwegian as their mother tongue. The numbers of pupils represented in the tests are thus 44 from Nylund School and 51 from the control schools.

Based on some of the most salient data from the interviews and observations, a presentation of how English has been taught in the represented classes in Nylund School and the control schools will be provided. The test results will then be compared as aggregate percentage scores for each of the three schools.

Results

Nylund School

The classrooms in Nylund School were rich in environmental print in both Norwegian and English, with desks arranged in groups for the various learning centres. Each classroom was equipped with at least four computers. There was a common area where the pupils could sit on the floor for whole class gatherings at the beginning and end of lessons and for the teacher learning centre. Each classroom was further equipped with its own class library of all the titles in at least five levels of the Wings series of books. These are the same books read by Australian children in their mother tongue, although the Australian pupils would read the corresponding books at a younger age than their Norwegian peers. Four copies were available of each title to allow homogeneous groups to read the same book. The levels were staggered from year to year to accommodate variation of reading ability within a given class. A classroom in Grade 3, for instance, would be equipped with levels 1 to 5, and a fourth grade classroom with levels 2 to 7. The school also had a well-furnished school library with a selection of other books in English in addition to the Wings series. At times there would be queues of pupils at the library waiting to take out books in both English and Norwegian. A typical learning centre session lasted for one and a half hours. It always started with the class in plenary for about 5 to 10 minutes, for example singing some songs together and the teacher providing information about the day's activities. Instructions were given in English but often repeated in Norwegian. In groups of three to four, depending on the size of the class, pupils then rotated between the different centres, which the teacher had prepared in advance, spending about 10 to 15 minutes at each. As a rule, Nylund School used five learning centres in addition to the one led by the teacher. Three of these were always silent reading in the reading corner, writing, for example sentences about a picture, and vocabulary practice on computers. Other centres included oral activities, such as role-play, games activities and vocabulary practice activities. At the end of the session there would be a second plenary gathering at which the teacher summed up the day's lesson.

At the teacher centre each pupil usually read aloud from a Wings book they had been reading at home, which was normally a quick process since the books at the lowest levels are relatively short. The teacher kept records of which books each pupil had read. Midway through the fourth grade, most of the pupils were between levels 2 and 4 on the Wings series, with some moving on to level 5. The pupils read between one and three books a week at home with parental help, reading each book several times to increase reading fluency. Before leaving the teacher centre pupils would choose a new book or books to take home to read. The last activity in the teacher centre was usually the teacher reading aloud a book unfamiliar to the pupils and asking them questions about it.

Pupils seemed enthusiastic and focused at most of the learning centres. They were extremely enthusiastic about reading the books, both the Wings series and other books. However, speaking activities, such as role plays, did not seem to work as well as the other activities in the learning centre sessions, with some pupils appearing to be confused, switching easily to Norwegian, and finishing with time to spare. The teachers generally expressed satisfaction with the way the learning centre model worked, but pointed out how demanding it was for them to prepare all the activities in advance. In addition, they constantly needed to monitor the composition of groups, as pupils who developed faster or slower than others needed to be moved to a higher or lower level group. It was also frustrating for the teachers not to be able to detach themselves from the teacher centre if pupils needed assistance when working at one of the other learning centres. Alternating between the learning centre approach and other approaches was considered a positive strategy as it allowed for a greater degree of flexibility in the teaching. In this way the pupils were able to experience, for example, the dynamics of whole class oral activities, such as dramatising stories together. It also provided a finer balance between oral and written training.

The control schools

The classrooms in C1 had desks arranged in rows and contained environmental print that was mostly in Norwegian. A large proportion of the time was spent on whole-class teaching, although the class was sometimes split into two large groups, for example one working on computers, which the pupils seemed to enjoy, and one led by the teacher, for example, working on a language game. The pupils worked with computers about once a month, although the teacher would have preferred even more time spent on them as she considered them to provide effective and enjoyable practice in English. The computers were located in a separate computer room and in the library. The teacher did not use a textbook and few readers were available. As a consequence, she made up her own materials from lesson to lesson. The school had thus far not decided to invest in an English course-book for each grade. However, the teacher suggested that using a course-book with its accompanying listening materials would have facilitated her role as an English teacher.

Typical activities included choral repetition of structures and vocabulary, pupils reading dialogues in groups and in class, and simple writing activities, such as completing sentences. The teacher normally gave instructions in both English and Norwegian, and translated the content of texts and individual words into Norwegian. Although oral language had been given priority up to the third grade, the teacher reported that the oral and written skills were equally prioritised in the fourth grade, mainly because both modes were reflected in the competence aims of the new curriculum. However, many pupils had experienced the transition to more reading and writing in the fourth grade as extremely difficult and demanding. Apparently one of the major challenges was the enormous range of mixed ability in each class.

The classroom in C2 had desks arranged in groups, a common area around the blackboard with benches and cushions, an English corner, and a comfortable reading chair for the teacher. It contained a good deal of environmental print in both English and Norwegian. There was one computer, although it had thus far not been used in English teaching. The teacher used a course-book, which was the policy of the school, but stressed the importance of having other materials in addition. These included a songbook, picture cards, posters and some readers. If the school had been able to afford it, she would willingly have increased the stocks of readers and supplementary teaching materials.

The teacher used primarily English, even when giving instructions to the pupils, translating the odd word into Norwegian when necessary. Typical activities were reading stories aloud to the pupils, choral repetition of words and structures, simple reading and writing activities connected to the course-book, and singing. Time was divided more or less equally between listening, speaking, reading, writing and vocabulary and language practice.

A workshop scenario was used for one of the two English lessons a week, during which pupils were divided into three large groups of seven to nine pupils, which rotated between three different activities. One activity would be teacher-led, for example reading a picture book to the group, practising pronunciation and asking questions about the text's content and vocabulary. Other workshop activities included writing, for example about a picture or text, or a listening comprehension exercise. The teacher considered the workshop as one of the most positive aspects of English lessons. As in C1, she stressed the enormous challenge of providing suitable and meaningful materials and activities for pupils of different ability levels in a mixed ability class. Those pupils who struggled with their Norwegian inevitably struggled with English as well.

Assessment of language skills

Figure 8.1 shows the results of the first Cambridge Starters tests at the end of the spring semester of 2006. The scores are presented as aggregate percentages for the three schools.

The differences between the schools on the first test results were relatively minor with all schools scoring between 56% and 68% on each test. Nylund School had a slightly lower score on the listening test than both the control schools (64% compared to 66% and 68%, respectively). Its score on the oral test (58%) was higher than C1 (56%), but lower than C2 (66%). Nylund School and C2 had equal scores of 62% for the reading and writing test, which was 5% higher than C1.

All three schools made progress from the first to the second test at the end of the autumn semester 2006, as indicated in Figure 8.2.

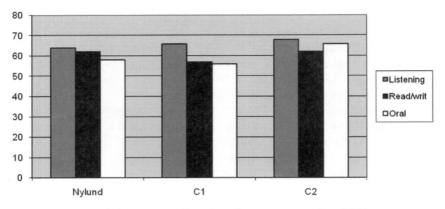

Figure 8.1   Pupils' scores on Test 1 in three tests, spring 2006

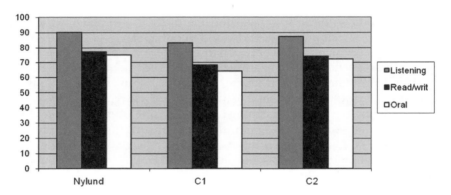

Figure 8.2   Pupils' scores on Test 2 in three tests, autumn 2006

Scores ranged from 64% to 90% on the different tests. However, whereas Nylund School had had the lowest listening score and the second lowest oral score on the first test, it now scored highest on all three tests. Its scores increased to 90% (listening), 77% (reading and writing) and 75% (oral). The scores for C2 were exactly 3% lower than Nylund School for each test, with C1 scoring lower than the other two schools on all three tests.

As Figure 8.3 shows, the rate of progress made by the Nylund School pupils from the first to the second tests was higher than the pupils in the two control schools, especially in the listening and oral tests.

The rate of increase for the Nylund School pupils was 26% in the listening test, 17% in the oral test and 15% in the reading and writing test. The rate of increase in the listening test was 9% higher than C1 and 7% higher

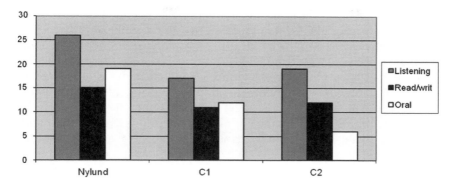

Figure 8.3 Pupils' rate of progress in three tests from Test 1 to Test 2

than C2. In the oral test the progress of the Nylund School pupils was 5% higher than C1 and 11% higher than C2, which was significant ($p < 0.001$). The reading and writing tests showed the lowest rate of increase, with Nylund School outperforming C1 by 4% and C2 by 3%.

Implications and Conclusions

There were numerous differences in classroom organisation, materials, facilities and practices in the schools represented in the study. Some of these differences were determined by school policies and financial constraints, and to a certain extent affected teaching. Nylund School's implementation of the EYLP approach necessitated it having a rich supply of books and several computers in each classroom. In addition, each classroom was rich in environmental print and was organised to accommodate the learning centre model. C1 had virtually no books, either readers or course-books, and few supplementary materials, although its pupils had at least monthly access to computers in EFL teaching. There was little environmental print in English and the desks were arranged in rows. C2 used a course-book, had one computer in the classroom, which was not used in English teaching, and only a few readers. Nevertheless, the classroom environment stimulated literacy through its environmental print and English corner, was organised in a similar way to Nylund School, and the teacher seemed to make good use of the materials at her disposal.

There were also different practices in the teachers' use of the target language from school to school. The teacher who used English most consistently and resorted the least to Norwegian was probably the one in C2. In both of the other schools the teachers had a tendency to repeat, for example, instructions in Norwegian. Attitudes to reading stories to pupils also varied. The teacher reading stories aloud to pupils was basic to the EYLP approach in Nylund School, and was also regularly practised by the teacher in C2. In contrast the teacher in C1 did not read stories aloud to her pupils.

As for effectiveness of the EYLP approach at Nylund School, only tentative conclusions may be drawn about it thus far since the study is in its preliminary stages. One is that Nylund School has demonstrated that it is actually feasible to implement an adapted version of the EYLP into the young learners' foreign language classroom. Not only is it feasible, but the rate of progress made by the Nylund School pupils from the first to the second test in all skills was higher than the two control schools, resulting in the highest scores in all tests. The considerable gains made in the oral skills are especially interesting. However, it is difficult to determine the exact influence that the EYLP model had on these results, since it was not the only form of teaching to which the pupils were exposed. Progress could have been partly due to the increased opportunities for oral practice that were provided when the learning centre model was not used.

However, since the control schools spent at least as much time on oral practice as Nylund School, time alone does not explain why the Nylund School pupils made greater progress on their listening and oral tests than their peers. Despite the fact that a number of factors, especially the teacher, may contribute to learner performances, it seems likely that the substantial amounts of reading done by the Nylund pupils, which was one of the major differences between the approach at Nylund School and the two control schools, was instrumental in enhancing their oral skills. Similar effects have been noted in book-flood projects, such as the one conducted by Elley and Mangubhai (1983) in Fijian schools. In contrast, the Nylund School pupils' rate of improvement in reading and writing skills was not as great as that of their oral skills, although still greater than the pupils in the two control schools. However, since the Nylund School pupils regularly read substantial amounts in both English and Norwegian, gains in their reading and writing skills are likely to manifest themselves over a longer period of time. Since the approach has been instrumental in enhancing pupils' L1 literacy levels in Australia and Norway, there is good reason to assume it can do the same for pupils' L2 literacy development.

One of the greatest merits of the EYLP model is that it caters for pupils at their level of ability through differentiated groups, differentiated tasks, and differentiated materials. Each pupil is also given individual attention by the teacher during a typical learning centre session. The teachers in the control schools found mixed ability classes to be one of the greatest challenges in their English teaching, without having any specific strategies to deal with the problem.

In spite of its merits and popularity among pupils, numerous challenges follow implementing the EYLP model. First, it requires a commitment at the school level. It presupposes that all classes, at least at the same year level but also throughout the school, adopt the model, preferably in several subjects, so that pupils are familiar with how it functions. In doing so, it presupposes a considerable financial investment in supplying classrooms with large supplies of books, such as the Wings series, and several computers. Second, it requires commitment, great effort and a high level of skill on the part of the teacher. Organising and designing differentiated tasks for learning centres, assessing pupils' reading, and interacting with pupils when reading aloud to them all require a certain level of expertise on the part of the teacher. Finally, parental cooperation and involvement is a necessary component, but one which cannot be taken for granted. Some parents need reminding of their role and responsibility in the process.

The EYLP model in English teaching at Nylund School will continue to be monitored in the coming years, during which time a more complete picture of its pros and cons will hopefully be acquired. If it proves to be as effective as the initial results indicate it potentially can be, the approach may be incorporated into teacher training programmes in Norway, and possibly be of interest for foreign language teachers and teacher educators in other countries. In addition to using the Cambridge Young Learners tests, it would be interesting, through interviews or questionnaires, to assess the effects the model has on pupils' reading attitudes and habits. It would also be interesting to compare how the pupils at Nylund School and the control schools perform in written production tasks. One would then be able to weigh up the overall benefits of the approach with the commitment, effort and cost that it entails.

References

Bonnet, G. (ed.) (2004) *The Assessment of Pupils' Skills in English in Eight European Countries. The European Network of Policy Makers for the Evaluation of Educational Systems*. On WWW at http://cisad.adc.education.fr/reva. Accessed 23.2.07.

Cambourne, B. (1986) Process writing and non-English speaking background children. *Australian Journal of Reading* 9 (3), 126–138.

Cambourne, B. and Turbill, J. (1987) *Coping with Chaos*. Rozelle, Australia: Primary English Teaching Association.

Clay, M.M. (1993) *Reading Recovery: A Guidebook for Teachers in Training*. Aukland, New Zealand: Heinemann Education.

Crévola, C.A. and Hill, P.W. (1988) Evaluation of a whole-school approach to prevention and intervention in early years. *Journal of Education for Students Placed at Risk* 3, 133–157.

Drew, I. (2004) Comparing primary English in Norway and the Netherlands. *Språk & Språkundervisning* 2/2004, 18–22.

Elley, W.B. and Mangubhai, F. (1983) The impact of reading on second language learning. *Reading Research Quarterly* X1X (1), 53–67.

Hafiz, F.M. and Tudor, I. (1989) Extensive reading and the development of language skills. *ELT Journal* 43, 4–11.

Hellekjær, G.O. (2005) The acid test: Does upper secondary EFL instruction prepare Norwegian students for the reading of English textbooks at college and universities? Unpublished doctoral dissertation, University of Oslo.

Hill, P.W. and Crévola, C.A. (2006) Key features of a whole-school, design approach to literacy teaching in schools. On WWW at http://www.sofweb.vic.edu.au/eys/pdf/hillcrev. Accessed 5.1.07.

Krashen, S. (1984) *Writing: Research, Theory and Applications.* Oxford and New York: Pergamon Press.

Lagerström, B.O. (2000) *Kompetanse i Grunnskolen. Hovedresultater 1999/2000. Statistisk Sentralbyrå 2000/72.* [Competence in Compulsory School. Main Results 1999/2000. Central Statistics Bureau 2000/72]. Oslo: Central Statistics Bureau.

Lancy, D. (ed.) (1994) *Children's Emergent Literacy.* Westport, CT: Praeger.

Lehmann, T. (1999) Literacy and the tertiary student: Why has the communicative approach failed? Unpublished doctoral dissertation, University of Bergen.

Seda, I. and Abramson, A. (1990) English writing development of young, linguistically different learners. *Early Childhood Research Quarterly* 33 (4), 379–391.

Stanovich, K.E. (1992) The psychology of reading: Evolutionary and revolutionary developments. In W. Grabe (ed.) *Annual Review of Applied Linguistics* 12 (pp. 3–30). Cambridge: Cambridge University Press.

Teale, W.H. and Sulzby, E. (eds) (1986) *Emergent Literacy: Writing and Reading.* Norwood, NJ: Ablex.

Vygotsky, L. (1978) *Mind in Society.* Cambridge, MA: Harvard University Press.

Chapter 9

The Age Factor and L2 Reading Strategies

RENATA ŠAMO

Introduction

A wide range of theoretical approaches to learning foreign languages has changed our understanding of reading in a second language (L2 reading), and probably the most important change resulted from the so-called cognitive revolution in the 1980s. One of its first influential presentations in literature on L2 acquisition refers to Anderson's (1983, 1985) production systems, which view language as a complex cognitive skill and cognitive skill acquisition as a process divided into cognitive, associative and autonomous stages. Making a clear distinction between the two basic types of human knowledge, Anderson sees this three-stage acquisition as a shift from declarative (generally represented by definitions, rules or facts) to procedural (considered to be more or less automatic) knowledge. In other words, the process of learning starts with the conscious investment of mental energy and the conscious use of necessary rules, whereas automatic data processing replaces the behaviour under the learner's supervision as the process of learning is becoming more and more successful. According to O'Malley and Chamot (1990), who did not only point out the interaction between language and cognition but also provided a comprehensive analysis of the two learning theories (cognitive theory and language acquisition theory), Anderson's model is to be recognised as a framework for the process of learning languages with an emphasis on knowledge compilation, controlled processing and automatic processing.

This model considers language comprehension implying active and complex processes during which meaning is constructed. In order to explain the mental processes necessary for understanding text (both written and aural), Anderson differentiates three inter-related processes: perceptual processing, parsing and utilisation. Taking into account the comprehension of meaning as the ultimate aim of reading, one of the basic aims of this chapter, we are going to describe each of them in the context of written text.

During perceptual processing, we pay attention to the text while its segments, that is, sequences of words, are retained in our short-term memory, but not longer than a few seconds because of the limited capacity of short-term memory. However, the analysis of language can begin while the text is still in short-term memory, as our selective attention helps us transform text segments into meaningful forms, directing us to those aspects of the task that could make understanding easier, such as punctuation or paragraphs. It is also possible to pay attention to contextual factors considering, for example, our reading aims or text types. In the second phase of parsing, we use words and phrases to construct meaningful mental representations of text while the segmentation of language material into words and phrases is considered crucial to define text meaning. In other words, Anderson saw meaning as the main key to parsing during the process of understanding, which is dependant on the interaction between different types of reader's knowledge. The last utilisation phase connects the mental representations of text meaning to the declarative knowledge stored in the reader's long-term memory enabling the connection between what is already known and the data that is completely new.

Perceptual processing, parsing and utilisation can be therefore associated with word recognition, syntactic analysis and text understanding, traditionally known as the three basic levels of reading, while the new approach to this complex linguistic skill, born within the cognitive theory of learning, has broadened its scope by presenting cognitive, metacognitive and socio-affective aspects of reading. Consequently, it introduced a strategic dimension that seems to be of great importance in considerations of how to achieve the 'proceduralisation' of knowledge efficiently and successfully.

Much of the recent research in the field of reading comprehension has concentrated on the knowledge and control of reading strategies. According to Garner (1987), a reading strategy is an action (or a series of actions) that is employed in order to construct meaning. Readers who know what strategies are, how to use them and when they are helpful are generally considered to be strategic readers (Paris *et al.*, 1983). However, almost all discussions on the use of reading strategies are centred on whether the idea of a strategy necessarily includes the notion of purposeful, conscious effort. Anderson (1980), for example, reported that readers may use strategies without being aware of using them, particularly when the material is not very difficult, whereas Paris *et al.* (1983) insist on the intentional and purposeful behaviour on the part of the strategic learner. It is widely accepted that readers need to use strategies in order to overcome their difficulties upon encountering obstacles to their comprehension. In the study presented here, reading strategies are seen as deliberate means of constructing meaning from a text when comprehension is impeded.

Aims of Study

The main aim of the present research was to analyse reading strategies used by good and poor learners of English as a foreign language on the sample of three L2 passages and to see whether there is a significant difference in their usage between the two groups. The research questions are as follows:

(1) Are learners with longer English learning histories better L2 readers than those who have learnt the language for a shorter time?
(2) Do good L2 readers use a wider range of reading strategies?
(3) Do good L2 readers use a wider range of reading strategies more frequently than their poor L2 reader peers?

Method

Participants

The sample included 37 primary-school pupils from Pula (Croatia), aged 13–14, who were divided into two groups: Group 1 learnt English for eight years (n = 19) and Group 2 for five years (n = 18) at the time of the study.

Instruments and procedures

Prior to the crucial research tasks, the participants were administered a standardised English proficiency test, as we first needed to divide them into good and poor learners of English. Afterwards, three different cloze tests (every fifth word omitted, only the first and last sentences unchanged) were individually administered to each participant as the main reading tasks. We applied this type of task believing that the cognitive processes involved in cloze, for example, imagining, reasoning, evaluating, judging and problem-solving, are the processes that are essential in reading. Besides, this cloze procedure was used more than once to enable us to collect more data and to help the participants increase their awareness of the comprehension strategies they were using while trying to figure out what the passages meant. Cloze performance data were compared with self-report data, as recommended by Ericsson and Simon (1980). While reconstructing the three texts and filling in the gaps (22, 32 and 38, respectively), the participants were instructed to verbalise their thoughts, which were recorded on audio-tapes and resulted in verbal protocols (n = 111 from 37 participants × 3 cloze-tests) whose transcripts were first coded and then analysed qualitatively and quantitatively. In other words, the strategies were identified and the frequency with which each strategy was used was scored for each passage. A score was also calculated for the total strategy use, which was made up of the number of times any strategy was mentioned. Multiple strategy use was often reported; when this happened, each strategy mentioned was included in the coding and analysis, revealing that readers often used more than one strategy to construct meaning. As for the applied classification scheme, we should mention that it was developed by considering processing strategies suggested by Anderson *et al.* (1991). Table 9.1 contains the list of all strategy types we included in this analysis in order to provide insights into how readers had arrived at their interpretations at a level of detail, main idea, inferred meaning or evaluation judgement.

Table 9.1   Classification of strategies used in study

Number	Category	Strategy
1.	Supervising strategies	Referring to the experimental task (e.g. Can I use the same word twice?)
2.		Recognising loss of concentration/memory problem (e.g. Wait a little bit … something has just occurred to me but … I've forgotten what)
3.		Stating failure to understand (a portion of) text (e.g. I couldn't understand everything)
4.		Stating success in understanding (a portion of) text (e.g. I've understood the first sentence)
5.		Adjusting reading style/rate to increase comprehension (e.g. *She told me that she has bought two tickets for …* continues murmuring while reading the rest)
6.		Formulating a question (e.g. *… it was a difficult operation but it was …* what operation?!)
7.		Making a prediction about the meaning of a word or text content (e.g. *… and this however* – it could be some place where there is the campsite or …)
8.		Referring to lexical items that impede comprehension (e.g. I'm not quite sure what *snail* means – if I can't understand one word, it's more difficult to me then)
9.		Confirming/disconfirming an inference (e.g. *Snail*, yes! There it *is*! / No, it can't be written here)
10.		Referring to the previous passage (e.g. We have before *where he walked* …)

(Continued)

Table 9.1   (*Continued*)

Number	Category	Strategy
11.		Responding affectively to text content (e.g. Yeah, it will be more interesting later)
12.	Support strategies	Skipping unknown words (e.g. Well, I'm going on and getting back to this later)
13.		Expressing a need for help/clarification (e.g. Is this different – *hotel* and *hostel*?)
14.	Paraphrase strategies	Using cognates between L1 and L2 to comprehend (e.g. *Campsite* ... reminds me of <u>kamp</u> or something like that)
15.		Breaking lexical items into parts (e.g. Five-star ... five is 5, star is a star)
16.		Paraphrasing (e.g. *Campsite* ... field for camping)
17.		Translating a word/a phrase into L1 (e.g. ... *to hospital*, <u>u bolnicu</u> ...)
18.		Extrapolating from information in the text (e.g. ... *he just puts ... his tent*, which means that he camps)
19.	Strategies for establishing coherence in text	Rereading (e.g. *He stopped at* (...) let me get back to the first paragraph to see if ...)
20.		Using context clues to interpret a word/a phrase (e.g. ... *walking*, so it is some man)
21.		Reacting to author's style or text surface structure (e.g. If there weren't this *too*, it would be *quite* ... / *It was a difficult operation* ... I need a noun as this is the adjective – *difficult* – *operation* ...)
22.		Reading ahead (e.g. *He loves being* ... let's go on ... *he doesn't stay* ...)
23.		Using background knowledge (e.g. ... *and took him to hospital* ... where did she take him ... injured people are usually taken to hospital, so it's – *hospital*)
24.		Acknowledging lack of background knowledge (e.g. I don't know where he flew ... where ...)
25.		Relating stimulus sentence to personal experiences (e.g. *Dire Straits!* I've never listened to them)
26.	Other strategies	Changing an answer (e.g. (...) *which was crossing a road, the road* ...)

The data collection lasted from November 2002 to March 2003, following the training on reading strategies and think-aloud procedure, while the analysis of the obtained results lasted until mid-January 2006.

Results and Discussion

Although we do not intend to present the standardised test results in this chapter, we should mention that each test element had different parameters, so we transformed the results into a standardised Z-scale, indicating 21 good learners and 16 poor learners. As the results based on the reconstruction of sample passages are of our current concern, particularly the ones emphasising the main differences between the abovementioned groups of learners, we present them first.

Statistically significant differences between the two groups in all the three cloze-tests (see Table 9.2) supported the assumption that good learners achieve significantly better results than poor learners. As we recorded a greater number of correct responses (both syntactically and semantically acceptable) in their cloze-tests, we could point out their better ability to construct meaning and to reconstruct text more accurately and completely. This would not have been possible if they had not been able to understand text globally, as well. Their knowledge of English as a foreign language should be additionally taken into account. So, it must be particularly emphasised that the participants, initially identified as good or poor learners of English, are to be seen as good/poor L2 readers until the end of this analysis. In order to see whether learners with longer learning history of English are better L2 readers than those who learnt it for a shorter time, we decided to take the years of learning as a relevant variable in our considerations.

As the statistically significant difference considering the number of good readers between the two groups of learners was not found this time (see Table 9.3), the assumption that Group 1 (longer exposure to English) included better L2 readers than Group 2 cannot be supported, despite our expectations about the significant difference to the benefit of the former group of learners. We suppose that the main reason lies in the fact that Group 1 had changed four teachers since they started learning English in

Table 9.2 Means, standard deviations and *t*-test results for cloze performances by good and poor learners

Cloze-tests	Good learners	Poor learners	t	p
No. 1	27.19 (6.93)	9.93 (8.31)	−6.88	0.000
No. 2	38.47 (10.37)	17.25 (11.08)	−5.98	0.000
No. 3	50.66 (9.75)	23.06 (13.63)	−7.18	0.000

Table 9.3 Differences between good and poor readers according to how long they learned English as a foreign language

Years of learning	Good readers	Poor readers
Five (5)	12	6
Eight (8)	9	10
Total	21	16

$\chi^2 = 1.40$; $df = 1$; $p < 0.23$

the first grade, while Group 2 had shared their English learning experiences with a single teacher since they began in the fourth grade. This change most probably resulted in a gradual decline of students' language learning motivation, which must have been also affected by the necessity to get adjusted to different teaching styles and evaluation criteria, which must have also had an impact on the quality of relationship between the teachers and the learners.

Also, Group 1 recorded less good achievements in other subjects, and their general achievement was getting worse from grade to grade. Talking to their English teacher about the possible reasons, we also discovered that many changes had happened in some families and the family situation in certain cases was difficult. It made us conclude that the learning process depends on a variety of factors, among which nonteaching ones are of particular importance, as the teaching context within a formal school system cannot be isolated from a wider social environment and atmosphere burdened with many challenges and doubts of contemporary living. Finally, it should be added that Group 2 was better in terms of the general success they made through schooling, which can be also related to the increase in their motivation to achieve good results. Trying to relate these findings to language learning strategies, let us mention Oxford's (1990) key points about them and their use for practical purposes. Among other things, Oxford explains that all the strategies (included in her classification) do not affect the learning process equally but they (both direct and indirect ones) are equally important in relation to expecting the desired results, as they support learning directly as well as indirectly. Besides, these are influenced by a variety of factors, among which we emphasise here the following: level of learning, teacher's expectations, age, learning styles and learning motivation.

Statistically significant differences between the two groups in all the three sets of verbal protocols reveal that good readers used a significantly greater number of strategies when reading the passages, whereas poor readers used significantly fewer strategies while solving the same cloze passages (see Table 9.4).

Table 9.4 Means, standard deviations and *t*-test results for L2 reading strategies reported by good and poor L2 readers

Verb. protocols	Good readers	Poor readers	t	p
No. 1	34.38 (20.34)	9.67 (6.96)	−4.50	0.000
No. 2	50.57 (23.40)	28.13 (24.53)	−2.78	0.009
No. 3	36.62 (21.09)	16.93 (16.91)	−3.00	0.005

The differences between participants identified as good and poor L2 readers in using the reading strategies on the sample of 111 verbal protocols are also graphically presented (see Table 9.5).

As can be seen in Table 9.5, statistically significant differences characterize the following strategies: reader recognises the loss of concentration or memory problem (No. 2), reader formulates a question (No. 6), reader confirms or disconfirms an inference (No. 9), reader translates a word or a phrase into L1 (No. 17), reader extrapolates from information presented in the text (No. 18), reader rereads (No. 19), reader reacts to author's style or text surface structure (No. 21), reader reads ahead (No. 22), reader acknowledges the lack of background knowledge (No. 24) and reader changes an answer after suggesting one (No. 26). It should be added that all these differences were recorded to the benefit of good readers, who used them significantly more frequently than poor readers.

More specifically, good readers realised that successful text comprehension required self-supervision over the process of reading by: recognising the loss of concentration and problem of memory; formulating questions, quite often to themselves, for clarifications; and confirming or disconfirming inferences. According to their strategy use, establishing coherence in text is also a kind of guarantee for good text comprehension, which they tried to achieve by rereading, reading ahead, reacting to author's style or text surface structure and acknowledging their lack of background knowledge. They also showed the significant advantages of extrapolation from information presented in the text, word or phrase translation into L1 and paraphrases.

On the other hand, poor readers supervised their own reading mainly by referring to lexical items that impeded comprehension and by making a prediction about the meaning of a word or text content, so that this self-supervision was closely connected to asking for help or clarification viewed as a kind of needed support. In order to establish text coherence, they generally tended to read ahead or simply acknowledged the lack of background knowledge. Only in the first task did they adjust their reading rates in order to increase comprehension and refer to the task. Other strategies

Table 9.5 Differences in L2 reading strategy use between good and poor readers on verbal protocols

Strategy number	Good readers	Poor readers	t	p
1.	3.42 (2.80)	3.87 (3.46)	0.41	0.678
2.	2.09 (1.67)	0.40 (0.50)	−3.79	0.001
3.	1.23 (1.44)	1.26 (1.16)	0.06	0.950
4.	0.33 (0.57)	0.33 (0.61)	0.00	1.000
5.	4.04 (3.96)	3.20 (5.11)	−0.56	0.579
6.	3.38 (2.49)	0.66 (0.97)	−3.98	0.000
7.	13.42 (12.67)	6.13 (9.85)	−1.86	0.072
8.	5.00 (3.74)	5.60 (5.34)	0.39	0.694
9.	6.57 (6.32)	1.33 (1.87)	−3.10	0.004
10.	0.14 (0.47)	0.00 (0.00)	−1.15	0.257
11.	0.28 (0.56)	0.06 (0.25)	−1.40	0.169
12.	2.61 (4.42)	0.53 (0.91)	−1.79	0.082
13.	4.80 (4.27)	5.80 (6.71)	0.54	0.592
14.	0.23 (0.43)	0.26 (0.45)	0.19	0.851
15.	0.19 (0.51)	0.00 (0.00)	−1.43	0.160
16.	5.42 (8.66)	2.20 (4.07)	−1.33	0.190
17.	8.38 (8.10)	1.60 (2.41)	−3.13	0.004
18.	4.52 (3.55)	1.53 (1.88)	−2.96	0.006
19.	3.61 (2.59)	1.40 (2.09)	−2.73	0.010
20.	0.23 (0.53)	0.06 (0.25)	−1.13	0.263
21.	8.14 (9.25)	1.46 (2.64)	−2.70	0.011
22.	27.61 (9.91)	9.73 (8.09)	−5.74	0.000
23.	1.52 (1.80)	0.60 (0.98)	−1.79	0.082
24.	9.14 (5.27)	4.80 (6.87)	−2.14	0.039
25.	0.33 (0.65)	0.13 (0.35)	−1.07	0.292
26.	4.80 (4.15)	1.73 (2.91)	−2.46	0.019

from the classification scheme were rarely used by poor readers or they did not use them at all.

Conclusion

The qualitative and quantitative analyses of the verbal protocols collected in two groups of Croatian teenage learners of English with five and eight years experience of learning EFL revealed that good and less successful readers approach reading tasks differently. Starting from the research questions, we found out that the learners identified as good L2 readers used a wider range of L2 reading strategies and they did so more frequently than poor L2 readers. These findings support the claim that good readers are more verbal, make better use of their limited working memory and verbalise more efficiently the things they do in a think-aloud task. Also, they identify and remember important information, monitor their reading and evaluate their reading. As Afflerbach (2001) states, the detailed description of good readers, resulting from the protocol-based research, can also inform us about how to teach less accomplished readers by incorporating this information into instruction on strategies and other knowledge that readers who are not so constructively responsive need to become expert in.

One of the research questions relates to how early and later starters of EFL perform on reading tasks. The results cast a 'shadow' on age being one of the most influential factors in the process of learning foreign languages, as the outcomes indicate that the learners who started learning English earlier and studied it for a longer period were not better L2 readers than those who learnt it for a shorter period. Therefore, the age when the process of learning a foreign language starts should be taken into account together with other factors to find out to what extent it predicts success and favourable outcomes. The starting age should be combined with special teaching conditions, mostly dependant on the teacher's ability to motivate learners and guide them towards expected outcomes even through training in learning strategies as well as with learning conditions among which learners' family situation can be particularly influential as a segment of wider social support and framework where the language learning process is conducted. The results have led us to the conclusion that an earlier start does not necessarily produce significantly better results in learning English, which fits into Singleton and Ryan's suggestion that the notion of an age factor should be rejected and we should start thinking '... in terms of a range of age-related factors ...' (Singleton & Ryan, 2004: 227).

References

Afflerbach, P. (2001) Verbal reports and protocol analysis. In P. Pearson, M. Kamil, P. Mosenthal and P. Barr (eds) *Handbook of Reading Research* (3rd edn). New York: Longman.

Anderson, J.R. (1983) *The Architecture of Cognition.* Cambridge, MA: Harvard University Press.

Anderson, J.R. (1985) *Cognitive Psychology and Its Implications.* New York: Freeman.

Anderson, N.J., Bachman, L., Perkins, K. and Cohen, A. (1991) An exploratory study into the construct validity of a reading comprehension test: Triangulation of data sources. *Language Testing* 8 (1), 41–66.

Anderson, T.H. (1980) Study strategies and adjunct aids. In R.J. Spiro, B.C. Bruce and W.F. Brewer (eds) *Theoretical Issues in Reading Comprehension* (pp. 483–502). Hillsdale, NJ: Erlbaum.

Ericsson, K.A. and Simon, H.A. (1980) Verbal reports as data. *Psychological Review* 87, 215–251.

Garner, R. (1987) *Metacognition and Reading Comprehension.* Norwood, NJ: Ablex.

O'Malley, M. and Chamot, A.U. (1990) *Learning Strategies in Second Language Acquisition.* Cambridge: Cambridge University Press.

Oxford, R. (1990) *Language Learning Strategies: What Every Teacher Should Know.* Boston: Heinle & Heinle Publishers.

Paris, S.G., Lipson, M.Y. and Wixson, K.K. (1983) Becoming a strategic reader. *Contemporary Educational Psychology* 8, 293–316.

Singleton, D. and Ryan, L. (2004) *Language Acquisition: The Age Factor* (2nd edn). Clevedon: Multilingual Matters.

Chapter 10

A Study of FL Composing Process and Writing Strategies Employed by Young Learners

ELENI GRIVA, HELEN TSAKIRIDOU and IOANNA NIHORITOU

Introduction

This chapter reports on an attempt to explore the writing strategies of young learners and to identify their composing strengths and weaknesses. The study bases its theoretical rationale on theories about 'writing' (Dyson & Freedman, 1991; Hayes & Flower, 1986; Susser, 1994), which is defined as (a) a process-oriented, goal-directed and problem-solving process, which involves the writer's awareness of the composing process and the teacher's or peers' intervention at any time needed; (b) 'a recursive, non-linear cognitive process in which the writer moves back and forth between prewriting-idea generating, writing, revising and editing until he/she is satisfied with his/her creation' (Susser, 1994: 39). Furthermore, writing is regarded as a socially situated, communicative act (Flower, 1994), a complex process that demands knowledge of the topic, language skills, ability to address to the audience using the right style and tone, to organise information, to use the right words and syntax, and to evaluate the final 'product' (White & Arndt, 1997).

A lot of researchers explored writing behaviours, by focusing on studying and understanding the process of composing (Zamel, 1982). Understanding what writers do involves thinking not just about what texts look like when they are finished but also about what strategies students employ to produce the texts and to develop some skills for generating, revising and editing texts. Thus, the instruction should be concerned with identifying and recording: what students can do while writing, how to assess ability and knowledge, how to deliver useful feedback appropriate for the student and how to develop writing strategies and subskills.

Students could be trained to utilise a range of strategies (Oxford, 1990), to gain metacognitive awareness (Chamot, 1987; O'Malley & Chamot,

1990; Rubin, 1987), and to monitor writing (Carrell & Devine, 1988; Raimes, 1987). Research has indicated that the use of appropriate strategies can result in achievement in specific skill areas (Oxford *et al.*, 1993). As students develop their awareness of the writing process, employ certain strategies and gain experience, many of the lower-level processes (such as forming letters and spelling) become automatic and unconscious and high-level skills are developed involving self-regulation and metacognitive control (Flower, 1990), such as planning, monitoring, revising and evaluating.

The Study

Aims

In Greece, there is an absence of a corpus of research data concerning FL composing processes of young learners within the framework of state primary education. This served as a starting point for the specific study, which can be considered as an attempt to provide a source of insight into the procedures and strategies employed by children while writing in English.

In particular, the basic objectives of the study are:

- to elicit information about young learners' writing process;
- to identify and describe the strategies employed when they write a task;
- to examine their views on their usual approach to writing;
- to record their perceived difficulties; and
- to explore the problems encountered by young learners.

Research questions

The aims of the study are restated as research questions. In particular, the main research questions the study seeks to answer are as follows:

(1) How do young learners plan a writing task?
(2) How do young learners organise ideas for composing a piece of writing?
(3) How do young learners draft and redraft a writing task?
(4) Which strategies do they employ while writing?
(5) What are the difficulties and problems young learners face?
(6) Which strategies do they employ to overcome difficulties?

Participants

The sample consisted of 184 Greek-speaking students (52% of them were females and 48% were males), aged 12, and enrolled in the sixth grade of state primary schools in North-Western Greece. All students have a four years' English learning experience in state primary schools. Most of the participants have been attending English language classes in private language schools for five years (5%), for four years (53%) and for three years (20%). In Greece, English as a foreign language is part of the state primary school curriculum (it is taught at the third, fourth, fifth and sixth grades). However, private language schools are for services that complement those offered at state primary schools. The participants' language level was estimated to range between sufficient (55%), average (26%) and low (19%) according to the results of an English test administered to them. The test was based on London Tests of English for Children (Breakthrough), equivalent to the A2 Level of Common European Framework.

Instruments and procedures

Multiple methods were used to collect data for the study, so that triangulation can help establish validity and reliability. Self-report questionnaires were used to gather information about the participants' composing process, writing strategy use and writing difficulties. Provision was made to include questions of the closed form or restricted types (Brown, 2001; Verma & Mallick, 1999; Wallace, 2000), using a three point Likert-type scale. The respondents had to rank the 32 items of the questionnaire in (a) frequency scales (frequently–sometimes–rarely), (b) scales of importance (most important–fairly important–least important), (c) difficulty scales (most difficult–fairly difficult–least difficult). The reason which determined the choice of this type of questions was to obtain specific responses from the largest possible number of students. However, using questionnaires has some limitations; students may not remember the strategies they have used in the past (Chamot, 2004: 3) or they say they use some strategies that in fact they do not use. In order to obtain a more complete indication of a learner's written ability and strategy use, verbal reports (think-aloud protocols) and retrospective interviews were used.

Verbal report data was collected from 20 12-year-old students (seven females and 13 males) while they were planning and writing their essays. A task was given at the beginning of the interview with the intent of observing how each child would approach the task. While composing, the students were asked to think aloud all the techniques and procedures used to perform the writing task. All their thinking aloud was done in L1 (Greek) in order to promote as much verbalising of thoughts as possible. After the think-aloud sessions, semi-structured interviews were conducted with the twenty students individually to gain further insight into their usual approach to writing, writing problems, their strategies and their perceptions on abilities and weaknesses. These sessions were tape-recorded, transcribed and analysed.

Data analysis

Data derived from the questionnaires was analysed by using descriptive statistical methods. Frequencies and percentages for all items of the questionnaires were obtained. Moreover, Chi-square-test (χ^2) was used to test possible differences between male and female students and between more proficient and less proficient language learners.

The verbal data underwent the following two procedures: Data reduction involved first and second level coding as well as pattern coding, which involves giving descriptive or conceptual names (Papadopoulou, 1999). Codes resulted in groups of categories, 'labelled' by a specific name (Miles & Humberman, 1994), which were developed from theories based on relevant literature (Chamot, 2004; Flower, 1990; Hedge, 1997; Susser, 1994; Tribble, 1997; Wenden, 1993) and Oxfords' strategy classification, which includes two major types: (a) direct, that is cognitive, memory and compensation strategies, (b) indirect strategies, which include metcognitive, social and affective strategies (Oxford, 1990). Then similar concepts with common characteristics were clustered into themes, so as to reduce the number of categories. The data was tabulated and displayed on individual tables and in crosschecking formats.

Results

Questionnaire data

Pre-planning a writing task

While pre-planning a task, an important group of young learners (67%) – regardless of their language level – reported that they try to generate raw material and they think about organising the content. However, 10% of the participants declared they rarely pre-plan their writing carefully in order to be able to organise their task. A significant difference was found ($\chi^2 = 11.688$, $df = 2$, $p < 0.005$) with male students rarely using this subprocess (67%) and female students thinking, frequently, about planning a written task (55%).

However, it is remarkable that a limited proportion of the sample (19%) declared they often try to identify the purpose of writing a task. On the contrary, an important percentage of the respondents (40%) ranked this subskill 'rarely' and the rest 41% 'sometimes' on the frequency scale. A lack of concern for identifying purpose was more evident in female students (53%) as opposed to male students (77%) who ranked special preference by ranking it as 'frequently' used ($\chi^2 = 8.731$, $df = 2$, $p < 0.05$). For the majority of young learners, the focus of the pre-planning sessions was semantic grouping of vocabulary and concepts, as they were concerned about identifying and selecting the appropriate vocabulary (59% chose 'frequently', 28% chose 'sometimes') (see Figure 10.1).

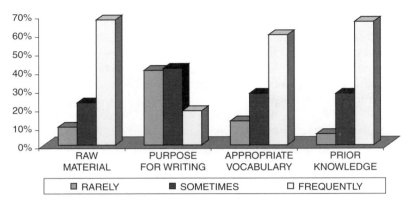

Figure 10.1 Pre-planning a writing task

Moreover a number of the participants showed preference for drawing on prior knowledge (content knowledge, language system knowledge and context knowledge) to make sense of the topic they are writing about and to generate ideas (62% 'frequently' and 28% 'sometimes'). Besides, the more proficient learners preferred activating their prior knowledge (62%) more often than the intermediate and low level ones (36%) ($\chi^2 = 8.156$, $df = 4$, $p < 0.05$).

Pre-planning activities

The participants were willing to be engaged in pre-writing activities, in brainstorming and pre-planning sessions. More precisely, the young learners (irrespective of their language level) showed a major preference (35% sometimes and 30% frequently) for having the opportunity to read a text as a model for the particular function. In addition, fewer than half of the total number of the participants (30%), irrespective of their language level, frequently preferred discussing with the instructor, while about the same percentage of the participants (32%) stated that they rarely preferred this activity (see Figure 10.2).

Moreover, they had preference for cooperating with peers to brainstorming the topic (39%). The poor writers showed a major preference for employing this subskill, since 28% considered it to be 'most important'. The more competent writers regarded 'brainstorming' as fairly important (58%) ($\chi^2 = 9.597$, $df = 4$, $p < 0.05$). However, almost half of the respondents (44%) stated that they rarely prefer being provided with a list of useful words and only 27% of the total number of students scored 'provision with a list of appropriate words' as a frequent one (see Figure 10.2, Appendix). The results indicated that there was a significant difference between the male students (70% 'sometimes'), and the female students

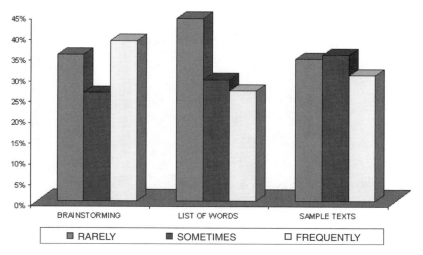

Figure 10.2   Pre-writing activities

who showed a greater preference (59% 'frequently') ($\chi^2 = 9.619$, $df = 2$, $p < 0.01$).

Composing a writing task

While writing a draft, *translation* of ideas into written words involves a lot of subprocesses. The majority of the respondents expressed more local processes dealing with 'spelling words' and 'sentence structure'. Regarding their primary concern, 'spelling of words' attracted most students' preference (81%). Significant differences were revealed between female and male students. The majority of male students (86%) declared that they do not pay any attention to spelling, as opposed to female students (51%) who ranked it as 'most important' ($\chi^2 = 8.924$, $df = 2$, $p = 0.05$). Furthermore, the more proficient students (61%) were more concerned than the poor writers, who paid no attention (43%) ($\chi^2 = 9.619$, $df = 2$, $p < 0.05$).

The selection of the appropriate vocabulary was viewed of highest importance for the great majority of students (73%) (see Figure 10.3). There were significant differences between the more competent writers, who paid much attention to using the appropriate vocabulary (59%), and the less competent ones who declared that they rarely focus on choosing the appropriate words (88%) ($\chi^2 = 23.390$, $df = 4$, $p < 0.001$).

The majority of participants reported that their second concern, while writing a draft, was to write grammatically and syntactically correct sentences (75% frequently and 22% sometimes) (see Figure 10.3). The more proficient students declared that they often pay special attention to grammar and syntax (63%), opposed to less sufficient ones who stated that their

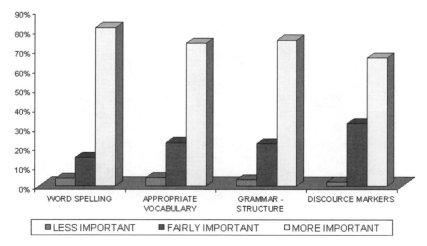

Figure 10.3   Writing at sentence level

attention was rarely drawn on grammatical accuracy (50%) ($\chi^2 = 18.818$, $df = 4$, $p < 0.005$).

At *text level*, a great percentage of learners (64%) – regardless of their language level – emphasised the fact that they were concerned with presenting and organising ideas in a correct sequence, so that coherence was achieved. Moreover a great percentage (72%) of the total number of students wondered how to start writing the draft, although a considerable number of the low level students (67%) stated they never follow this sub-skill (see Figure 10.4).

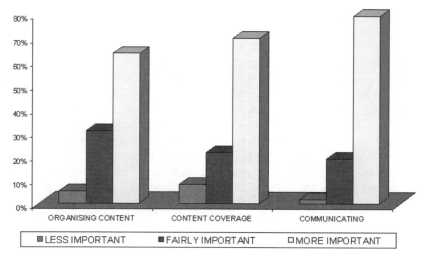

Figure 10.4   Composing at text level

Furthermore, most of the students (70%) appeared to stress on covering the main points of the content. However, there were significant differences between male students (87%), who in their vast majority did not pay any attention to including the relevant ideas, and the female students (50%) who were especially interested in incorporating all the necessary information and covering all the essential points ($\chi^2 = 7.452$, $df = 2$, $p < 0.05$).

It is worth mentioning that the vast majority of the participants (79%) were in favour of communicating their ideas, so that the text is clear for the reader. It seemed to have a higher incidence of use with the more competent students (59%) ($\chi^2 = 9.276$, $df = 4$, $p < 0.05$).

Difficulties

Most of the students, regardless of their language level, identified some problems and difficulties encountered and presented the strategies employed to solve them. The frequency distribution of the data showed that the most difficult subskills are considered to be the following. 'Finding and using the appropriate words' was of high difficulty for a certain number of the students (33%), and of medium difficulty for half of the participants (51%) (see Figure 10.5). There was a significant difference between the competent students, who rated 'finding and using the appropriate words' low in difficulty (53%), and the poor writers (47%) ($\chi^2 = 15.438$, $df = 4$, $p < 0.005$). However, only 30% of the students declared that they face great difficulty in structuring a sentence. For struggling writers, writing correct and effective sentences was a significant problem (53%) as opposed to more competent writers ($\chi^2 = 25.184$, $df = 4$, $p < 0.001$).

It is noteworthy that the participants were partly in agreement when facing difficulties in including and developing the main points adequately

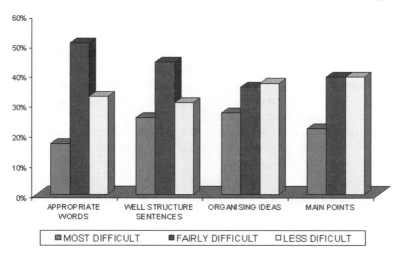

Figure 10.5 Difficulties

(40%, most difficult, 40% fairly difficult) (see Figure 10.5). 'Developing the content adequately' constitutes a major difficulty for the low level (56%) and average (46%) students' writing ($\chi^2 = 9.487, df = 4, p = <0.05$). Moreover, a great number of the students faced difficulties in formulating/organising ideas (36% very difficult, 37% fairly difficult). Most of the poor (53%) and less efficient (48%) writes struggled to a high degree with grouping ideas into paragraphs ($\chi^2 = 16.969, df = 4, p < 0.005$).

Overcoming difficulties

In order to overcome the problems and difficulties, the students stated that they employ the following strategies. The most frequently cited strategy used was translation from L1. The participants admitted they think either frequently (49%) or sometimes (36%) in L1 and then translate into English and write down the ideas in English. Moreover, a significant number of young learners (59%) stated they frequently use mother tongue patterns and rules while writing in FL. A considerable number of students stated that they tend to simplify their word usage (36% frequently) when meeting a difficult phrase or word or sentence. However, they (43%) occasionally cross out words or look for substitutes. Only 19% of the total number of the participants ranked 'skipping the difficult parts' as a high priority, as opposed to male students, who in their vast majority (74%) preferred using this strategy frequently ($\chi^2 = 7.343, df = 2, p < 0.05$).

Moreover, a significant percentage of the participants accepted the idea of regression and 'recombining' while they are writing, as 42% of the students found 'adjusting the meaning of a phrase-sentence' a better way of facing some problems, while (31%) of the total sample preferred using it sometimes. However, only 19% of the total number of the participants ranked 'skipping the difficult parts' as a high priority (see Figure 10.6).

For the majority of young learners 'cooperating with peers' is regarded as a very helpful way to overcome difficulties and they frequently employed this strategy (39% sometimes, 38% often). Most of the boys (73%) agreed in perceiving 'cooperating with the peers' as very helpful, as opposed to girls, who rarely follow this social strategy (54%) ($\chi^2 = 8.451, df = 2, p < 0.05$). Furthermore, 'asking for clarification' is of high importance for the vast majority of the students, as the participants declared that they think highly of this way of overcoming difficulties and use it either frequently (46%) or sometimes (42%).

Interview and Verbal Report Data

Rich insights to the composing process and writing strategies were provided through think-aloud process and retrospective interviews. The data, after being coded, resulted into 37 codes, which were grouped into 14

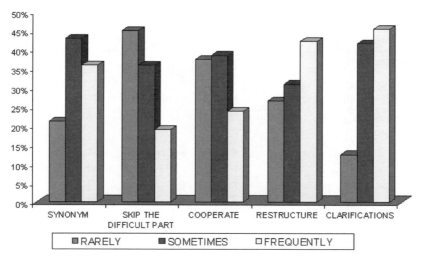

Figure 10.6 Overcoming difficulties

categories classified into four basic themes: (a) Composing process, (b) Writing difficulties, (c) Direct strategies, (d) Indirect strategies (see Table 10.1).

Composing process

The students appeared to be able to articulate their composing processes reasonably fully and it was revealed that more than half of the young writers tried to devise some kind of preplanning and ideas generated by brainstorming and activating their prior knowledge. More competent writers agreed that outlines are a good technique to plan ideas and avoid some problems with organisation. However, poor writers did less preplanning; they generated little content and organised it poorly.

While writing, most of the students reread the text to assess correctness and pinpointed some weak points, they changed or corrected some words and revise the sentence structure. Very few students wrote nonstop about the topic for a given time, not pausing to edit for appropriateness or correctness. Better writers preferred rereading and revising 'paragraph by paragraph'. They reorganised some sentences, threw out or changed some words and they were more able to evaluate and revise their work. However, the poor writers revised their work at a superficial level; they centered on vocabulary and grammatical aspects, such as the right words, right tenses and prepositions, as their primary concern was to translate thoughts into words and sentences. The majority of them got distracted by punctuation, formatting and they were often overwhelmed – discouraged by the demands of writing. Three less experienced writers,

Table 10.1 Themes, categories and codes

Themes–Categories	Codes
1. Student profile	School grade Male/female Age English language level
(a) Composing process	
2. Pre-writing phase	GETHEL = Getting help GENIDE = Generating ideas ORGIDE = Organising ideas
3. While-writing phase	DRAF = Drafting REDRAF = Redrafting – refining DRAFED = Drafting/editing
(b) Writing difficulties	
4. Vocabulary	RIGWOR = Right words MEANG = Meaning SPELG = Spelling
5. Sentence	SENSTR = Sentence structure GRAMM = Grammar
6. Text	PLACON = Planning content ORGCON = Organising content
7. Anxiety	ANXVOC = Anxiety vocabulary ANXSPE = Anxiety about spelling ANXGRA = Anxiety about grammar/ structure ANXCON = Anxiety about the content ANTIMAN = Anxiety about time management
(c) Direct strategies	
8. Memory	PLANW = Placing new words in a context
9. Cognitive	USRES = Using resources TRANSL = Translating TRANSF = Transferring RECOMB = Recombining
10. Compensation	ADJMES = Adjusting the message USSYN = Using a synonym/circumlocution
(d) Indirect strategies	
11. Metacognitive strategies	LINKNM = Linking with already known material PLATAS = Planning for a language task PAYATT = Paying attention SELEVCO = Self-evaluation/correction PEECOR = peer-correction SELMON = Self-monitoring

continued

Table 10.1   (continued)

Themes–Categories	Codes
12. Affective strategies	REWAR = Rewarding ENCYOU = Encouraging yourself
13. Cooperating with teacher	ASKCLA = Asking for clarification ASKCOR = Asking for correction
14. Cooperating with peers	ASKHEL = Asking for help GIVHEL = Giving help

being unable to think of the right word, midsentence, stopped writing and tried to find what word to use halfway. As for organising ideas, three very poor students showed ignorance of how to organise their thoughts into separate paragraphs.

Young learners' writing was interrupted midsentence by a language concern, whether spelling, grammar, word choice or struggle of putting ideas into coherent English and doubt about the meaning conveyed. In fact, they were aware of their own difficulties in generating language at sentence level (25 references) and text level (24 references). They described some factors that constrained them from performing writing tasks effectively:

(1) limited lexical knowledge; the majority of the participants faced difficulties in remembering and selecting appropriate words and rated 'finding and choosing appropriate vocabulary' highly in difficulty, causing them a lot of anxiety (18 references). Moreover, the majiority of the poor and average students had difficulty with spelling (14 references) especially of compound words;

(2) use of grammatical forms; they believed that the 'main source of grammatical error is the use of mother tongue patterns and rules, which leads to an error or inappropriate form in the target language';

(3) sentence structure; they encountered difficulties in sentence structure (subject–verb agreement, verb–tense consistency) (14 references) and they reflected their concern for making their writing cohesive as the sentence structure is 'all messed up' and 'the content is not always well-developed';

(4) inadequate knowledge of how to organise ideas clearly. Most of the students stated that they faced the highest degree of difficulty in planning (13 references) and organising (11 references) the piece of writing.

Strategies

Participants used direct strategies and indirect strategies. Certain direct strategies like, 'placing new words in the context', 'using resources', 'translating', 'recombining', 'using a synonym or circumlocution' occurred with greater frequency than others. The most frequently *memory* strategy used was 'placing words in the context' (18 references), as students declared that they place some new words or phrases, taught in the previous lessons, into the context of composing.

Concerning *cognitive* strategies, 'looking up every word in a dictionary', was considered to be the most useful and the most frequently used strategy by the majority of students (19 references), who consult bilingual dictionaries for word meanings and for checking spelling mistakes. Word-for-word (verbatim) 'translation' from mother tongue was a frequent occurrence among students (18 references), irrespective of their FL level. A considerable number of participants (12 references) declared that they apply knowledge of words and structures from L1 to English in order to produce an expression in the new language. Some students (8 references) relied on the strategy of 'recombining' to produce a sentence. While redrafting they linked one phrase with another in a whole sentence, reconstructing a meaningful sentence by putting together some items in new ways.

Furthermore, young learners employed two basic *compensatory* strategies to overcome limitations and noticeable weaknesses in FL: (a) 'using a synonym', and (b) 'adjusting/approximating the message'. Almost all participants commonly used another word or phrase in order to convey the intended meaning and they provided strong reasons for doing this. Half of them (10 references) declared they write some expressions slightly different which mean almost the same thing when they cannot come up with the right expression.

As for indirect strategies, the majority of young learners could not manage to employ certain affective strategies, as they were in a state of anxiety about 'coming up with the appropriate words or phrases' (18 references), spelling, grammar and structure and time management. It is remarkable that the less-competent writers experienced a higher level of anxiety, as they did not show complete control and mastery of the language structures.

Although students experienced some uncertainty and anxiety when they attempted to compose a task in English, most of them believed that self encouragement through positive statements could change their feelings and could reduce performance anxiety. However, only a few of the participants adopted some strategies to reduce anxiety, such as 'self-encouragement' (8 references) and 'rewarding themselves' while performing a writing task in English (3 references).

They showed preference to learning interactively by asking the instructor questions for clarification, or verification, or for help in translating words (20 references) or asking for correction (7 references). Furthermore, most of the writers, especially the less competent ones, liked cooperating with other peers in order to clarify some ambiguities when encountering some problems (12 references). However, six competent writers showed preference for writing alone because they declared that they manage better by themselves.

As regards metacognitive strategies, 'linking with already known material' was a strategy frequently used by more than half of the participants (13 references), who drew upon previous experience to facilitate new knowledge and to generate ideas. A large number of students (16 references) showed positive attitude towards evaluating their own writing, and an important proportion of them (especially more efficient learners) got involved in the process of identifying difficulties and problems, and self-correcting. It is remarkable that eight of the more competent students tried to monitor their difficulties; some others preferred correcting the last draft with their peers by reviewing their drafts, noting the style and content, comparing their writing with that of their peers, and commenting on each other's drafts. Only a few children preferred using the strategy of 'paying attention' (6 references); four of them paid attention to specific aspects of language, such as 'how to use specific expressions and how to use tenses'.

Discussion

Rich insights into young learners' strategies, preferences and writing subprocesses in the specific learning context were gained from the verbal data and the questionnaires. The research instruments complemented each other by providing partly similar data; the results of the questionnaires have contributed to the listing of the subskills and strategies young learners use as well as to the recording of their writing deficiencies. The participants' verbal descriptions and comments on writing, which were more spontaneous than their answers on the questionnaires, provided a further indication of the writing sub-processes, strategies and weaknesses.

While the emergence of clear and sigificant differences in strategy use and writing process is important, it must be noted that there were similarities too, as think-aloud protocols, interviews and questionnaires showed both competent and less competent learners, both male and female learners employing similar strategies and following about the same subskills. There was a general agreement among all participants that writing is a difficult skill which requires effort and demands knowledge of vocabulary, correct use of connectives, punctuation, and sentence structure, as well as textual organisation. Most of the young writers activated prior knowledge to generate ideas (although a few learners overlooked the importance of prewriting process), attempted to produce a first/rough draft and redraft it, translated, switched to mother tongue, looked up words in a bilingual dictionary, used a synonym or changed the sentence structure when composing was not proceeding smoothly and they sometimes revised and proofread the draft. The students were aware of their weaknesses and they showed a positive perception of their need to improve writing skills.

Some differences between the efficient and the less efficient writers in the perception and use of strategies for planning, organising and evaluating were highlighted. The better writers held a broader view of their own writing problems, the requirements of the writing task and had a rather positive self-concept as writers. More efficient writers employed and utilised a greater number of strategies than the less efficient ones, and followed some high-level writing processes (like generating content, planning and revising) to a certain degree. They agreed that when assessing their text, they rethink ideas and revise them if necessary and then proofread.

In contrast, the less competent writers had a more limited knowledge of the writing task (Arndt, 1987; Zamel, 1982). They used fewer strategies and used them less frequently (Cumming, 1989; Wenden, 1993). The failure to sufficiently employ cognitive and metacognitive strategies is likely to result in less efficient writers being overdependent on local processes (dealing with spelling of words, punctuation and finding the appropriate vocabulary). They sometimes failed to monitor their writing and they lost the meaning of sentences as soon as they focused on spelling or finding the appropriate words, and they made little or no attempt to revise.

Conclusion

The study attempted to 'establish an understanding' of a particular group of FL young writers, to examine the way in which they compose a piece of writing and to investigate the strategies they employ in order to overcome writing difficulties. It succeeded in describing the writing process and categorising a large number of the strategies used by the particular group of young writers. The study indicated that most of young learners showed some understanding of the control they have over their own cognition while writing. Moreover, they appreciated the need to orientate themselves to the specific requirements of a writing task and they see the need to improve their writing subskills and to participate interactively in the process of writing.

The interpretation of data provides the opportunity for some possible directions for pedagogical research to be highlighted. However, because of the limited sample size, the findings can be regarded as suggestive rather than definitive and some implications for classroom instruction are discussed. The results (a) provided a means for teachers to increase their understanding of how students write in response to assigned writing tasks and the possibility of identifying a number of areas where the learners' knowledge was inadequate or limited, and (b) suggested that students need guidance, explicit instruction, which should aim at developing effective writing skills (both high-level and lower-level skills) and strategies and at developing students' awareness of the strategy they use. The basic purpose is to make students skillful and independent writers through process-oriented and self-regulated writing instruction, so that they use more effective strategies for planning, organising ideas, drafting, revising and reviewing the content. More precisely, children should be encouraged to have their own ideas about content, to write multiple drafts, as rewriting techniques help students how to plan, to collaborate, to reflect on and revise their work and to begin to be self-critical and edit their work and to focus on spelling, grammar, punctuation, choice of appropriate words and sentence linking.

Within this perspective, the teacher's role is to foster students' development of a variety of strategies, help them compose through modeling and scaffolding, develop their awareness of the writing process and help them make writing purposeful and contextualised whenever possible (Ellis & Brewster, 1991: 57) in an instructional context which: (a) aims at developing both organisational skills, such as the use of outlines to plan out a writing text, and revision skills, such as the ability to critically read and analyse one's own writing, (b) includes interactive writing and incorporates prewriting activities in order to encourage students to brainstorm and think about the key vocabulary, to activate prior knowledge so that they have ideas ready, to set the purpose for writing, and to think about the text type and layout, and (c) provides young learners with sample texts and exposes them to various types of writing (Brewster *et al.*, 1992), so that they have knowledge of a variety of forms or genres for writing, and they use that knowledge to help them generate content and organise their writing. Such an instructional context should also encompass writing frames that can help young writers learn to write quickly and acquire writing skills and strategies and should encourage students to correct, refine and improve their own texts.

References

Arndt, V. (1987) Six writers in search of texts: A protocol-based study of L1 and L2 writing. *ELT Journal* 4, 257–267.

Brewster, J., Ellis, G. and Girald, D. (1992) *The Primary English Teachers' Guide*. Harmondsworth: Penguin.

Brown, J.D. (2001) *Using Surveys in Language Programs*. Cambridge: Cambridge University Press.

Carrell, P.L. and Devine, J. (1988) *Interactive Approaches to Second Language Teaching*. Cambridge: Cambridge University Press.

Chamot, U.A. (1987) The learning strategies of ESL students. In J. Rubin and A. Wenden (eds) *Learner Strategies in Language Learning*. London: Prentice Hall International.

Chamot, U.A. (2004) Issues in language strategy research and teaching. *E.J.F.L.T* 1 (1), 14–26. On WWW at http:/e-flt.nus.edu.sg/v1n12004/Chamot.htm. Accessed 5.9.06.

Council of Europe (2006) *Common European Framework of Reference for Languages*. Cambridge: Cambridge University Press.

Cumming, A. (1989) Writing expertise and second language proficiency. *Language Learning* 39 (1), 81–141.

Dyson, A. and Freedman, S. (1991) Writing. In J. Flood, J. Jensen, D. Lapp and J.R. Squire (eds) *Handbook of Research on Teaching in the Language Arts* (pp. 54–68). New York: MacMillan.

Ellis, G. and Brewster, J. (1991) *The Storytelling Handbook for Primary Teachers*. London: Penguin.

Flower, L. (1990) The role of task representations in reading to write. In L. Flower, V. Stein, J. Ackerman and M. Kantz (eds) *Cognitive Process in Writing* (pp. 31–50). Hillsdale, NJ: Lawrence Erlbaum Associates.

Flower, L. (1994) *The Construction of Negotiated Meaning: A Social Cognitive Theory of Writing*. Carbondale, IL: University of Southern Illinois Press.

Hayes, J.R. and Flowers, L.S. (1986) Writing research and the writer. *American Psychologist* 41 (10), 1106–1113.

Hedge, T. (1997) *Writing*. Oxford: Oxford University Press.

London Tests of English for Children. Pearson language assessments. On WWW at http://www.pearsonlanguage.assessments.com. Accessed 5.9.06.

Miles, M. and Huberman, M. (1994) *Qualitative Data Analysis*. London: SAGE Publications.

O'Malley J.M. and Chamot, A.U. (1990) *Learning Strategies in Second Language Acquisition*. Cambridge: Cambridge University Press.

Oxford, R. (1990) *Language Learning Strategies: What Every Teacher Should Know*. New York: Newbury House Publishers.

Oxford, R., Park-Oh, Y., Ito, S. and Sumrall, M. (1993) Learning a language by satellite: What influences achievement? *System* 21, 31–48.

Papadopoulou, C.O. (1999) Teachers' conceptualization and practice of planning in the Greek EFL context. Unpublished thesis, University of Oxford.

Raimes, A. (1987) Language proficiency writing ability and composing strategies: A study of ESL college student writers. *Language Learning* 37, 439–465.

Rubin, J. (1987) Learner strategies: Theoretical assumptions, research, history and typology. In A. Wenden and J. Rubin (eds) *Learner Strategies in Language Learning* (pp. 15–30). New Jersey: Prentice Hall.

Susser, B. (1994) Process approaches in ESL/EFL writing instruction. *Journal of Second Language Writing* 3, 31–47.

Tribble, C. (1997) *Writing*. Oxford: Oxford University Press.

Verma, G. and Mallick, K. (1999) *Researching Education: Perspectives and Techniques*. London: Falmer Press.

Wallace, M. (2000) *Action Research for Language Teachers*. Cambridge: Cambridge University Press.

Wenden, A. (1993) Strategic interaction and task knowledge. In J.E. Alatis (ed.) *Proceedings of the Georgetown University Roundtable of Languages and Linguistics*. Washington: Georgetown University Press.

White, R. and Arndt, V. (1997) *Process Writing*. London: Longman.

Zamel, V. (1982) Writing: The process of discovering meaning. *TESOL Quarterly* 16 (2), 195–209.

Chapter 11

How do 9–11-Year-Old Croatians Perceive Sounds and Read Aloud in French?

VANDA MARIJANOVIĆ, NATHALIE PANISSAL
AND MICHEL BILLIÈRES

Introduction

Supercalifragilisticexpialidocious! You must have recognised Mary Poppins' famous magic word, but do you know what it means? Even if you do not really know the meaning of this word, you are able to read it, in a silent way or aloud. If this is the first time that you encounter this word, you would not probably succeed in articulating it very quickly: *su-per-qua-li-fra-gi-li-stic-ex-pi-a-li-do-cious*. What if somebody asks you to say it backwards? Would you be able to do so, as Mary did in her song? *Dociousaliexpilisticfragicalirupus*? So, try to imagine what happens in the head of a child starting to learn a foreign language. They face a new sound system, sometimes even a new alphabetic code, and may or may not already be expert readers in their mother tongue.

The aim of the chapter is to find evidence for phonological representations of French sound units in Croatian early learners' interlanguage. The experimental study on Croatian novice readers examines how children apply the grapheme–phoneme correspondence rules of their mother tongue while reading when facing the opaque French language. Children were given different tasks and the authors expected them to be most accurate in a Repetition task, less so in a Reading Aloud task and the least accurate in a simultaneous task of Listening and Reading Aloud task. Examining the phonological loop factor, they supposed that due to a cognitive load, the reading task will imply longer reaction times than the two other tasks.

All writing systems transcribe the units of spoken language. The basic units of an alphabetical writing system are graphemes, which transcribe the phonemes of the spoken language, and all phonological systems include consonants and vowels. The ease of reading acquisition, however, is assumed to depend on the degree of transparency between graphemes and phonemes, which varies across languages (Rieben *et al.*, 1997; Rieben & Perfetti, 1989). We can also add that most of the differences between phonological and orthographic structures are related to vowels. Similarly to English and German, the French language contains 20 to 24 phonemes for 50 to 60 graphemes (Sprenger-Charolles *et al.*, 2006). Yet, the Croatian language is completely transparent: 25 phonemes for 25 graphemes (Babić *et al.*, 1991). We consider this discrepancy in orthographic transparency between the Croatian and the French language as of utmost importance; particularly, when the difficulty in L2 acquisition is intensified by the introduction of phonological structures subjacent to the oral language, but non-existent in the L1.

The main characteristic of all writing systems, with the exception of Chinese, is that two reading routes can be used to grasp written-words: a lexical reading route, relying on a large set of meaningful units and a sublexical one, relying on a small set of meaningless units. The sublexical (direct) reading route – a general principle – depends on the degree to which the writing system represents the spoken language it encodes. In other words, learning to read depends on the consistency of grapheme–phoneme correspondence rules in the writing system, but also on the quality of a child's phonological representations, especially at the phonemic level (Goswami & Bryant, 1990; Rieben & Perfetti, 1989).

One important concept in all reading theories is automaticity, as it was thoroughly explained in Ecalle and Magnan (2002). The written-word identification process does not require specific attentional resources and it will be rapid, precise and automatic for expert readers. Novice readers' lexical access is, on the contrary, controlled. The processes involved in written-word identification are specific to reading, whereas those involved in reading comprehension are generally thought to be amodal, that is, similar for spoken and written language. Thus, comprehension depends on the automaticity degree of so-called low-level mechanisms, such as written-word identification, which allows us to allot a large part of our cognitive capacity to comprehension (Sprenger-Charolles *et al.*, 2006).

The goal of reading is to understand what is being read. However, this should not conceal the fact that the reading problems are primarily due to the difficulty identifying written words, more precisely to the lack of automaticity in written-word identification for novice Croatian readers in L2 French. As we can peruse in Ecalle and Magnan (2002) the dominant model of word identification in expert reading presupposes the coexistence and collaboration of two different ways of access to internal lexicon: by addressing (direct way) or by assembling (indirect way). The indirect way permits us to read unknown words, such as *supercalifragilisticexpialidocious*, by transforming the visual information into phonological information via the grapheme–phoneme correspondence rules. Hence, the activity of reading implies a word identification (lexical access) and double extraction of written material: pronunciation and meaning, which infers subsequently orthographic and semantic representations. The process of word identification is thus related to the existence and development of the metalinguistic competence (child's phonological representations) and the working memory efficiency (Gathercole & Baddeley, 1993; Goswami & Bryant, 1990; Sprenger-Charolles *et al.*, 2006).

We have already mentioned the importance of the child's phonological representations. In this context, we would like to define the term 'phonological awareness' (Goswami & Bryant, 1990). Phonological awareness is the capability of perceiving, manipulating and thinking through the speech sounds. Its functioning relies on the co-activation of lexical units and not really on their physical properties. Some experimental results allow several abstraction levels: awareness of phonological chains, that is, identification and segmentation of syllables; phonetic awareness, that is, identification that speech is a sequence of minimal units permitting perceptive differentiation, and phonemic (phonological) awareness. We know that phonological awareness' training makes reading quicker and easier, not only is phonological awareness a good predictor of reading competence (Gathercole & Baddeley, 1993; Sprenger-Charolles *et al.*, 2006), but it also continues its development in reciprocal causal relationship with reading (Sprenger-Charolles *et al.*, 2006).

Alan Baddeley (Baddeley, 1992, 2003a, 2003b) considers working-memory as a low-capacity system, responsible for manipulation of information during many cognitive activities, such as learning, reading, vocabulary acquisition, language comprehension and others, and at the same time, it handles the passive, temporary storage of this information. Working memory is composed of a central executive system whose function is to manage two slave-systems: the phonological loop, responsible for verbal information and the visuo-spatial notebook, responsible for visuo-spatial information. The phonological loop is comprised of two components: the phonological store which represents material in a phonological code decaying with time. The second component involves a process of articulatory rehearsal (or *subvocalisation*) which serves to refresh the representations in the phonological store in order to uphold memory items in the short-term store. The phonological loop is also used to recode visual, nonphonological inputs such as printed words or pictures into their phonological form so that they can be held in the phonological store. Knowing that, with the increasing development of automatic processes, working memory resources will be employed to a lesser extent, we may expect that the study of working memory, and particularly the impact of the phonological loop (Majerus *et al.*, 2001) could indeed reveal low-level processes in reading.

We would like to insist on this well-founded postulation stating that the components of working memory play a crucial role in language perception and production. Likewise, this is the reason why we can consider that the mnesic capacity underlies the possible transfer between L1 and L2 processing mechanisms. L1 can influence L2 production and perception in the transfer of L1 procedures. In the case of lexical encoding and decoding, the transfer will take place through conceptual, syntactic, morphological and phonological transfer. The latter one, which happens to be quite complex in both L2 perception and production, is the one that interest us the most in this study. Even advanced learners frequently substitute L1 phonemes for similar but nonidentical L2 phonemes. Moreover, we could observe that L2 learners, and in particular the beginners, use L1 rules when encoding L2 linguistic items (e.g. regarding the reading activity, this hypothesis was affirmed in this study). Furthermore, not only the L1 'imprints' itself in these processes, but leaves also its marks in the articulation. We may presume that L2 speakers have one kind of an articulatory *habitus*, that is, their articulation reposes on a set of specific and automatised articulatory movements which can explain why the acquisition of L2 phonological features can sometimes be difficult even for highly advanced L2 speakers (Kormos, 2006). To illustrate this remark, we can think of a native French speaker for whom it is very difficult to pronounce the English phoneme /θ/, like in *path* /pæθ/. All of those who have been learning English will think with nostalgia of their teacher saying the famous: 'Bite your tongue!'-instruction. On the contrary, native English speakers will probably be in difficulty when striving to articulate the famous French phoneme /R/ as in *Paris* /paRi/.

Hence, the role of automaticity in both L1 to L2 transfer and L2 acquisition is central. Indeed and broadly speaking, this ability to retrieve the information automatically is an important bond between perception, working memory and long-term memory. In relation with reading processes, we might observe that in the absence of automaticity of the low-level processes, the working memory capacity will engage the totality of the attentional resources required in order to simply apply grapheme–phoneme correspondence rules. In her recent publication, Kormos (2006) provides a synthetic list of automaticity characteristics: fast, ballistic, load-independent, effortless and unconscious. Yet, we know that L2 novice readers' competence is *a fortiori* slow, intentional, effort-demanding, and conscious. Besides, it implies a heavy cognitive load. Knowing that the development of automatic processes does not require much of our working memory resources, we may imagine that the study of working memory could reveal low-level processes, and in particular the impact of the phonological loop (Baddeley *et al.*, 1998; Majerus *et al.*, 2001). Because, '... the phonological loop should facilitate language acquisition in two ways: the store should provide relatively unconstrained temporary representation for new phoneme sequences, and the articulatory system should facilitate learning through rehearsal ...' (Baddeley, 2003b: 833). In other terms, in order to obtain some valuable indications on reading acquisition, we would like to make a thorough study of written-word identification processes, which are in fact a fundamental stage that permits us to connect two distinctive levels of representations: sublexical and lexical level, by concentrating on one of the working memory's slave-systems: the phonological loop.

The Study

In this chapter, we present the aims and the most significant results of our first experiment related to our short overview of the literature in what we hope to be a meaningful and helpful discussion for language teachers.

Aims

The primary objective of this study was to find evidence for phonological representations of French sound units in Croatian early learners' inter-language. The complexity of such an experimental protocol could not permit the evaluation of all the sounds of the French language. Besides, it is a well-known fact that the French consonant system does not represent any major problems to Croatian speakers. Therefore, we have decided to focus exclusively on vowels, and in particular on nasal and mid vowels. They appeared to us as the most interesting for two reasons. First of all, nasal vowels do not exist in the Croatian phonological system, neither the opposition between close and open vowels, such as /e/-/ɛ/ and /o/-/ɔ/. Second, the mispronunciation of these vowels often provokes misunderstanding.

We wanted to observe the specific linguistic phenomena performed by Croatian novice readers while in contact with the unknown French language. Moreover, the influence of the phonological loop on the storage, rehearsal and retaining of new lexical items is also a well-established fact. We have stipulated that the reaction–time measures should permit us to shed light on this short-term memory component.

Considering all of these elements together, we hypothesise that Croatian novice readers when facing the opaque French language (Jaffré, 2003) will apply the grapheme–phoneme correspondence rules of their mother tongue while reading. We have postulated as well that the pronunciation accuracy will vary between tasks. It will be more accurate in a Repetition task, less accurate in a simultaneous task of Listening and Reading Aloud, and the least accurate in a Reading Aloud task. As for the phonological loop factor, we have presupposed that due to a cognitive load, the reading task will undoubtedly imply longer reaction times than the two other tasks.

Research protocol
Participants

Participants in this experiment were Croatian children, aged from 9 to 11 years of age, not presenting any specific cognitive or linguistic deficits and disorders. All 42 participants were school children, beginners in French. At the time the experiment started, they had had about six hours of French lessons and their skills may be evaluated at the time as corresponding to the very beginning of A1 level of the Common European Framework of Reference for Languages (Conseil de l'Europe, 2001). In relation with their reading competence, we consider that they are expert readers in Croatian, yet novice readers in L2 French.

Stimuli

We have extracted seven phonemes from the complete set of 16 French vowels-one high vowel /y/, four commonly named 'mid' vowels: /o/, /ɔ/, /e/, /ɛ/ and two nasal vowels: /ɔ̃/ and /ã/. We identify this factor with seven modalities as a *'phoneme factor'*. We observe conjointly the vowel position in the word which includes three modalities (initial, middle and final), that is a 'position factor'. Moreover, the stimuli are presented in two different conditions: isolated item and item in context. This factor with two modalities (isolated and in context) is named an 'isolated vs. context factor'. Therefrom, we created three different stimuli-lists each containing 21 bisyllables where seven phonemes appear three times, in word-initial (e.g. *usage* /y-zaʒ/), word-middle (e.g. *virus* /vi-Rys/) and word-final position (e.g. *début* /de-by/). The stimuli list continues with 21 sentences where each of the 21 words appears embedded in context (e.g. *Elle connaît son usage.* /ɛl-ko-ne-sɔ̃-ny-zaʒ/; *Il a un virus.* /i-la-ɛ̃-vi-Rys/; *Le film est au début.* /lə-film-e-to-de-by/). Three stimuli lists correspond to three different tasks, that is, three different fashions of stimuli presentation. This '(presentation) modality factor' thence includes three modalities: auditive, visual and audiovisual.

The words were picked in the NOVLEX lexical data-base which contains 9300 written-language lexical entries, excerpts from French children's literature (Lambert & Chesnet, 2001). The syllabic structure criterion was respected: all isolated stimuli-items are bisyllable words, and the sentences are composed of between four and seven syllables. Meanwhile, we have also observed a grammaticality criterion: stimuli-items are concrete nouns without possible homonymy with verbs. In addition, the frequency of stimuli items was evaluated and we proposed 31 unknown words, and 32 words for which the meaning was supposed to be transparent to Croatian children (e.g. *police, orbite, pilote*). This familiarity was evaluated on the basis of their presence in textbooks used in class (Batušić & Montani, 1992; Montani & Batušić, 1996; Vrhovac, 1992, 2003).

Procedure

This psycholinguistic study, conducted in a heteroglossic environment, lasted for four weeks during which three tasks were administered to the participants. Each task lasted approximately six minutes and included a different stimuli list. The materials used for the stimuli manipulation were a laptop computer, two speakers and a digital voice player/recorder. The software used for the manipulation of stimuli was Histrion 251-0SX-et-WIN, developed by Pascal Gaillard (Laboratory Jacques-Lordat, University of Toulouse). Each one of the three tasks that we gave learners corresponds to one perceptive modality:

Task 1: In the Repetition task, the participant was sitting in front of the speakers, listening to the stimuli and repeating them immediately. The instruction was as follows: *You will now hear a sequence of words and sentences in French. You just have to repeat what you hear, like a parrot. Ready?* Isolated items were appearing within a five-second interval and items in context within a 12-second interval. This appearance interval was the same in all three tasks and the guidelines were always given in Croatian.

Task 2: In the Reading Aloud task, the child was sitting in front of the laptop screen and stimuli appeared on the screen. The instruction in this task was: *A list of words and sentences will appear on the screen. Please read aloud what you see. Ready?*

Task 3: In the Simultaneous Listening and Reading Aloud task, the pupil was sitting in front of the laptop screen and speakers and stimuli were appearing simultaneously on the screen and out of the speakers. *Today, you will hear and see on the screen at the same time a list of words and sentences. Please read aloud what you see. Ready?*

Forty-two children took part in the experiment, though the results are based on the production analysis of only 36 children. We have eliminated productions of six children because they were not always present in school, and thus did not accomplish the totality of tasks contained in the research protocol. The data was collected in September and October 2005, in four primary schools in Zagreb (Croatia). The experiment took place in the institution, during children's school-hours. Taking into account tiredness and accommodation effects, the experimenter took special care to wait at least four days before soliciting the children for the following task. The productions were recorded on Edirol's R-1 digital sound device and photographs were taken of each classroom where the experiment was conducted.

The data analysis was undertaken in Toulouse. It consisted of Vowel Pronunciation assessment and measurements of children's Reaction Times to the given stimulus. As for vowel pronunciation, we have evaluated children's productions as 'accurate' or 'inaccurate'. The third 'no response' category concerned the cases in which the child either did not respond to a stimulus, or when her/his production did not correspond at all to the given stimulus (e.g. when the child created some kind of an unreal French sound sequence). The reaction time measures were processed with Amadeus software and calculated in milliseconds.

Results

As this is a preliminary experiment with a qualitative aim, a descriptive analysis of Pronunciation Performance was carried out, according to tasks and in percentages of accurate and inaccurate productions. As to Reaction Times, a quantitative analysis will be presented in the second part of this chapter.

The main idea of this article is to present to the community of Foreign Language Teachers the most pertinent findings about the phonological proficiency of Croatian Early Learners in pronunciation, as well as in written-word identification, of specific French vowels. For that reason, we will not present the detailed statistical analysis of the totality of collected data (4536 entries) and will zoom-in on the most revealing data.

Pronunciation assessment

All this considered, in this chapter we will concentrate only on the most relevant result, those concerning the phonemes /y/,/ɔ̃/ and /ã/ (see Figures 11.1–11.3 for performances in isolated environment and Figures 11.4–11.6 for items in context):

(a) Isolated items. While in the French graphophonological system the grapheme U corresponds to the phoneme /y/ (e.g. *sud* /syd/), in Croatian system grapheme U transcribes the phoneme /u/ (e.g. *sud* /sud/). Phoneme /u/ exists in French and matches to the grapheme OU (e.g. *soul* /sul/) that turns out in /ou/ in Croatian (e.g. *soul* /soul/). Furthermore, as we have already reported, the phoneme /y/ does not exist in the Croatian phonological vocalic system. Thus, we may expect that the first difficulty for Croatian learners will be to perceive this new sound.

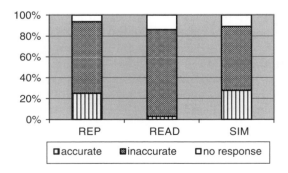

Figure 11.1 Pronunciation of isolated /y/ across tasks

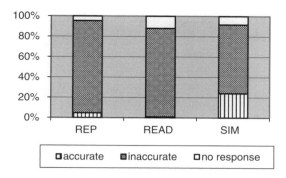

Figure 11.2   Pronunciation of isolated /ɔ̃/ across tasks

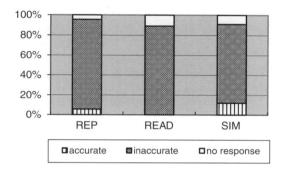

Figure 11.3   Pronunciation of isolated /ã/ across tasks

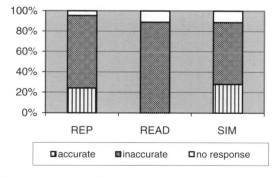

Figure 11.4   Pronunciation of /y/ in context across tasks

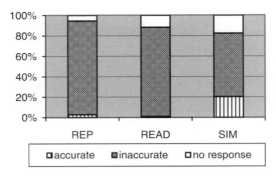

Figure 11.5 Pronunciation of /ɔ̃/ in context across tasks

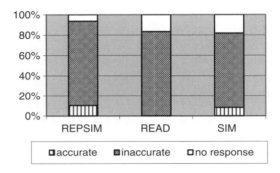

Figure 11.6 Pronunciation of /ã/ in context across tasks

Subsequently, they will find themselves in a situation where they will be asked to produce this sound. And during reading activity, they will tend to pronounce the French U grapheme – /y/ as a Croatian U – /u/.

In Figure 11.1, we may observe the pronunciation performances of phoneme /y/ in Repetition (Task 1), Reading Aloud (Task 2) and Simultaneous Listening and Reading Aloud (Task 3). Out of 108 productions (phoneme /y/ appearing three times in each task performed by 36 subjects), the percentages of correct pronunciations in Tasks 1, 2 and 3 are respectively 25%, 3% and 28%. Among incorrect pronunciations, respectively 69%, 82% and 61%, the massive answer was /u/. This confirms our first hypothesis: Croatian readers apply the grapheme–phoneme correspondence rules of their mother-tongue. We may also notice close scores of accurate and inaccurate pronunciations in Task 1 – Repetition and Task 3 – Simultaneous Listening and Reading Aloud. Nevertheless, with respect to the 'no response' realisations, the percentages (respectively 6%, 15% and 11%) show slightly better performance scores in Task 1 – Repetition. We may suppose then that the simple task of Repetition with only one input modality, an auditive one, was less inhibitive to process than the double input of audiovisual modality of Task 3.

As to the phoneme /ɔ̃/ (Figure 11.2), the results also corroborate our first hypothesis. The majority of children were not successful at pronouncing it. This nasal vowel was submitted to the children in different graphical representations: ON, OM, EM. In this case, the already well-developed phonological awareness of Croatian learners actuates the pronunciation of nasal consonants: /on/, /om/, /em/. In the Reading Aloud task, we observe 4% of accurate pronunciations, 4% of 'no response' to stimuli and 92% of inaccurate answers. In this task, we may notice 1% accurate responses, 87% inaccurate responses and 12% 'no responses'. In the Simultaneous Listening and Reading Aloud task, we got 24% accurate pronunciations, 68% inaccurate pronunciations and 8% 'no responses'. Although the slight difference of 'no response' answers in Tasks 1 and 3 tend to reveal a greater cognitive load in processing the double information input, the discrepancy in the results in pronunciation accuracy in these two tasks make us reconsider our second hypothesis of pronunciation accuracy tendency. We hypothesised that pronunciation will be more accurate in the Repetition task than in the Simultaneous Listening and reading Aloud task. All the results suggest the contrary: the pronunciation is more accurate in Task 3.

We obtained almost identical results with the phoneme /ɑ̃/ (Figure 11.3), except for the percentage of accurate pronunciations in Task 3 (12% compared to 24% of phoneme /ɔ̃/). This could imply that Croatian learners have even more difficulty with the pronunciation of this nasal vowel. The comparison between the phonological realisations of these two phonemes leads us also to the following remark: the French grapheme AN corresponding to the phoneme /ɑ̃/ is often pronounced as /ɔ̃/ by Croatian speakers.

(b) Items in context. Figure 11.4 illustrates the children's performance in pronouncing the phoneme /y/ embedded in context. As the results are 24% accurate, 72% inaccurate pronunciations, and 4% 'no-responses' in Task 1, the children's performance appears to be the same as on isolated items. Our principal hypothesis is confirmed once again by the performances in Oral Reading task: 0% accurate pronunciations. Besides, comparing the Simultaneous Listening and Reading Aloud task and the Repetition tasks, we noticed the global tendency of greater number of 'no-responses' in the Simultaneous Listening and Reading Aloud task than in the Repetition task (11% and 4%, respectively), but also a higher percentage of accurate pronunciations (28% and 24%, respectively).

Analysing the 'isolated vs. context' condition, the results presented in Figures 11.5 and 11.6 show a trend: the pronunciation accuracy of stimuli inserted in sentences is comparable to the one beheld in the case of isolated items. In addition, the higher percentages of 'no-response' answers in 'context' condition explain the minimally lower percentages of inaccurate pronunciations. Our hypothesis concerning better performance in the pronunciation of isolated items than of items in context is thus partially attested.

Assessment of reaction times

An ANOVA statistical analysis was conducted on reaction times, calculated in milliseconds. Several factors were taken in consideration: seven 'phonemes', three 'presentation modalities' and three 'vowel position in the word' condition and all of them were examined in two 'isolated vs. context' conditions:

(a) Isolated items. The results suggest a significant effect of the 'phoneme' factor $[F(6.198) = 2.26; p < 0.04]$ and the Tukey test demonstrates that the performance of the phoneme /ã/ (960 msec) is degraded in comparison to the other phonemes (between 815 and 890 msec; see Figure 11.7).

The variance analysis confirms the effect of the 'presentation modality' factor $[F(2.66) = 42.53; p < 0.00]$. The Tukey test has permitted to set forth a performance degradation in visual modality (circa 1600 msec) and a performance equality of auditive and audiovisual modalities (circa 400 msec; see Figure 11.8).

In contrast, the variance analysis did not allow us to establish a significant effect of the 'vowel position in the word' factor $[F(2,66) = 0.31; p < 0.73]$: the reaction time performances are situated around 850 msec in all three modalities-initial, middle and final positions.

(b) Items in context. A variance analysis was also performed on reaction times measured in the 'context' condition. Only the 'presentation modality' factor represents a significant effect $[F(2.68) = 5.73; p < 0.05]$, that is, reaction time increases in visual modality (mean-time of 2894 msec) and there is a

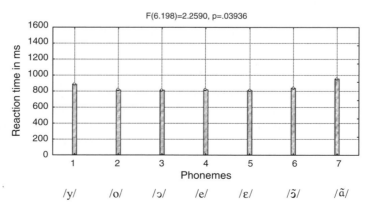

Figure 11.7   Reaction times – 'phoneme' factor

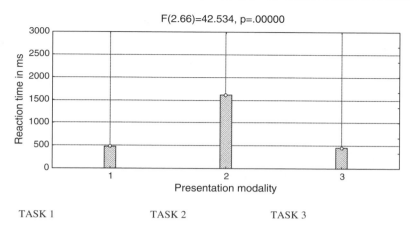

Figure 11.8   Reaction times – 'presentation modality' factor across tasks

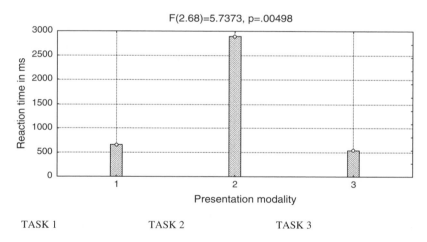

Figure 11.9   Reaction times – 'presentation modality' factor across tasks

statistical equivalence of reaction times in auditive and audiovisual modality (respectively, 665 msec and 546 msec), as is shown in Figure 11.9.

Summary

From a psycholinguistic point of view, the mental (or *internal*) lexicon is comprised of representations of all words belonging to a particular language. These representations can be phonological, orthographical, morphological, syntactic and conceptual. Two main research issues related to the internal lexicon concern its organisation and the procedures involved in lexical access, that is, a set of operations that are necessary for associating the sensory representations (auditive or graphic) of linguistic items to their mental representations. Aware of the impact that L1 might have on L2, it is not surprising that this research field is highly relevant for L2 acquisition research.

Many research studies attested the existence of working memory system, and the role played by working memory in cognitive processes is today irrefutable (Baddeley, 1992, 2003a, 2003b; Ecalle & Magnan, 2002; Gathercole & Baddeley, 1993; Goswami & Bryant, 1990; Majerus *et al.*, 2001; Rieben & Perfetti, 1989; Sprenger-Charolles *et al.*, 2006). It is probably even more obvious when talking about the acquisition of mechanisms that enable the lexical access because the matching of mental and sensory (auditive or visual) representations takes place precisely during the temporary storage of information in working memory. Among all components of this multicomponent system, the phonological loop is probably the most investigated one. Despite all of these investigations, the study of the phonological loop's impact on phonological encoding in L2 need to be taken further because of the multitude of unanswered questions, in both L1 and L2 acquisition studies. It is one of the aims of this study to tackle these unanswered questions: in what way do we process L2 phonological representation that does not have its correspondent in L1? Moreover, we wish to explore to what extent these processes become automatised. The study of L2 Reading Acquisition through the lens of phonological loop appeared as an appropriate context while reading activity implies several high- and low-level cognitive processes, such as written-word identification and comprehension, which are necessarily supported by the phonological loop, as it is responsible for the graphophonological recoding of written input.

Taking into account the results obtained in the qualitative Pronunciation Assessment, and with the aim of comparing it with the Reaction Times, we have restricted the analysis to the three most contrastive phonemes – /y/, /ɔ̃/ and /ɑ̃/. In isolated conditions, the results suggest better performances in pronunciation for phoneme /y/ than for the nasal vowels. We are also able to affirm that the pronunciation of the phoneme /ɑ̃/ was the least well-performed. On the other hand, the comparison of statistical analysis results in 'isolated vs. context' conditions, does not seem to confirm our hypothesis inferring that the pronunciation performance will decay in a 'context' environment notwithstanding the higher percentage of 'no-responses' for words appearing in sentences. We supposed that the pronunciation of longer sequences will raise the cognitive load because of the increasing number of items retained in working memory, and thus, that the pronunciation will be impaired. This might be a justification for numerous 'no-response' events in 'context' condition. Yet, two cases can be distinguished. Either the participants were inhibited and did not respond at all to the given stimuli, or they proposed the same ratio of accurate pronunciations as in the 'isolated' condition. One possible explanation for this could be that the memory span capacity of some participants was not indeed affected because of the absence of semantic representations. Nevertheless, these results show the importance of automaticity in the activation of L1 phonological representations: the pronunciation of phonemes inexistent in Croatian was the least well-performed.

With regard to the written-word identification, the results obtained in Task 2 (Reading Aloud) support our first hypothesis that Croatian novice readers in L2 French apply the grapheme–phoneme correspondence rules of their L1 Croatian. Indeed, the pronunciation performances recorded in this task show the lack of L2 phonological sensitivity because of the automatic processing of grapheme–phoneme correspondence rules in L1 Croatian. Even if, in the Repeating task, some participants manage to reproduce some French phonemes inexistent in Croatian, they are no longer able to produce them in the Reading Aloud task. The only possible retrieval from the mental lexicon is the one of L1 phonological representations and the attentional processing of L2 cannot be activated because of the automaticity in L1 grapheme–phoneme recoding.

The Reaction Time measures permitted us to sustain this hypothesis, both in 'isolated' and 'context' condition: Reading Aloud takes approximately four times longer than Repetition (Task 1) or Simultaneous Listening and Reading Aloud (Task 3). Furthermore, these measures indicate longer reaction times in pronouncing the phoneme /ã/ that appears clearly as the most challenging for Croatian early learners and clarifies our vision of their interlanguage (*cf.* Aims). That is, when the children who master Croatian transparent GPC code are facing incomprehensible French items, they cannot rely on the double extraction of written material – pronunciation and signification. Aware of the alphabetical principle, they can proceed to phonological recoding, but their articulatory processor (a phonological loop component) cannot find the matching phonological representation in the long-term memory because dealing with an unknown visual code. And unlike in the Repeating task, there is no auditive print in the working memory's short-term store that could potentially permit them to retrieve the right information. The working memory attempts to reach the long-term memory require then all of their attentional resources and hence, the start of production takes much longer. Furthermore, the developed automaticity in reading implies the activation of what already exists, that is, L1 Croatian phonological representations that are the most resembling to the L2 French visual stimuli.

With regard to the concepts of phonological awareness and the phonological loop, we may state that the initial idea of the importance of phonological representations has been confirmed by these results: Croatian beginners took much more time to process auditive and visual information that is not latent in their long-term memory. Worded differently, we may again pinpoint the phonological loop, device responsible for the processing of visual and phonological information (e.g. written-words), as the essential agent in reading as well as in the acquisition of reading. Thus, this experiment should be followed by another experiment with a more didactic aim. We would like to conduct a comparative study of several strategies of reading acquisition in L2 French through phonological awareness' training. This second experiment will allow us to evaluate different teaching practices and, hopefully, to distinguish the most appropriate ones in order to optimise reading instruction in L2 French.

References

Babić, S., Brozović, D., Moguš, M., Pavešić, S., Škarić, I. and Težak, S. (1991) *Povijesni pregled, glasovi i oblici hrvatskoga književnog jezika* [Historical review, sounds and structures of standard Croatian language]. Zagreb: Globus, Nakladni zavod – Academia scientiarum et artium Croaticae.

Baddeley, A. (1992) *La mémoire humaine. Théorie et pratique* [Human memory: Theory and practice]. Grenoble: PUG.

Baddeley, A. (2003a) Working memory and language: An overview. *Journal of Communication Disorders* 36, 189–208.

Baddeley, A. (2003b) Working memory: Looking back and looking forward. *Nature Reviews – Neuroscience* 4, 829–839.

Baddeley, A., Gathercole, S. and Papagno, C. (1998) The phonological loop as a language learning device. *Psychological Review* 105 (1), 158–173.

Batušić, I. and Montani, K. (1992) *Parlez comme nous, niveau A – udžbenik* [Speak like us, A level – textbook] (11th edn). Zagreb: Školska knjiga.

Conseil de l'Europe (2001) *Un cadre européen commun de référence pour les langues: Apprendre, enseigner, évaluer* [Common european framework of reference for Languages: Learning, teaching, assessment]. Paris: Les Editions Didier.

Ecalle, J. and Magnan, A. (2002) *L'apprentissage de la lecture* [Learning to read]. Paris: Armand Colin.

Gathercole, S.E. and Baddeley, A.D. (1993) *Working Memory and Language*. Hove and New York: Psychology Press Ltd (Erlbaum).

Goswami, U. and Bryant, P. (1990). *Phonological Skills and Learning to Read*. Hove: Lawrence Erlbaum Associates.

Jaffré, J-P. (2003) La linguistique et la lecture-écriture: De la conscience phonologique à la variable 'orthographe' [Linguistics and reading-writing: From phonological awareness to the «orthography» variable]. *Revue des Sciences de l'Éducation* 1 (29), 37–49.

Kormos, J. (2006) *Speech Production and Second Language Acquisition*. Mahwah, NJ: Lawrence Erlbaum Associates Publishers.

Lambert, E. and Chesnet, D. (2001) *NOVLEX: Une Base de Données Lexicales pour les Elèves de Primaire* [NOVLEX: Lexical data-base for primary school pupils]. On WWW at http://www.mshs.univ-poitiers.fr/lmdc/pagespersos/lambert/novlex/. Accessed May 2005.

Majerus, S., Van der Linden, M. and Belin, C. (eds) (2001) *Relations entre perception, mémoire de travail et mémoire à long terme* [Relationships between perception, working memory and long-term memory]. Marseille: SOLAL.

Montani, K. and Batušić, I. (1996) *Parlez comme nous, niveau B – udžbenik* [Speak like us, B level – textbook] (14th edn). Zagreb: Školska knjiga.

Rieben, L. and Perfetti, C.A. (1989) *L'apprenti-lecteur: Recherches empiriques et implications pédagogiques* [Learning to read: Basic research and its implication]. Lausanne-Paris: Delachaux et Niestlé.

Rieben, L., Fayol, M. and Perfetti, C.A. (eds) (1997) *Des orthographes et leur acquisition* [Learning to spell]. Lausanne-Paris: Delachaux et Niestlé.

Sprenger-Charolles, L., Colé, P. and Serniclaes, W. (2006) *Reading Acquisition and Developmental Dyslexia* (1st edn). Hove-New York: Psychology Press.

Vrhovac, Y. (1992) *Parlez comme nous, niveau A – radna bilježnica* [Speak like us, A level – exercise book] (7th edn). Zagreb: Školska knjiga.

Vrhovac, Y. (2003) *Parlez comme nous, niveau B – radna bilježnica* (Speak like us, B level – exercise book) (9th edn). Zagreb: Školska knjiga.

Chapter 12

Differences Between the Processes and Outcomes in Third Graders' Learning of English and Ukrainian in Hungarian Schools in Beregszász

ILONA HUSZTI, MÁRTA FÁBIÁN and
ERZSÉBET BÁRÁNYNÉ KOMÁRI

Introduction

This chapter reports on the first phase of a longitudinal investigation aiming to explain the reasons why ethnic Hungarian schoolchildren achieve better results in English as a foreign language than in Ukrainian as a second language. The study was conducted in Beregszász, a small provincial town in Transcarpathia, the south-western part of the Ukraine. Hungarians live in minority; 48% of the town's population is Hungarian (Molnár & Molnár, 2005). In this community five schools teach Hungarian in Beregszász: four teach elementary learners between the ages of six and 10. Besides Hungarian, all institutions teach Ukrainian as the state language, and English as a foreign language.

Since Ukrainian became the official language in the Ukraine in 1991, it has been an obligatory subject in all schools. But many teachers of the Ukrainian language in Hungarian schools are either not qualified teachers of Ukrainian, or they do not speak the learners' mother tongue (Hungarian) and thus, are unable to draw learners' attention to similarities and differences between the two languages (Báránýné Komári, 2004; Milován, 2003).

Little has been written about English language teaching in Transcarpathian Hungarian schools. There are some studies (e.g. Beregszászi, 2004; Huszti, 2005; Orosz, 2004), but they do not focus on teaching English in elementary classes in particular. A study (Fábián *et al.*, 2004) surveyed learning and teaching conditions of English in 39 Transcarpathian Hungarian schools: 48 teachers, including 27 primary-school teachers, of English filled in a questionnaire about the circumstances in their schools. Their main concern was the lack of appropriate textbooks in Hungarian schools. They used a book (Plakhotnyk & Polons'ka, 1997) based on the grammar-translation method with a lot of translation and reading exercises, but hardly any listening or speaking activities. They felt these facts prevented them from achieving better results in language teaching.

Povhan (2003) states that Hungarian learners' knowledge of the Ukrainian language depends on their social status, the Ukrainian environment, language practice opportunities outside the school, language use in the family and influence of the mass media. Findings of her study indicate that only 10% of Hungarian elementary-school learners have the possibility or need to communicate in Ukrainian within their family or with their friends. Based on these findings, Povhan enumerates some essential tasks of Ukrainian teachers in Hungarian elementary schools: motivate learners to study Ukrainian, enrich their vocabulary with age-appropriate words and expressions that meet learners' needs, and so on.

The Study

Aims

The aim of the present study is to get insights into how children with Hungarian as a first language (L1) learn English and Ukrainian in this specific educational context. Our hypothesis, based on our teaching experiences, is that learners achieve better results in English than in Ukrainian. This can sound paradoxical, as the learners are Ukrainian citizens living in the Ukraine. This experience motivated an empirical investigation into the processes and outcomes of language learning at these schools. We formulated our research questions as follows:

- Do learners achieve better results in learning English than in Ukrainian?
- What are the main differences between teaching EFL and Ukrainian to Hungarian learners in a minority context?
- What might cause these differences?

Participants

In the present study participants were 76 eight-year-old third graders (29 boys – 38% and 47 girls – 62%). They took a test measuring their listening, speaking, reading and writing skills in four schools where the language of instruction is Hungarian. Learners had been learning English for more than one year (starting in second grade) with the exception of one school where they started in first grade. All learners had been studying Ukrainian for the third year, as learning the Ukrainian language in Transcarpathian Hungarian schools starts in first grade with an introductory oral period. This corresponds to the general practice of teaching foreign languages to young learners, as early programmes usually focus on oral skills (Nikolov & Curtain, 2000).

The teacher participants of our study were six teachers of English and four of Ukrainian. They were all women, except for one male teacher of English. The mean age of the English teachers was 27.33 years (age range 24–31), whereas that of the Ukrainian teachers was 37.75 (age range 33–43). In the case of the first group, teachers' general teaching experience ranged between 3–12 years (mean: 5 years), whereas in the latter group between 12 and 21 years (mean: 16.25 years).

Teachers of Ukrainian were asked about their nationality and native language. One of the four teachers was a native speaker of Ukrainian, two were native speakers of Russian qualified to teach Russian, but after the collapse of the Soviet Union in 1991 they began to teach Ukrainian. One teacher was a Ukrainian-Hungarian bilingual. As for their qualifications, five of the English teachers had college degrees, one had a qualification issued by a two-year intensive English training course, two teachers of Ukrainian had university degrees in Russian and two teachers were qualified elementary-school teachers.

Instruments

A test battery was designed to assess learners' levels of knowledge of English and Ukrainian. The English tests had a parallel version in Ukrainian. The battery contained four sections focusing on the four language skills. Every correct answer scored one point. The total sum was 33 plus the number of appropriate utterances a learner produced in Section 4 on the speaking test. In the listening task, learners had to put down in their mother tongue names of colours they recognised in sentences like 'The rose is red.' In the reading section, learners were presented a short text about a classroom and they had to answer five comprehension questions in Hungarian, based on the text (e.g. 'Are there four windows in the classroom?'). The writing section contained two parts (Part A: filling in the missing letters, e.g. 'b.ok'; Part B: unjumbling sentences, e.g. 'name/is/Kate/My'). The vocabulary of the tests corresponded to the language material in the National Curriculum for Foreign Languages (Bekh *et al.*, 2001) and the Ukrainian Curriculum for Hungarian schools (Babych, 2003).

Besides the language tests for children, interviews were conducted with teachers of English and Ukrainian in their mother tongue to avoid misunderstandings: thus, six interviews were conducted in Hungarian, two in Russian and two in Ukrainian. In general, our questions concerned the teachers' perceptions, opinions and views about the way the language (English or Ukrainian) is taught in the elementary classes in Beregszász Hungarian schools (see the Appendix).

A contrastive analysis was conducted on the textbooks used for teaching English (Karpiuk, 2002, 2003) and Ukrainian (Kryhan *et al.*, 2003a–c). The aim of textbook analysis was to describe and compare their contents and the structure of the syllabi. We wanted to explore to what extent and how the textbooks encouraged learners to communicate. Also, we aimed to examine how the contents of the books might account for the differences in learners' knowledge of Ukrainian and English. The two curricula (Babych, 2003; Bekh *et al.*, 2001) were also analysed to get deeper insights into their nature and contents. We hoped to get further explanations for the differences between learners' knowledge of Ukrainian and English.

Procedure

The investigation was carried out in three phases. During September and October 2006 the English and Ukrainian tests were administered to the learners. First, the Ukrainian tests were filled in by the 76 learners in the four schools; then, the English ones were given to learners three weeks later to avoid the practice effect (Nunan, 1992). Three weeks was thought to be enough for the learners to forget the items in the Ukrainian test. Teacher interviews were conducted in November 2006. The interviews were tape-recorded and transcribed to make the analysis easier. The teachers were willing to participate in our research and very helpful during the interviews. Finally, analyses of the documents (English and Ukrainian curricula and textbooks) were conducted in December 2006.

Findings

Results of interviews with teachers of English

All interviewed teachers agree that the curriculum is communication-oriented and emphasises development of learners' speaking skills. It is topic-based and the topics are relevant for learners. The curriculum focuses on communication rather than grammar. Conversation models are given to every topic in the book. Language functions are also required by the curriculum such as 'Introducing oneself', 'Greetings', 'Asking for help', and so forth. All the interviewees claim that they teach similar functions. The textbook helps them as each unit contains tasks practising these functions. Learners like learning functions especially in dialogues. However, some teachers consider the number of lessons to be insufficient for fulfilling the requirements of the curriculum and for teaching communicative skills. All teachers agree that the textbook helps them in developing communicative competence.

Results of the interviews with teachers of Ukrainian

When asked about the Ukrainian Curriculum, the teachers pointed out that it does not focus on developing the learners' speaking skills, as it is rather grammar-based. Learners need to analyse and learn grammar in details: separate lessons are devoted to phonetics, spelling, word structure and syntax. All teachers claimed that the Curriculum does not contain any statements on teaching language functions. They believe that learners can only achieve good results in Ukrainian, if they live in bilingual families and in a community where they hear and use Ukrainian every day.

Test results

The results of the test administered in third grade are summarised in Table 12.1.

Judging from the means, the data do not prove our hypothesis. In all skills, except for listening comprehension ($t = 0.0018$, $p < 0.05$), better results have been achieved in Ukrainian than in English (writing: $t = 0.05$, $p < 0.05$; reading: $t = 0.37$, $p > 0.05$; speaking: $t = 4.99$, $p < 0.05$). Therefore, at the given stage of language learning, Hungarian schoolchildren living in the Ukraine performed better on the tests in the state language than in English in reading, writing and speaking, although the difference in reading is not significant.

In the Ukrainian language learners' proficiency in the productive skills is better developed than in English. Participants achieved the highest scores, in both languages, on the writing tasks, whereas the results in reading were lowest. The biggest difference in favour of Ukrainian was found on the speaking test. The difference between the results of listening was significantly higher in English than in Ukrainian (English means: 4.96, standard deviation: 2.02; Ukrainian means: 3.47, standard deviation: 2;

Table 12.1 Descriptive statistics of the proficiency tests taken by third grade learners ($n = 76$) (maximum scores for each skill are indicated in parentheses)

Skills	English		Ukrainian	
	Means	*Standard deviation*	*Means*	*Standard deviation*
Listening (13)	4.96	2.02	3.47	2.00
Reading (5)	1.48	1.22	1.68	1.05
Writing (15)	4.93	2.57	6.15	3.96
Speaking (10)	1.68	1.37	4.55	2.30

Table 12.2 The number of lessons per week

	First grade		Second grade		Third grade	
School	English	Ukrainian	English	Ukrainian	English	Ukrainian
A, B, D	0	2 (oral course)	1	3	2	4 (2 language, 2 reading classes)
C	1	2	2	3	2	4

$t = 0.0018$, $p < 0.05$) in spite of the fact that the learners have some contact with the Ukrainian language in their everyday life. Performances on the speaking tests showed that while communicating in English and Ukrainian, children switch to their native tongue in case they understand the question but cannot convey the message they are eager to tell in the target language.

The number of lessons and the starting age are considered to be important factors in language learning. Table 12.2 shows the weekly number of lessons in English and Ukrainian. The number of lessons is much higher in Ukrainian than in English and the learning process begins a year earlier in all schools. Furthermore, School C is also different because it starts teaching English a year earlier than the other schools. In comparison to the other schools, the results of the English tests in School C were better than in the other schools.

Textbook analysis

The English textbooks (Forms 2 and 3)

The English textbook used in Grade 2 in the Hungarian schools was written for Ukrainian learners (Karpiuk, 2002). The book consists of six units containing altogether 66 lessons, with a lesson lasting 45 minutes. At the back of the textbook, there is an English-Ukrainian vocabulary which includes all the unfamiliar words in the units. The vocabulary contains three columns: the first column presents the word, the second column shows its pronunciation and the third column contains the Ukrainian translation of the word.

The book is based on a framework story with characters appearing throughout the book. The central character is Miss Mary Poppins whose task is to introduce learners to the world of English. There are four children whose presence is essential in the book as English is presented through life situations taken from the lives of these imaginary children. All the four language skills are developed. There are various activity types in the textbook focusing on vocabulary, grammar, listening, reading, speaking and writing. All the instructions are presented in two languages (English and Ukrainian). The activities should be carried out individually, in pairs, or in groups. The book is full of attractive coloured pictures. Most of the lessons contain a section called 'Playtime', where various rhymes, poems, songs and games are presented which have a motivating effect on children to learn English in a more effective way. In summary, the textbook meets the demands of modern language teaching. It corresponds to the requirements set out in the curriculum (Bekh *et al.*, 2001). The only drawback from the point-of-view of Hungarian learners is that the vocabulary section does not contain Hungarian translations. Otherwise, the book seems to be motivating and challenging both for learners and teachers.

English 3 (Karpiuk, 2003) also consists of six units containing 10 lessons each and an introductory unit in which the language material of English 2 is revised briefly. There is a vocabulary section at the end of the book with English words organised in alphabetical order. The inside cover of the textbook contains Ukrainian explanations of different English grammatical structures (e.g. the present progressive). The book is full of lively coloured pictures. The section titled 'Playtime' also appears in the book and it contains authentic English Mother Goose rhymes, songs and different games. The topics the book covers are all interesting and close to the lives of the learners (e.g. hobbies, (pen)friends, personal qualities, food and eating). All the four language skills are developed in the book, with a focus on listening and speaking. Another positive feature is that it teaches modern colloquial real-life vocabulary, for example, kid, computer, Barbie, hamburger, pizza, coke, toaster. In addition, the book meets the needs of eight-year-old children by presenting their favourite cartoon characters (e.g. Winnie-the-Pooh, The Little Mermaid, Cinderella). All these features make the book easy and pleasant to use both for learners and teachers.

Ukrainian Primer for second grade, Reader for third grade, Ukrainian for third grade

The Ukrainian Primer for Grade 2 (Kryhan *et al.*, 2003b) was written for Hungarian schools and learners. It starts with an introductory chapter which presents pictures about various topics (greetings, school, classroom, toys, colours, seasons, garden, family and folk traditions). This is followed by the presentation of the letters of the Ukrainian alphabet. Pupils are presented sample phrases, sentences and texts for developing their reading skills. The book contains only those elements of grammar that are essential for learners at this level of study, for example, discrimination of the spirant *г* and the plosive *ґ*, pronunciation of the sound cluster *шч*, the discrimination of vowels *u, i, e*, and so on. One of the essential drawbacks of the book is that for Hungarian learners it is difficult to understand

Ukrainian folk tales in it because their language is beyond their level of proficiency.

The third grade Ukrainian Reader contains 12 units with topics covering 'Folk wisdom', 'The fruitful golden autumn', 'The book is the source of knowledge', 'Family', 'Ukraine – our motherland' and others. However, levels are problematic, as they are difficult for Hungarian learners: texts require excellent knowledge of Ukrainian. Also, the topics are not relevant for the age group: they do not raise the learners' interest, they are boring and too abstract for young learners.

The third grade Ukrainian Language textbook (Kryhan *et al.*, 2003c) is a grammar book of five units focusing on topics like 'The vowel and consonant system of the Ukrainian language', 'The sentence and its types', 'Principal and secondary parts of the sentence' and 'The word and its meaning'. The reading and writing skills are developed, but learners' speaking and listening skills are not improved, as the book does not aim at teaching learners to communicate in Ukrainian.

English Curriculum

The foreword of the new National Curriculum for Foreign Languages emphasises that foreign language teaching aims to develop communicative language competence and therefore, the contents of the curriculum are renewed. The editors (Bekh *et al.*, 2001) of the curriculum claim that it was prepared on the basis of the *Common European Framework of Reference for Languages* (2001) and by the end of the third year of study (age 10) learners are to achieve A1 level. The document integrates basic principles of communicative teaching, learner autonomy, integrated teaching of language functions and developing various learner competences.

Ukrainian Curriculum

The Ukrainian Curriculum (Babych, 2003) distinguishes between two periods of language learning: the alphabet period, when pupils are getting acquainted with the letters of the Ukrainian alphabet (second grade) and the post-alphabet period, when pupils are considered literate in Ukrainian and able to read and write in this language (third and fourth grades). The main topics are subdivided into four sections along the four language skills. The speaking section is subdivided into two subsections: lexical material and information about the language. In the lexical material section, there are two groups: (1) words and expressions that learners need for active use, and (2) words and phrases for passive acquisition. The part on 'Information about the language' contains grammar and structures that learners must acquire. A positive feature of the curriculum is that it indicates the tentative number of lessons to be spent on a topic, for example, the topic 'My family' should be taught in 12 lessons.

Discussion

Teachers' views on curricula and materials

In the interviews we asked teachers to what extent textbooks contain tasks that focus on communication. The Ukrainian teachers complained about the fact that the textbook does not contain a large number of such activities. Therefore, it does not help teachers in developing learners' oral skills.

Concerning the English textbook, the teachers found that it centred on communication. On the one hand, they underlined the importance of pictures in it. Two of them mentioned picture-based tasks as their favourite ones because they think children remember words more easily when they can connect them with a picture image. Children's most favourite activities from the textbook have a creative character: acting out dialogues, colouring and drawing. On the other hand, the number of examples for introducing a new topic and exercises aimed at practising grammar (e.g. the use of *am, is, are*) are considered to be inadequate. The English-Ukrainian vocabulary at the end of the book provides unfamiliar words and expressions to each topic but it was found useless for Hungarian children. The Ukrainian teachers, when asked about their favourite task types, stated that they preferred gapped words, the analysis of sound-spelling correspondences and picture descriptions or talking about pictures.

A reading task in English includes reading the text in chorus followed by individual reading and a simple reading comprehension task, with true of false answers. Most teachers focus on sounds and phonetic transcription. According to their experiences, gifted learners acquire them with ease, while others need more practice; their general opinion is that learners at this age have no difficulty in learning the transcription signs and in pronouncing the sounds represented by them. Teachers consider reading aloud essential at this age, and they seem to prefer the phonics approach (Slattery & Willis, 2001) to teaching reading.

Teachers gave an account of how they practice writing: writing 'lines' of letters and words, copying crosswords, filling in missing letters into gapped words and dictation. In general, learners enjoy writing tasks, especially crosswords. Wordsearch was mentioned as the most popular type of crossword. Checking and correcting each other's homework is among the most favourite activities. Teachers noticed that learners sometimes confused Ukrainian and English words. They also claimed that while constructing dialogues either in English or in Ukrainian, the words come into children's minds first in English.

As can be seen, both the English curriculum and the textbook are based on communicative methodology, whereas the Ukrainian materials follow a more traditional grammar-based approach. In teachers' views, as the results of the interviews show, because of these reasons, learners develop more positive attitudes to language learning in English classes.

Test results

The reasons of the good results in the writing section of the test in both languages we consider to be: (a) the same types of writing tasks; (b) good and sufficient amount of practice in doing such exercises; (c) children had enough time. This is explained by Kubanek-German (1998) who states that writing is easier than speaking because children have more time to think. The interview data also prove that teachers pay more attention to writing in the teaching process. Also, writing tasks were easy: gap-filling and unjumbling sentences.

The high score in listening might be due to the relatively easy task and the children's good ability to recognise and distinguish sounds. The poor results in reading are most probably influenced by the limited number of reading tasks in both the English and the Ukrainian course books; long, boring and inadequate texts in Ukrainian, short but too few texts in English; hardly any reading comprehension questions; frequent reading aloud and translation, especially in Ukrainian classes.

In the speaking test, most children managed to talk about themselves: 'I live in the Ukraine/Beregszász.', 'I have dogs', 'I don't like cats/flowers/ strawberries/school.' Their performances were better on questions requiring a short 'Yes' or 'No' answer, as speaking skills need longer time and more practice to develop than listening.

The main reasons why the results were better in Ukrainian include an earlier starting age, more lessons and some extracurricular exposure to the state language in everyday life. On the other hand, the reasons why learners seem to prefer English to Ukrainian and seem to acquire it more quickly are as follows: methods, textbooks and the content of the syllabus are more age-appropriate and learners' attitudes and motivation are more favourable.

Thus, we came to the conclusion that although participants in the study achieved better results in Ukrainian, they seem to acquire English at a faster pace than Ukrainian and have more positive attitudes to it. The reasons are supposed to be related to the teaching methods (communicative vs. grammar translation), the quality of the textbooks and the content of the teaching materials.

Textbooks

Comparing the English textbooks and the Ukrainian ones, the difference in their scope becomes evident at first glance. The English books focus on speaking and communication, while the Ukrainian books are centred on grammar, reading and translation. In the English textbooks, words are not translated but taught through pictures or definitions. This way is more effective because when learners concentrate on the clues and guess meanings in context, meanings will be remembered more easily than in the case when the translation is immediately provided.

The English books aim at developing socio-cultural competence by pointing out certain differences between the English and the Ukrainian way of life, culture, and so on. Unfortunately, such differences between the Ukrainian and the Hungarian culture are not pointed out either in the primer, or the reader. In sum, the Ukrainian textbooks provide knowledge about the language, whereas the English textbooks promote practice and competence in language use.

Curricula

Comparing the two curricula, the English curriculum recycles the material by repeating and extending the scope of a given topic over years, whereas the Ukrainian curriculum follows a linear approach. Another advantage of the English curriculum is that it pays special attention to learners' competences; the Ukrainian curriculum focuses on linguistic competence only. Unlike the English curriculum, the Ukrainian one presupposes the learners to have a good basis for studying Ukrainian, which the learners evidently do not have. The curriculum covers a wide range of grammar structures that, in the teachers' view, learners find difficult to grasp.

Conclusions

The results of the proficiency tests in English and in Ukrainian refuted our original hypothesis, as learners performed better on the parallel test in Ukrainian than in English, most importantly in their productive skills. This could be explained by learners' closer and more frequent contact with Ukrainian than with English.

The participating teachers of English are mainly satisfied with the contents of the curricula and the textbooks (Karpiuk, 2002, 2003). However, they believe more lessons could help learners acquire the target language better. Half of the Ukrainian teachers do not find any problems with the curriculum or the textbooks.

In sum, the situation is controversial. Although learners have access to English, a foreign language, only in the classroom, the focus is more on communication; whereas Ukrainian is taught as a second language, learners' exposure in the classroom is limited to grammar and translation. Further research is needed including classroom observation sessions to prove the above statement empirically. Obviously, at the very early stages of language learning children have an advantage in the Ukrainian language compared to English. Further research is needed to see whether this advantage remains with the learners at later stages of language learning. Therefore, we will conduct a similar proficiency test both in English and in Ukrainian with the same learners to see if differences continue to exist. Also, we intend to investigate the learners' attitude and motivation to learn English and Ukrainian.

Pedagogical Implications and Limitations of Study

Although motivation was not the focus of our research, we assume that language learning attitudes and motivation need to be explored, as most probably they play an important role. As it turned out in the interviews, two Ukrainian teachers were inappropriately trained for the age group they taught. For these teachers, it would be beneficial to participate in in-service teacher training courses to upgrade their methods and techniques of language teaching. This is necessary, as their pupils achieved lower scores in Ukrainian than the pupils whose teachers are better qualified. Classroom observations and inquiries into children's individual differences are necessary to find out more about the reasons.

One of the factors believed to predict language learning success is the number of lessons per week. Two English lessons a week in third grade, according to the teachers, do not seem to be enough to teach the target language vocabulary and the four skills. Therefore, stakeholders (headmasters of these schools) should consider how they could increase the number (provided the quality of teaching is high, as more weekly hours cannot guarantee better quality of language education).

Finally, the curriculum and textbook in the Ukrainian language need revision, as presently their focus is narrow and they do not reflect learners' needs. Changing classroom practice, however, will take a long time.

We are fully aware of limitations of our study. First, classroom observations were not carried out to triangulate the relevance and adequacy of the teachers' answers in the interview and their classroom practices. Second, affective factors were not explored; therefore, it is possible that what teachers perceive as different is motivation. Third, the quality of teaching and learners' development over time were not researched. These are issues to be examined in the following stages of our long-scale research.

References

Babych, N.I. (Бабич, Н.І.) (2003) *Календарно-тематичне Планування Навчальних Предметів у 1–4 Класах для Шкіл з Угорською Мовою Навчання* [Syllabi of School Disciplines in Forms 1–4 for Schools with Hungarian Language of Instruction]. Ужгород: Інформаційно-видавничий центр ЗІППО.

Báránymé Komári, E. (2004) Az ukrán nyelv oktatásának problémái és feladatai a kárpátaljai magyar iskolákban [The problems and tasks of teaching Ukrainian in the Hungarian schools of Transcarpathia]. *Közoktatás* 4 (5), 15–16.

Bekh, P. (gen. ed.) (Бех, П. / гол. ред.) Akulova, O., Birkun, L., Burenko, B., Vasylenko, M., Kalinina, L., Karpova, T., Kovalenko, O., Samojlyukevych, I., Sychyvytsia, L. and Shylova, N. (eds) (Акулова, О., Біркун, Л., Буренко, В., Василенко, М., Калініна, Л., Карпова, Т., Коваленко, О., Самойлюкевич, І., Сичивиця, Л., Шилова, Н. – ред.) (2001) *Програми для Загальноосвітніх Навчальних Закладів: Англійська Мова (2–12 Класи)* [Curricula for Elementary, Primary, and Secondary Schools: English (Forms 2–12)]. Київ: Міністерство освіти і науки України. Шкільний світ.

Beregszászi, A. (2004) Idegennyelv-oktatásunk gondjairól és feladatairól szocio-lingvisztikai nézőpontból [About the problems and tasks of our foreign language teaching from a socio-linguistic point of view.]. In Huszti, I. (ed.) *Idegennyelv-oktatás Kisebbségi Környezetben* [Teaching Foreign Languages in Minority Context] (pp. 10–20). Ungvár: Poliprint.

Common European Framework of Reference for Languages: Learning, Teaching, Assessment (2001) Cambridge: Cambridge University Press.

Fábián, M., Huszti, I. and Lizák, K. (2004) *Az Angol Nyelv Oktatásának Helyzete Kárpátalja Magyar Tannyelvű Iskoláiban* [The State of English Language Teaching in Transcarpathian Hungarian Schools.]. Paper presented at the *4th National Conference on Education*, 20–22 October 2004. Budapest: Hungarian Academy of Science.

Huszti, I. (2005) English language teaching in the upper primary classes of Transcarpathian Hungarian schools: Problems and solutions. In Huszti, I. and Kolyadzhyn, N. (eds) *Nyelv és Oktatás a 21. Század Elején* [Language and Education at the Beginning of the 21st Century] (pp. 182–186). Proceedings of the international conference *Language and Education at the Beginning of the 21st Century* held at the II. Rákóczi Ferenc Transcarpathian Hungarian College in Beregszász. Ungvár: PoliPrint.

Karpiuk, O.D. (Карп'юк, О.Д.) (2002) *Англійська Мова: Підручник для 2 Класу Загальноосвітніх Навчальних Закладів* [English Textbook for Form 2]. Київ: Навчальна книга.

Karpiuk, O.D. (Карп'юк, О.Д.) (2003) *Англійська Мова Підручник для 3 Класу Загальноосвітніх Навчальних Закладів* [English Textbook for Form 3]. Київ: Навчальна книга.

Kryhan, S.G., Keresteny, I.S. and Sergiychuk, Yu.P. (Криган, С.Г., Керестень, І.С., Сергійчук, Ю.П.) (2003a) *Буквар. Підручник для 2 Класу Загальноосвітніх Навчальних Закладів з Угорською Мовою Навчання* [Primer: A Form 2 Textbook for Schools with Hungarian Language of Instruction]. Чернівці: Букрек.

Kryhan, S.G., Maidan, A.P. and Serhiychuk, Yu.P. (Криган, С.Г., Майдан, А.П., Сергійчик, Ю.П.) (2003b) *Книга для Читання. Підручник для 3 Класу Загальноосвітніх Навчальних Закладів з Угорськоіо Мовою Навчання* [Reader: A Form 3 Textbook for Schools with Hungarian Language of Instruction]. Чернівці: Букрек.

Kryhan, S.G., Maidan, A.P. and Serhiychuk, Yu.P. (Криган, С.Г., Майдан, А.П., Сергійчик, Ю.П.) (2003c) *Українська Мова. Підручник для 3 Класу Загальноосвітніх Навчальних Закладів з Угорською Мовою Навчання* [Ukrainian: A Form 3 Textbook for Schools with Hungarian Language of Instruction]. Чернівці: Букрек.

Kubanek-German, A. (1998) Primary foreign language teaching in Europe: Trends and issues. *Language Teaching* 31, 193–205.

Milován, A. (2003) Az ukrán nyelv oktatása Kárpátalja magyar tannyelvű isko-láiban [The teaching of Ukrainian in schools educating in Hungarian in Kárpátalja]. *Kisebbségkutatás* 11 (4), 984–989.

Molnár, J. and Molnár, D.I. (2005) *Kárpátalja Népessége és Magyarsága a Népszámlálási és Népmozgalmi Adatok Tükrében* [The Population and the Hungarians of Transcarpathia through the Mirror of Consensus and Demographic Data]. Beregszász: KMPSZ.

Nikolov, M. and Curtain, H. (eds) (2000) *An Early Start: Modern Languages in Europe and Beyond*. Strasbourg: Council of Europe Publishing.

Nunan, D. (1992) *Research Methods in Language Learning.* Cambridge: Cambridge University Press.

Orosz, I. (2004) Nyelvoktatás – kinek, mikor, hogyan? [Language teaching – whom to, when, how?]. In I. Huszti (ed.) *Idegennyelv-oktatás Kisebbségi Környezetben* [Teaching Foreign Languages in Minority Context] (pp. 53–68). Ungvár: Poliprint.

Plakhotnyk, V.M. and Polons'ka, P.A. (Плахотник, В.М., Полонська, П.А.) (1997) *Англійська Мова: Підручник для Першого Класу* [English Textbook for Form 1]. Київ: Перун.

Povhan, K. (Повхан, К.) (2003) Українська мова у школах національних меншин: Проблеми і перспективи навчання державної мови учнів-угорців [The Ukrainian language in schools of national minorities: Problems and perspectives of teaching the state language to Hungarian learners]. *Українська Мова і Література в Школі* 8, 52–55.

Slattery, M. and Willis, J. (2001) *English for Primary Teachers: A Handbook of Activities and Classroom Language*. Oxford: Oxford University Press.

Appendix

Teacher interview protocol
(English version)

1. Age.
2. Degree.
3. Number of students in the group.
4. How long have you been teaching English?
5. How long have you been teaching in primary classes?
6. Does the current curriculum, in your opinion, pay enough attention to developing the learners' speaking skills? If yes, how?
7. What is the learners' attitude to learning English? Do they study it with pleasure or only because it is compulsory?
8. To what extent does the third grade English syllabus focus on communication?
9. Does the syllabus require teaching language functions? (e.g. introducing oneself, greeting, asking for help, giving directions giving information, expressing opinion).
10. Do you teach similar functions in third grade?
11. How much does the coursebook you use help you in teaching functions? Does it contain tasks aimed at developing communicative skills?
12. What coursebook do you use?
13. What is your favourite exercise type in the book?

14. What is the learners' favourite exercise type?
15. What do you find lacking from the book?
16. How do you teach target language reading and writing in the third form?
17. Do children in your opinion acquire the language in general easily or with difficulties? Why?

Chapter 13

The Growth of Young Learners' English Vocabulary Size

ANDREA OROSZ

Introduction

Vocabulary is an essential component of competence in a foreign language and the Hungarian *National Core Curriculum* (2003) sets standards for the scale of English vocabulary acquisition during the course of the study in schools. We have no data, however, to tell us whether these targets are met and whether the progress learners make in learning vocabulary is satisfactory in terms of achieving the communicative goals of the curriculum. This study seeks to fill this void of information by testing the vocabulary sizes of learners in the first four years of English study at a Hungarian primary school. The results show that learners make good and regular progress, at least equivalent to similar learners in other countries, and exceed the vocabulary targets specified in the curriculum.

Aims of the study

The purpose of the investigation reported in this study is to measure the English as a foreign language (EFL) vocabulary size among young learners in the first years of English in Hungarian schools. Vocabulary is an essential element of foreign language learning which contributes at every level to communication and comprehension in the target language. Measuring and monitoring this element of knowledge is hoped to contribute to our better understanding of the learning process and allow us to make better judgements about the likely levels of success for learners.

Background, context and literature review

Background and context

Vocabulary size refers to the total number of words that a person knows (Read, 2004). Although vocabulary size development seems to be one of the most important goals of language learning and scholars have been aware of its importance for a long time, until recently there have been no standards or widely-used tools for measurements in this area. Only in the last few years has computer technology and the development of corpus linguistics made it possible to make a good estimate of a learner's vocabulary size. The existence of such tests make it possible to measure vocabulary knowledge at different stages of learning and calculate how much vocabulary is needed to take milestone exams such as school-leaving exams at secondary schools and international exams such as TOEFL and IELTS.

The growth of vocabulary size should provide a lot of information about foreign language learners' development. If the input is appropriate, foreign language vocabulary should develop gradually and if vocabulary knowledge were to stop increasing then it would be a concern that progress generally might be halted. As vocabulary size is closely related to other language skills, measuring vocabulary size should provide insight into students' overall language development. The standard vocabulary size tests which are used for giving information about foreign language learners' vocabulary size appear very suitable for measuring young learners' vocabulary uptake. It is particularly important to know how much vocabulary young learners acquire because it is the foundation on which later learning can be built. Additionally, it should provide teachers with a picture of the efficiency of their teaching and enable judgements to be made about the expansion of students' vocabulary size relative to older learners.

The decision to investigate young Hungarian students' vocabulary advancement was made after conducting a survey amongst teacher trainees who had just returned from English lesson observations and teaching practice in different schools in Hungary. The survey revealed that teachers appeared to spend very little time on vocabulary teaching both in the primary and secondary schools, but regularly tested whether their students had learnt the new words. There appeared to be a contradiction here. New materials were introduced without preparation and recycling of the vocabulary to facilitate memorisation. Despite this, teachers seemed to expect an enormous expansion in their students' vocabulary knowledge. Measuring young language learners' vocabulary size should make an interesting study, therefore, and should enable us to make better judgements about their English knowledge. It is especially important because it appears to be a commonly held belief that Hungarians are not able to learn languages well and our position in language learning is bad compared to other countries.

What does vocabulary size tell us about students' foreign language knowledge?

Vocabulary size is inevitably inter-related with learners' general language level. Vocabulary size, other language skills and knowledge of structures, correspond well among populations of learners. In brief, they depend on each other and this is frequently commented on in texts on language acquisition. For example, 'knowing a word involves how to use it in sentences' (Sinclair quoted in Nation, 2001: 106); 'In order to know a word it is necessary to know what part of speech it is and what grammatical patterns it can fit into' (Nation, 2001: 55). Vocabulary size corresponds with reading abilities, comprehension and writing abilities (Meara & Buxton, 1987). Also, knowing a word involves knowing what words it typically occurs with (Nation, 2001: 27). As vocabulary extends, other language skills also develop. All in all, it would be beneficial for teachers to know about the development of their students' general language level and a vocabulary size levels test might provide an alternative solution for this purpose.

How many words are taught in a lesson and how often are they tested?

In order to know more about how important teachers of English consider teaching vocabulary in primary schools to be, a cross-sectional survey was conducted. The survey conducted by students at the University of Szeged at the end of school year 2005/2006, involved 34 trainees who completed a questionnaire about their primary school lesson observation experiences concerning vocabulary teaching. Students usually start learning English at the age of nine, in Grade 3 and at the age of 12 they are in Grade 6. It was anticipated that the survey would help reveal the number of words taught to learners on average for this age group in one single lesson and how and how often teachers tested their students' vocabulary knowledge. The findings suggested that ten new words, on average, were introduced in each class. This is a believable number because eight to 12 productive items are considered to be the optimal number of new vocabulary items in one lesson, but they may not be retained (Gairns & Redman, 1986: 66).

The survey also suggested that teachers believe that they can promote their students' vocabulary learning by making them take vocabulary tests frequently. Assessing young learners' development on a regular basis might have a positive effect and students who are regularly assessed may achieve better results than those who are not. The survey showed that in 20 out of 34 schools students take a vocabulary test on the next lesson after learning the vocabulary items even in the lower primary classes. My observation on this is that while making students take tests can be part of good practice, the problem is that after the test they seldom return to the previously learnt vocabulary. The absence of recycling might make the newly learnt items hard to retain. This testing method may fail to reflect the long-term retention of vocabulary and the benefit of this effort in overall language ability. Grades are given on the basis of immediate vocabulary recall and not of long-term vocabulary knowledge.

Estimating Hungarian learners' vocabulary size

Knowing the input of vocabulary per lesson, and the number of lessons the learners take, it is possible to estimate the likely vocabulary size that students might gain during their studies. If we take into account only years 3–6, learners participate in the following number of lessons:

3rd grade: 74 (two lessons a week)
4th grade: 74
5th grade: 111 (three lessons a week)
6th grade: 111

This means that over four years the learners will have had altogether about 370 English lessons. If we suppose that students retain all the words they are exposed to (10 words a lesson) this would mean that they would know approximately 3700 words by the end of sixth grade, at the age of 12. This number corresponds with the B2 CEF level (Milton, 2006a: 202). It is a known fact that sixth graders do not reach the B2 CEF level. Nor do they reach it in the upper primary classes, and only some students' vocabulary knowledge might be expected to develop to this level at secondary school. Most probably, learners in primary do not retain all the vocabulary items they are exposed to and do not get to this level of vocabulary knowledge. However, we do not know what their vocabulary size is and how it compares with similar learners elsewhere.

What factors affect students' vocabulary knowledge?

Many factors may affect students' foreign language vocabulary growth. One factor is the vocabulary of the course books the students use. These, together with the word lists teachers give their students to learn, might be expected to be the primary sources of vocabulary input for most foreign language learners. Vocabulary input might include teacher talk, although the influence of this is an area almost entirely unresearched. Whether these words are retained might be affected by word learnability which includes qualities like the length of a word and its cognateness, which can affect whether a word can be retained in memory (Laufer, 1990). Similarly, the degree of recycling, the regular use of familiar vocabulary during classes, is likely to influence retention (Gairns & Redman, 1986). Vocabulary retention might be further influenced by the focus of teaching and the priority, and the time, devoted to vocabulary learning. Finally, whether vocabulary is easily learned might be a product of the learners' aptitude, individual learning strategies and styles (Meara & Milton, 2003: 10).

Vocabulary requirements in the National Core Curriculum *(2003)*

Even if we do not know exactly how many words learners will know after four years of learning, we do know that some of what they are taught will be forgotten, we do have information from the Hungarian *National Core Curriculum*. This document suggests how much active and passive vocabulary should be gained by students at the end of different grades in the primary and secondary schools. The figures are provided in Table 13.1.

Table 13.1 Hungarian *National Core Curriculum* vocabulary guidelines

	3rd grade	*4th grade*	*5th grade*	*6th grade*	*7th grade*	*8th grade*	*10th grade*	*12th grade*
Active vocabulary	200	350	500	600	800	1200	B1 CEF level (2750–3250)	B2 CEF level (3250–3750)
Passive vocabulary	150	150	200	250	300	400		
Active & passive vocabulary	350	400	700	850	1100	1600		

Source: Krizsán (2003)

The study reported in this chapter focuses on students' vocabulary advancement in Grades 3, 4, 5 and 6. The data in the chart suggest that after four years of English language learning students are expected to have an active knowledge of 600, and an additional passive knowledge of 250 vocabulary items. Active words refer to productive, whereas passive words refer to recognition vocabulary in addition to productive vocabulary knowledge. Altogether, by the end of sixth grade, learners are required to know 850 words. This is a much more realistic figure than 3700, the number learners may have been exposed to in four years. However, these targets appear rather inconsistently arranged in that they appear to suggest some 350 words might be learned in the third grade but only 50 the following year. It is unclear how these figures have been arrived at.

Vocabulary learning in other countries

The vocabulary knowledge and progress of 227 young learners has been measured (Milton, 2006b) in private EFL schools in Greece (called frontisteria). Every learner in a frontisteria was tested at the end of the school year using Meara and Milton's (2003) *X-Lex* test, which provides an estimate of the number of words known out of the most frequent 5000 words in English. The learners received 100 hours of classroom instruction per year over the first five years (Junior to level D) and 125 hours of input in years 6 and 7 (class E and the FCE class). Learners in this study, fairly consistently, appear to add about five new words to their vocabularies per contact hour of study. For the first four years, therefore, they are roughly equivalent in the amount of classroom lessons they receive to learners in Hungary, but the lessons in Hungary are shorter (see Figure 13.1).

These figures suggest that Greek learners of English learn approximately 500 words per year and after four years have a vocabulary size of some 2000 words. While this is smaller than the 3700 words to which Hungarian learners are exposed, it is considerably larger than the 850

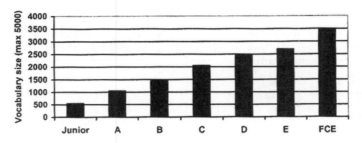

Figure 13.1   Lexical growth in learners of EFL in Greece (Milton, 2006b: 34)

word target identified in the Hungarian *National Core Curriculum* (2003). In the absence of evidence we do not know whether Hungarian learners do have vocabularies at the curricular level or at the more elevated levels of the Greek learners.

The figures reported in the Greek study are mean scores and, of course, there is considerable individual variation. An idea of the scale of the variation which occurs can be seen in Figure 13.2 which shows the spread of scores around the mean for the figures provided in Figure 13.1.

While most learners clearly make good and regular progress in their vocabulary development, it is also clear that many students do not. Some students make what appears to be spectacular progress. There is considerable overlap between the classes. The best students, these results suggest, can acquire over 1000 new lexical items in the first year and, subsequent figures imply, continue to make considerable progress thereafter. Some learners, at the end of this course of study, seem to have real knowledge of the vast majority of frequent words in English and are presumably well placed to read with understanding and communicate through English.

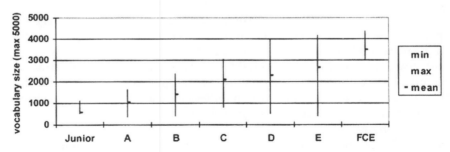

Figure 13.2   Spread of lexical size scores among learners of EFL in Greece (Milton, personal correspondence)

Not all students are so good, of course, and the lowest scoring students have estimated vocabularies in the region of 400 to 500 words across all the levels up to the FCE group (where the least able learners deemed unable to pass the exam, are excluded). Again, in the absence of evidence, we have no idea whether this kind of variation is a feature of vocabulary learning in Hungary.

Aims of Study

The purpose of the investigation reported in this study is to measure the English foreign language vocabulary size among young learners in the first years of English in Hungarian schools. This information will allow a number of specific objectives to be achieved.

(1) It will allow us to measure the progress of learners over time in this vital element of language learning.
(2) It will allow us to estimate vocabulary uptake per contact hour.
(3) It will allow us to compare participants' vocabulary size with that of the Greek learners whose knowledge and progress have been reported above, and with the targets set in the *National Core Curriculum*.

Participants

The participants were a convenience sample of 253 students in an average primary school in Szeged (a large town in the south of Hungary). Learners' ages ranged between nine and 12 (3rd–6th grades). Participants started learning English in grade three in two lessons a week (76 lessons a year). The same pattern of teaching is followed in the fourth grade. In Grades 5 and 6, learners study English in three lessons per week, a total of 111 lessons per year. Lessons are 45 minutes in duration.

Testing Instruments

The testing instrument was Meara and Milton's (2003) *X-Lex*; the same test was used in the Greek study reported above (Milton, 2006b) to allow a direct comparison of vocabulary knowledge between the two groups of learners. This test is a checklist test where learners are presented with 120 words, one at a time, and they are required to say whether they know the meaning of the word or not. One-hundred of these words are real words selected at random from each of the first 5000 word frequency bands provided in Nation's (1984) and Hindmarsh's (1980) lists. There are also 20 pseudo words, false words constructed to look and sound like real English words, whose purpose is to provide a check for guesswork and overestimation on the part of the test takers. The score on the real words allows a vocabulary size estimate, out of 5000, to be made. The score on the pseudo words allows this score to be adjusted for guessing. The adjusted score is the one reported in this study.

Procedures

The test was delivered in a paper and pencil version at the end of the school year 2005/2006 in order to minimise the disruption to classes and to represent annual progress. The test instructions, an example, and the first few lines of test items are shown in Appendix A. As Meara and Milton report:

> Since each response takes only a few seconds, the entire test takes only about 10 minutes. A further advantage of testing vocabulary using this YES/NO [checklist] method is that it is possible to test many more items than would normally be the case in traditional language tests. This means that the scores are likely to be more accurate and reliable than in tests with fewer items. (Meara & Milton, 2003: 2)

Another advantage is that even young learners can do it in a few minutes. The instructions and the example were given in Hungarian to ensure that the students could really understand what to do and nothing could disturb their understanding of the task.

The data collected is used in the following ways in order to provide answers to the questions raised. Firstly, the mean score for each year can be calculated and this information can be used to suggest progress from year to year. A learning rate per classroom hour can also be estimated for each year of study. Secondly, these scores can be compared with data from other countries and with the targets set by the *National Core Curriculum*.

Results

Growth in vocabulary size

The results in Table 13.2 indicate that Hungarian students' English vocabulary grows year by year, although this development is not always

Table 13.2   Mean vocabulary size estimates in Grades 3, 4, 5 and 6

	3rd grade	*4th grade*	*5th grade*	*6th grade*
Mean vocabulary knowledge estimate	348	696	1177	1457
Standard deviation	229	486	540	648
Vocabulary growth per year	348	348	481	280

completely smooth. The mean scores for each of the four grades, and the inferred growth per year, are given in Table 13.2.

An ANOVA confirms there is an effect between groups and that the differences in the mean scores for each grade are significantly different, $F(250) = 48.852$, sig. < 0.001.

Over the first three years of learning vocabulary uptake appears both very regular and impressively large. In Grade 5 in particular, nearly 500 new words are added. Only in the sixth grade does the rate of progress appear to diminish. However, these figures are complicated by differences in numbers of lessons taught in each grade. This kind of variation can be compensated by calculations of the vocabulary uptake per lesson and per contact hour.

Growth in vocabulary uptake per contact hour

Learners in this study had a total of 370 lessons in English over the course of their four years of English and about 277 hours in input. The vocabulary uptake of the learners is recalculated to show how many words on average are learned per lesson and per hour; the figures are shown in Table 13.3.

Some of the apparent inconsistencies of the mean vocabulary growth figures are ironed out here. In the first three years, vocabulary uptake appears to be consistent and very high at about six words per contact hour. Only in Grade 6 does this progress decrease but the rate of learning is still above three words per contact hour.

Comparison with Greek learners and with *National Core Curriculum* targets

These figures may be very useful in identifying the nature and amount of progress learners make in vocabulary, but they stand in isolation. Only when they are compared with other systems and with national targets do they begin to tell us whether progress is in line with the expectations of the *National Core Curriculum* and whether this progress appears satisfactory compared with learners elsewhere. Table 13.4, therefore, compares the annual vocabulary knowledge of learners with *National Core Curriculum* targets, and Table 13.5 compares annual progress and vocabulary uptake per hour against the figures for Greek learners presented above.

Table 13.3   Vocabulary uptake per hour and per lesson

	3rd grade	*4th grade*	*5th grade*	*6th grade*
Mean vocabulary gain per lesson	4.70	4.70	4.33	2.52
Mean vocabulary gain per hour	6.27	6.27	5.77	3.36

Table 13.4 Vocabulary growth compared with Curriculum targets

	3rd grade	*4th grade*	*5th grade*	*6th grade*
Mean vocabulary size estimate	348	696	1177	1457
National Core Curriculum targets	350	400	700	850

Table 13.5 Vocabulary growth compared with learners of similar background in Greece

	3rd grade	*4th grade*	*5th grade*	*6th grade*
Mean vocabulary size estimate Hungary	348	696	1177	1457
Mean vocabulary size estimate Greece	628	1141	1558	2279
Mean vocabulary gain per contact hour Hungary	6.27	6.27	5.77	3.36
Mean vocabulary gain per contact hour Greece	6.28	5.13	4.17	7.21

The observed progress of the learners in this study exceeds the targets of the national curriculum and the progress of the Greek children in a similar study, with the exception of Grade 6, where Greek learners learn over the double of what participants in our study learnt.

Discussion

At the outset of this chapter it was explained that we have no normative data to tell us how progress in vocabulary, an essential element of a foreign language, progresses during the course of English study in Hungarian schools. Such data can be enormously useful and can be used as a basis for comparison over time and to check the maintenance of standards. It can also be used for comparing learners at different levels of language knowledge and to provide targets for levels of knowledge for important milestone qualifications such as the new two-level school-leaving exams in Hungary. It can allow comparison of performance in different schools and different countries. This information would also be particularly useful in informing the debate over standards in Hungary given the prevailing belief often expressed by learners and teachers that the English language teaching system is not as good as elsewhere.

The results reported in this chapter suggest that progress in vocabulary learning in the first four years of English appears remarkably consistent up to Grade 6 at about six words per contact hour. This result is impressive and suggests a well prepared programme of study. It is not entirely clear what happens in Grade 6 where the rate of uptake decreases to about 3.4 words per contact hour. This may be due to the idiosyncrasies of the course books or, since this is a cross-sectional study, differences in the academic make-up of different years of study. It would be well worth repeating this study with different students and in a different school to see whether these results are generalisable to the whole system. If they are generalisable, then this kind of progress will be compared with vocabulary uptake noted in other schools and countries, with older learners, in Milton and Meara's (1998) review.

Notwithstanding this conclusion, the standard deviations reported in Table 13.2 suggest that the kind of variation in scores which was noted among Greek learners also occurs in Hungary. In the first year of English, the most able performers appear to learn approximately 1000 words which is a believable figure, since this kind of progress at the outset of learning is noted in both Greece and Britain (Milton, 2006a). The least able learners may have acquired only a handful of words in the same period. Rapid progress among the most able learners appears to continue, since in Grade 6 the most able learner scored over 3000 words in the vocabulary size test, while the least able continue to struggle with the lowest scoring learners knowing only a few hundred English words.

While the data presented does make this apparent, there is a clear frequency effect in the vocabulary acquired by the learners. The vocabulary in the most frequent vocabulary bands is much more likely to be acquired than that in the less frequent bands. That is probably good. As Milton (2006a) points out, this suggests the exposure to English the learners receive is pretty naturalistic and this should promote good coverage and maximise comprehension. If courses in Hungary were to unduly emphasise infrequent vocabulary this would deny learners the opportunity to develop their knowledge of structure, which requires knowledge of the most frequent vocabulary, and would inhibit comprehension. This effect is visible and can be seen when the results for each grade level are divided to show knowledge in the five frequency bands separately. This is shown in Figure 13.3.

The frequency effect is very clear even at the outset of learning in Grade 3 when the presence of infrequent, subject vocabulary, required to provide thematic content, might be expected to unbalance the kind of frequency effects normally seen in larger corpora. Again, this may be interpreted as an impressive feature of the vocabulary teaching system in Hungary. Milton (2006a) notes the absence of this feature in the foreign language acquisition of French in British schools, and connects this to the very low levels of vocabulary uptake among these learners.

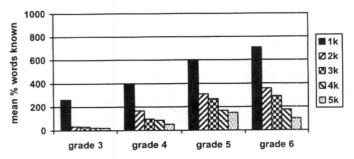

Figure 13.3   Word knowledge in the five frequency bands

Progress also appears rather good. The number of words learned is substantially greater than the vocabulary targets prescribed in the *National Core Curriculum*. It also appears better than similar Greek learners in Grades 3, 4 and 5 although less good in Grade 6. Overall, progress as assessed in terms of vocabulary uptake per hour is almost identical over four years of study to the learners in Greece. This should be reassuring to those teachers and administrators who believe English is not taught well in Hungary. Learning of vocabulary appears well ahead of target and Hungarian learners are at least as good, if not better, than learners of English in other systems. If vocabulary learning is good then this suggests general progress in passive knowledge of English will be good, as will progress in orthographic productive skills such as writing.

This conclusion has to be placed in context, as this estimate, a figure based on knowledge of the most frequent 5000 words in English, is likely to be an underestimate of learners' total word knowledge. Very infrequent lexis, included in lessons and teaching material to provide thematic content, have been omitted from this count.

Conclusion

This investigation of Hungarian primary school students was designed to provide insight into their English language vocabulary size development in Hungarian schools. Results show that in Hungary primary school students' vocabulary development has some impressive characteristics. Good progress appears to be made, especially at the outset of learning, although further study would be useful to test whether the decline in uptake towards the end of primary school is a general feature of learning and, if it is, whether this is a deliberate feature of the syllabus. Nonetheless, uptake over the whole period of four to five words per contact hour appears very good compared to learners elsewhere. The fact that learning appears so closely connected to word frequency is probably also an encouraging finding.

Now that we are in possession of this data it becomes legitimate to speculate how the results might change if students had better learning strategies and teachers had more effective teaching techniques. It should not be forgotten that part of the motivation for this study was doubt concerning the word repetition and recycling strategies (spaced and massed), which were noted in the surveyed teachers' vocabulary teaching practices described in the first part of this chapter. There may actually be room for improvement in these already good findings.

The testing project provides an insight into some inconsistencies of the *National Core Curriculum*. The surveyed primary school students performed much better than expected on the basis of the requirements of the curriculum. The vocabulary knowledge of Grade 6 learners corresponds with the *Common European Framework* A1 level at the time of the test. They are approaching A2 level, which is between 2000 and 2750 words. These numbers correspond with the secondary school intermediate-level school-leaving exam requirements. This is an unexpected conclusion and the *National Core Curriculum* requirements might usefully be reconsidered and, perhaps, better matched with the *Common European Framework* requirements in the future. Nevertheless, lower primary students are on the right track, as their vocabulary size level grows progressively and if they were to continue at this rage, their vocabulary they would reach the A2 level in the upper primary school.

It would be a mistake to let this study and its conclusions stand in isolation. In the future some further investigation is needed in order to test whether these findings are in line with vocabulary size growth in other schools in Hungary. This should provide a better understanding of English vocabulary size development in Hungary at different stages of learning, and across different schools and different regions. It is intended that this line of investigation will be continued in the future with a longitudinal study in order to investigate how individual students perform over a longer period. Future study might also include investigation into the phonological vocabulary size and learners' performance in order to attempt to assess Hungarian learners' oral fluency.

References

Gairns, R. and Redman, S. (1986) *Working with Words: A Guide to Teaching and Learning Vocabulary.* Cambridge: Cambridge University Press.

Hindmarsh, R. (1980) *Cambridge English Lexicon.* Cambridge: Cambridge University Press.

Krizsán, E. (2003) *Mozaik kerettanterv az általános iskolák számára. Angol nyelv 3–8. évfolyam.* On WWW at http://www.mozaik.info.hu/Homepage/NAT2003/Doc/Angol3-8doc. Accessed 29.1.08.

Laufer, B. (1990) Ease and difficulty in vocabulary learning: Some teaching implications. *Foreign Language Annals* 23 (2), 147–155.

Meara, P. and Buxton, B. (1987) An alternative to multiple choice vocabulary tests. *Language Testing* 4, 142–151.

Meara, P. and Milton, J. (2003) *X-Lex: The Swansea Levels Test*. Newbury: Express Publishing.

Milton, J. (2006a) Language Lite: Learning French vocabulary in school. *Journal of French Language Studies* 16 (2), 187–205.

Milton, J. (2006b) X-Lex: The Swansea Vocabulary Levels Test. In C. Coombe, P. Davidson and D. Lloyd (eds) *Proceedings of the 7th and 8th Current Trends in English Language Testing (CTELT) Conference* (Vol. 4) (pp. 29–39). UAE: TESOL Arabia.

Milton, J. and Meara, P. (1998) Are the British really bad at foreign languages? *Language Learning Journal* 18, 68–76.

Nation, I.S.P. (ed.) (1984) *Vocabulary Lists: Words, Affixes and Stems*. English University of Wellington, New Zealand: English Language Institute.

Nation, I.S.P. (2001) *Learning Vocabulary in Another Language*. Cambridge: Cambridge University Press.

National Core Curriculum (2003) Budapest: Ministry of Education.

Read, J. (2004) *Assessing Vocabulary*. Cambridge: Cambridge University Press.

Appendix A

An example of the *X-Lex* test format

English X_Lex Paper Version 1

2006 / Hungary

Kérlek olvasd el a következő angol, vagy annak látszó szavakat. Pipáld ki azokat, amelyeket ismersz, példa szerint:

dog   ✓

....

osztály

Segítségedet köszönöm, kellemes vakációt kívánok! ☺

that	Both	Cliff	sandy	lessen	Darrock
kennard	Before	Cup	normal	impress	Antique
dose	diversal	number	earn	reward	Grip

Chapter 14

Factors Influencing Young Learners' Vocabulary Acquisition

MAGDALENA SZPOTOWICZ

Introduction

Children enjoy learning new words in a foreign language (L2). Initially, when they are six, seven, or eight years old, they learn and remember the oral form of the words and store the phonetic representations of these words in their mental lexicons. Children's enthusiasm for getting to know more and more 'names for things' at this age encouraged me to inquire into the process of vocabulary acquisition. The larger study consists of two parts. The first qualitative part (Szpotowicz, 2000) was published in Research into Teaching English to Young Learners (Moon & Nikolov, 2000), whereas the present paper is based on the quantitative part of the larger study.

Aims of Study

The overall aim of the study was to investigate learners' vocabulary learning, memorising and their ability to retrieve words from memory after a period of time. The learning process was not supported by graphic representations of the words. The study attempted to scrutinise the following problems:

- the amount of lexical material available for retrieval after a period of three to five days;
- the relationship between the semantic category of words and their learnability;
- the relationship between the length and learnability of words;
- the influence of word pronunciation on its learnability (aural memory); and
- the relationship between vocabulary recall and recognition.

Background to Young Learners' Acquisition of Vocabulary

Children's L2 learning involves three dynamic processes: cognitive development, a continuing first language development and the relatively new process of second language acquisition. It is in this context that second language vocabulary acquisition needs to be presented.

An analysis of category types used in early childhood, both in first and second languages, has shown that 'the middle of a general to specific hierarchy is particularly significant for children' (Cameron, 2001: 79): children most commonly use words for basic level concepts. These vocabulary items are learnt before words which are higher or lower in the hierarchy. For example, the basic level words chair and dog are learnt before their superordinates (furniture; animal) and subordinates (rocking chair; spaniel).

Cameron (2001) claims that from the conceptual point of view words at the basic level represent objects which have similar shapes and it is possible to use one mental image for the whole category. Thus, in the foreign language classroom basic level concepts will be mastered before items on the superordinate and subordinate level. Cameron suggests that when teachers develop vocabulary around a topic or a lexical set for example, food or travel, they can begin from basic level items, such as bread or car and later proceed to more general vocabulary (vegetables or vehicles) and finally to more specific words (chili sauce or shuttle bus). This approach seems to be in line with what Verhallen and Schoonen (1993: 346) observed about how children acquire new words and new concepts.

Young children are familiar with words like 'rose', 'tulip', 'flower', 'plant'; this does not mean, however, that they are aware of the hierarchical relations between these concepts; its only later on that they learn the relationships between the words 'rose' and 'tulip' as coordinated concepts, both dominated and superordinated by the concept 'flower', with the concept 'plant' still higher in the hierarchy (Verhallen & Schoonen, 1993: 346).

Conceptual development across early school years has an important influence on vocabulary growth in children's foreign language learning (Cameron, 2001: 81). First of all, the types of words which children learn change with age. At the age of five, they only learn very concrete vocabulary related to objects they can handle or see. When they are older, they can cope with words and topics that are more abstract and remote from their immediate surroundings.

Cameron believes that teaching vocabulary to children has to include the recycling of words. Vocabulary knowledge has to be constantly expanded and deepened by frequent repetition, presenting words in different contexts and linking words in networks of meaning. It is also observed that children change in how they can learn new words. Very young learners will learn these as collections, whereas the older they grow the more their learning becomes organised. They make connections between the words and master the paradigmatic organisation of words and concepts to facilitate their learning.

Nation (1990: 51) lists basic techniques which teachers can use to explain the meanings of new words to young learners: (1) by demonstration or pictures, that is, using objects, cut-out figures, gestures, showing photographs, pictures from books, performing an action, drawings or diagrams on the board; (2) by verbal explanation, that is, using an analytical definition, putting the new word in a defining context or translating into mother tongue. Most of these techniques require some mental processing and thus help learners make stronger memory connections.

Another aspect of vocabulary learning that seems significant for both children and adults is the discrepancy between comprehension and production of words. Comprehension of vocabulary is usually far superior to lexical production. Yoshida (1978: 95) observed that a four-year-old child learning English as L2 scored 72% in a comprehension test, whereas only 34% of his responses were correct in a production test. Yoshida also noticed that 'among the words acquired by the subject, general nominals (concrete objects) indicated the highest score: 61%. Action words (verbs) showed the second highest: 13%, whereas the third was modifiers (adjectives, etc.): 10%'.

As far as the acquisition of semantic categories is concerned, children are especially interested in 'food and animals'. According to Ferguson (1974 cited by Yoshida, 1978: 97), these two categories have a universal frequency in child language samples. Yoshida claims that children learn those words in which they reveal interest. 'The contents of a child's vocabulary shows his world – his interests and preferences.'

A fascinating fact about children's vocabulary capacity is that a child's lexical knowledge is closely related to their academic achievement. 'Educators have long known that the size of children's vocabularies correlates with general intelligence scores, reading ability and school success' (Dickinson, 1984 quoted by Verhallen & Schoonen, 1993: 344).

Research Questions

Based on the aims of the study and a short overview of the literature the following research questions are addressed:

(1) How many words can young learners remember from one lesson to the next? What is the amount of retrieved material after a period of three to five days from the learning session?
(2) Which vocabulary items (semantic category) are easier to remember for participants?

(3)   Can children remember better one-, two- or three-syllable words?
(4)   What individual differences characterise students in their ability to remember the words?
(5)   Is there a difference between recognition and recall test results?

The first three questions could be answered by analysing the recall and recognition test results. This set of questions is scrutinised below and presents the analysis of the vocabulary test data from the researcher's perspective. The last two questions concern the correlation of vocabulary test results and factors observed by the teacher, such as attention focused on the learning task, general student performance during English lessons, parental support, motivation to learn English, and student attitude to English classes.

Participants

The study was conducted in five classes taught by four teachers and it involved a total of 67 children. It comprised students learning English as a foreign language in Poland learning in three different educational contexts: a big city fee-paying school, a village state school and a private language school afternoon course for children in a middle-sized town. All participants were first-grade pupils aged seven.

The four teachers (identified by their initials: AB, MG, BM and AC) had different qualifications and experience. Teacher AB who taught a group of 22 students in a state rural school lacked formal qualifications and preparation for teaching English to children. She also had no experience and confidence in what and how she was teaching. Teacher MG taught two classed of about 16 students in each and had a few years of experience. She was confident and enthusiastic about her job. Teacher BM taught another group of 16 at the same school; she was well experienced, had excellent qualifications to teach young learners and liked the students and her work. Teacher AC taught a group of about 12 students in a private language school. She was confident and reflective, interested in her student's progress and their achievements.

Instruments

The method used in the study was a quasi-experimental design of pre-test and post-test. Two main research instruments were used: vocabulary recall and recognition tests, and a questionnaire for teachers. Vocabulary tests consisted of the same items and were applied in the same way as in the qualitative research project (Szpotowicz, 2000: 361–362). In the productive vocabulary test (recall test) students were interviewed individually by the researcher; they were asked to name the objects shown on small cards. The researcher noted down and coded the quality of their production in the following way:

(1)   child could recall or recognise the word;
(2)   child could not recall or recognise the word;
(3)   child could recall word but mispronounced it;
(4)   child could remember only half of the word or a form that sounded similar, but would not be understood in communication.

In the receptive vocabulary test (recognition test) each set of words was tested separately, after the vocabulary was introduced and practiced by the teacher. Children were presented with a worksheet consisting of several pictures (the tested words and a distractor). Each picture had a slot for writing numbers. During the test the teacher read aloud the words and said what numbers they were. The students marked the pictures with the appropriate numbers the teacher called out. For example, T: 'Number one is a cat'. As the teacher was reading out the numbers, she was showing the students a number flashcard. This was done in order to exclude the possibility of a mistake because the child did not know the number in English.

The information about the students' regular class performance and behaviour was obtained from their teacher of English, who filled in an observation sheet for each child in her class. It was a source of additional information about individual learners, which was later used for interpreting the students' test results. It consisted of nine questions on the learners' attitude to English lessons, their internal motivation to work during English classes, parental support, general achievement in English, learners' focused attention on new vocabulary sets introduced in the experiment and their attentiveness during other English lessons.

Procedures

The four teachers taking part in the research project followed the same procedures (Szpotowicz, 2000: 360–373). The target words were presented in three groups of six lexical items. Within each group there were two monosyllabic words, two bi-syllabic and two tri-syllabic ones. In set one there were animals (set one: tortoise, hare, jaguar, rat, hamster, kangaroo), because children like this topic and it was assumed that they will be motivated to learn them. In this group of words two were cognates with Polish words, that is, jaguar and kangaroo, but there were no false cognates in this set.

The second group comprised words belonging to different semantic fields, but all were familiar and relevant to students because they were fairy tale characters or objects of everyday use which are meaningful to children (set two: angel, cottage, dwarf, stool, bathing-suit, roller-skates).

In this group of words there was one cognate with a Polish word, that is, roller-skates (Pol. rolki), and one false cognate (stool), which sounds similar to the Polish word stół (meaning: table).

The third group represented objects recognisable to children and known from their everyday experience. However, these words were potentially uninteresting, as they belong to the 'adult' world and cannot be played with (set three: lock, string, hanger, ladder, lawnmover, radiator). In this group of words there was no cognate, but the word lock was a false cognate with the Polish word lok (meaning: curl).

The words were introduced on a monthly basis. Each set of words was presented and practised in one lesson and tested on the following one. The procedure for introducing the words was as follows:

(1)   Teacher presents the flashcards with pictures, repeats the words and gets the students to repeat them chorally and individually.
(2)   The children practise the form and meaning of the words. One by one they come to the front and mime the words so that the others can guess the meaning.
(3)   Each student gets a set of cards with outline pictures to colour them in.
(4)   In pairs children ask each other about their pictures: 'What colour is your ...?'
(5)   Finally, pupils stick the pictures onto a sheet of paper following the order the teacher dictates the words.

At the beginning of the next lesson the students were tested first with the productive vocabulary test (individually) and later with the recognition test (the whole class). The tests were repeated three times in order to observe the process of learning and remembering lexical items that belong to different semantic groups.

Results

The first set of research questions attempted to find out which of the three vocabulary sets (animals, unrelated words, household equipment) were easier to remember, which words (regardless of the vocabulary set in which they were presented) were easier to remember, and the difference between recall and recognition test results.

How many words can young learners remember from one lesson to the next? What is the amount of retrieved material after a period of three to five days from the learning session?

The first question focuses on recall and recognition of different lexical sets. In order to find out which of the three vocabulary sets (animals, unrelated words, household equipment) was easier to remember, the mean test results of all participants were compared. The comparison was carried out by means of ANOVA (analysis of variance), where the mean results of the three vocabulary sets were compared (Figures 14.1 and 14.2).

The differences between the recall of the subsequent lexical sets were statistically significant, $F2$ (2.92) = 8.41 (F stands for F ratio which indicates the difference between two or more populations). The *post hoc* test revealed that the difference between mean test results in set one and set two was statistically significant. The difference between set two and set three was also significant. However, the difference between set one and set three was not statistically significant. As Figure 14.1 indicates, the growth of recall took place only in the second vocabulary set (unrelated words). After this increase, the ability to recall set three (household equipment) dropped considerably.

A similar tendency could be observed in recognition test results (Figure 14.2). The difference here was statistically less significant, F (2.92) = 2.74, and the *p*-value < 0.699. The *post hoc* test showed that the only difference that was statistically significant was between vocabulary set two and set three. It revealed that the recognition results for set one (animals) and set two (unrelated words) were on a similar level. The drop in the ability to recognise set three (household equipment) was noticeable, but not as steep as that for the recall results (Figure 14.1).

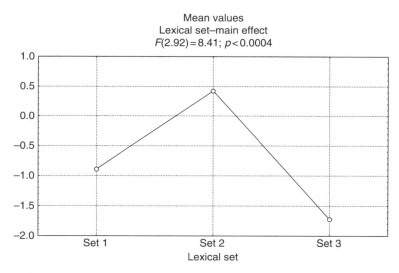

Figure 14.1 Comparison of mean results on the vocabulary sets in the recall test
Source: Szpotowicz, 2008, WUW

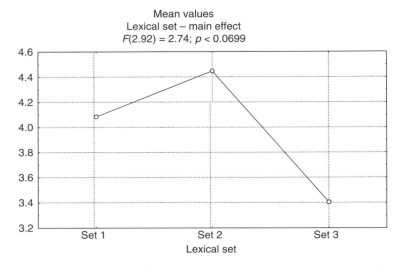

Figure 14.2 Comparison of mean results on the vocabulary sets in the recognition test
Source: Szpotowicz, 2008, WUW

Which words (regardless of the vocabulary set in which they were presented) were easier to remember?

The second question dealt with the learnability of words. The task was to determine which words were retained in memory after a period of time and how they were retrieved. As stated above, the participants' memory of words was researched in two ways, that is, both recognition and recall processes were observed. Thus, to determine which words were easy to remember it was necessary to analyse test results on the recall and the recognition tests separately.

The first test measured the number of lexical items the participants were able to recall after a few days. As the children's verbal productions were different (i.e. correct recall, incorrect recall, no recall) it was necessary to introduce the following measures. Values expressing positive figures represent data obtained from the correct answers; zero values denote incorrect answers, whereas negative figures represent no answer, that is, the inability to recall.

In order to measure the differences between the mean scores for individual words' recall it was necessary to use dependent sample t-test. This analysis provided the presentation of the recalled words according to their accessibility, that is, the ease of retrieval (Figure 14.3).

Analysis of p-values distinguished four approximate groups of words. The group of the easiest words comprised stool, roller-skates and lock. The difference between stool and roller-skates and lock was at the level of

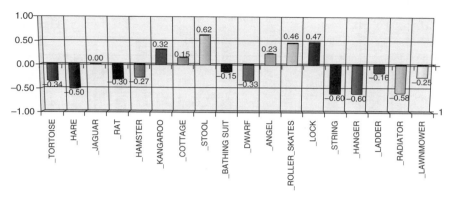

Figure 14.3 Means of the recall test (all tested words)
Source: Szpotowicz, 2008, WUW

a statistical tendency, and not significant; 0.19 between stool and roller skates and 0.18 between stool and lock. The second group of words consisted of kangaroo, cottage and angel, and was rather coherent, as there were no significant differences between the results of these words. The third group comprised all the other words except for the words string, hanger and radiator, which belong to another coherent group, as these were the most difficult words to recall.

An interesting example for interpretation was the word jaguar. As is shown in Figure 14.3, the value for the word's recall results is 0.00. This might indicate that all the children's answers had zero values, that is, were pronounced incorrectly. However, a very high standard deviation figure (SD = 1.01) suggests that the results were of different values and must have included a different proportion of various answers, which eventually were balanced into this result.

The differences between mean test results in the recognition tests were also analysed after the application of the *t*-test for dependent samples. The analysis distinguished a group of words which were the easiest to recognise (Figure 14.4). This group included the words: stool, roller-skates and jaguar. The second group of words comprised six words: cottage, bathing suit, angel, dwarf, kangaroo and hamster; these were on intermediate difficulty level. The last group comprised the remaining eight words (rat, hare, tortoise, string, hanger, radiator, ladder, lawn-mower) which turned out to be the most difficult of all the tested words in the recognition test.

Differences between recall and recognition

The third research question was concerned with the difference between the results obtained in the recall and recognition tests. Variance analysis

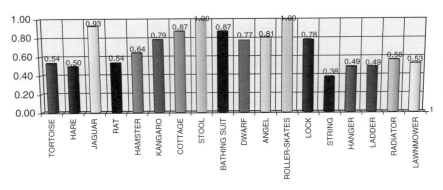

Figure 14.4   Means of the recognition test (all tested words)
Source: Szpotowicz, 2008, WUW

(ANOVA) of both types of tests for each of the tested vocabulary sets revealed that the differences were statistically significant.

In the first vocabulary set (animals) the difference between recall and recognition tests was statistically significant; F $(1.55) = 163.96$ (p-value < 0.000). The recall test results were considerably lower than the results in the recognition tests. In the second vocabulary set (unrelated words) the difference between recall and recognition tests was statistically significant; $F (1.60) = 113.17$ (p-value < 0.000), with recall test results being lower. In the third vocabulary set (household equipment) the findings were similar: the difference between recall and recognition tests was also statistically significant; F $(1.54) = 138.08$ and (p-value < 0.000). It can be stated that in all three vocabulary sets recognition test results were significantly higher than in the recall tests.

Correlation analysis of lexical test results and factors observed by the teacher

Following the analysis of lexical test results a question was put: which of the factors observed by the teacher correlated with these results? The data was obtained from the analysis of questionnaires filled in by the teachers about all young learners in their groups. The analysis aimed to find out if the children who had better test results were also better focused on the three sets of learning tasks. It also analysed if the students' performances on the tests were related to their typical classroom behaviour and achievements, the amount of parental support provided at home, the children's attitudes and motivation to participate and learn during English classes.

Table 14.1 shows the Pearson correlation coefficients between lexical test results and factors observed by the teachers. Correlations presented on grey background are statistically significant. They show that the young

Table 14.1 Correlation analysis of lexical test results and factors observed by teachers

	Set 1 recall test	Set 1 recognition test	Set 2 recall test	Set 2 recognition test	Set 3 recall test	Set 3 recognition test
Focused on set 1	0.741	0.511	0.314	0.353	0.570	0.589
	n = 54	n = 54	n = 58	n = 59	n = 53	n = 53
	p = 0.000	p = 0.000	p = 0.017	p = 0.006	p = 0.000	p = 0.000
Focused on set 2	0.666	0.511	0.437	0.477	0.618	0.535
	n = 52	n = 52	n = 58	n = 58	n = 52	n = 52
	p = 0.000	p = 0.000	p = 0.001	p = 0.000	p = 0.000	p = 0.000
Focused on set 3	0.598	0.380	0.103	0.307	0.603	0.491
	n = 47	n = 47	n = 52	n = 52	n = 50	n = 50
	p = 0.000	p = 0.008	p = 0.467	p = 0.027	p = 0.000	p = 0.000
Paying attention on lessons	0.540	0.456	0.464	0.519	0.530	0.560
	n = 54	n = 54	n = 58	n = 59	n = 53	n = 53
	p = 0.000	p = 0.001	p = 0.000	p = 0.000	p = 0.000	p = 0.000
General student performance	0.431	0.409	0.382	0.408	0.422	0.563
	n = 54	n = 54	n = 58	n = 59	n = 53	n = 53
	p = 0.001	p = 0.002	p = 0.003	p = 0.001	p = 0.002	p = 0.000
Parental support	0.389	0.260	0.288	0.256	0.418	0.170
	n = 54	n = 54	n = 58	n = 59	n = 53	n = 53
	p = 0.004	p = 0.058	p = 0.028	p = 0.051	p = 0.002	p = 0.222
Motivation to learn English	0.557	0.385	0.497	0.439	0.458	0.434
	n = 54	n = 54	n = 58	n = 59	n = 53	n = 53
	p = 0.000	p = 0.004	p = 0.000	p = 0.001	p = 0.001	p = 0.001
Attitude to English classes	0.462	0.290	0.317	0.455	0.556	0.297
	n = 54	n = 54	n = 58	n = 59	n = 53	n = 53
	p = 0.000	p = 0.033	p = 0.015	p = 0.000	p = 0.000	p = 0.031

Source: Szpotowicz, 2008, WUW

learners who focused more on the learning tasks achieved higher scores on their vocabulary tests. The strongest relationship was observed in the recall test in vocabulary set 1 ($r = 0.741$). This correlation coefficient indicates a rather strong positive relationship between being focused on the presentation and practice activities and the following recall test results, that is, the ability to recall words orally.

The children's focused attention on the lessons observed by the English teachers correlated well with their test results. The correlation coefficient ranged from $r = 0.456$ in the recognition test in set 1 and 0.563 in the same type of test in set 3. Similarly, the general good performance in English lessons correlated with the results of vocabulary tests obtained in all three lexical sets. Parental support, as observed by the teacher, correlated significantly only with recall test results and did not correlate with recognition test results.

Finally, children's motivation to participate in English classes and their positive attitude to lessons showed a positive relationship with the results of all vocabulary sets in both types of tests. Therefore, the young learners who put more effort into performing well on tasks and liked their lessons achieved higher results in vocabulary tests than those children who did not work hard or disliked activities in the English lessons.

Teacher variable

A close analysis of data obtained in the study revealed a relationship between the teacher factor and the students' results. The assumption was that teachers played an important role, but their role was not assumed to be critical. Variance analysis (ANOVA) showed that the teachers' role was of great importance in how much vocabulary the children in the research sample learnt in the three sets.

A two-factorial analysis revealed that the students' test results were in fact heterogeneous and strongly related to the teacher variable. As Figures 14.5 and 14.6 indicate, each of the four groups taking part in the experimental design study achieved different means.

Two-factorial analysis of teacher influence on the recall test results demonstrated that the results obtained in BM's group did not vary according to the vocabulary set. Similarly, AC's and AB's students achieved recall results at a level which did not show statistically significant differences between different vocabulary sets. The only teacher whose groups produced different results for each vocabulary set was MG. The difference between set one (animals) and set two (mixed words) was statistically significant, similarly to the difference between set two and set three (household equipment).

In the recognition test results there was only one statistically significant difference between vocabulary sets. As the *post hoc* test revealed, such

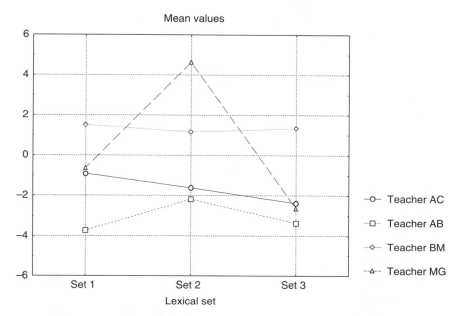

Figure 14.5 A two-factorial analysis of the teacher influence on the recall test results
Source: Szpotowicz, 2008, WUW

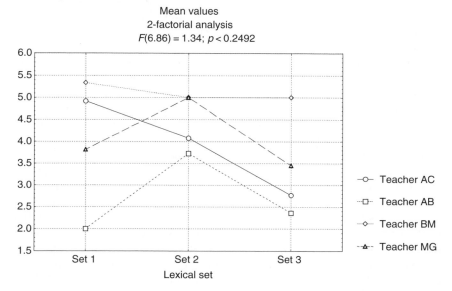

Figure 14.6 A two-factorial analysis of the teacher influence on the recognition test results
Source: Szpotowicz, 2008, WUW

difference was observed between set one (animals) and set three (household equipment) for the group taught by AC. A difference at the level of statistical tendency was noticed for the same two sets (one and three) for the group taught by AB. The relationship between the teacher variable and the vocabulary test results was observed in both recall (Figure 14.5) and recognition (Figure 14.6) test results, but it seemed stronger for recall than recognition results.

Discussion

I expected young learners to remember the vocabulary items representing animals better and score worse on a group of unrelated words, and to perform poorly on the lexical group of household equipment. My hypothesis did not prove to be entirely correct. Instead, the results showed that the second lexical set (unrelated words) was remembered best both in the recall and in the recognition test results. The increase in the second set can be explained by the fact that children got used to the techniques and felt more confident in the second round of the procedure. However, the assumption about the third set of vocabulary items being the most difficult to remember proved to be correct. The results in both recall and recognition tests dropped considerably in set three. This outcome can be interpreted, as in the assumption, by pointing out that these words are not appealing to children's imagination and not attractive enough to learn and remember. Also, the participants remembered the words more easily which sound similar to Polish and do not contain sounds unfamiliar for the Polish ear.

As stated above, in the statistical analysis of the data, the group of the easiest words in the recall test included: stool, roller-skates and lock, whereas in the recognition test the easiest words were: stool, roller-skates and jaguar. In light of these results the above hypothesis seems to be correct. The word stool is immediately associated with its Polish 'false friend' stół and the word roller-skates is easily associated with the word rolki, whereas the word lock sounds like the Polish lok. Finally, the word jaguar sounds similar to its Polish equivalent, but it contains an unfamiliar initial sound. This might be the reason why the word was one of the easiest to recognise, but more difficult to recall, where the correct pronunciation was required. This hypothesis can also be confirmed by the analysis of the most difficult words to recall (string, hanger and radiator) and to recognise (rat, hare, tortoise, string, hanger, radiator, ladder, lawnmower). None of these words sounds similar to Polish, or can be associated with Polish 'false friends'. All of them contain sounds alien to the Polish phonological system.

The hypothesis of a significant difference between recall and recognition scores regardless of the set of words being tested was fully confirmed.

In all the three sets of words the differences were significant: the recall test was always considerably more difficult than the recognition test.

The learners who scored better on vocabulary tests tended to focus more on the learning tasks, thus showing how teachers' observations of children's classroom behaviour coincided with young learners' performances on the tests. The teachers were asked to observe other factors such as: learners' general concentration on English lessons, their performance in English classes, the support they were given at home, motivation to participate in English lessons and their attitude to learning English.

Teachers' views on how much attention children paid on the lessons appeared to be an important factor determining high performance on vocabulary tests. It seems that the ability to focus attention was a stable characteristic for the participants, and those who were usually focused on English lessons also paid attention to the presentation of the new vocabulary sets. The children preceived by their teachers as good learners of English tended to achieve high on the vocabulary tests: the factor 'general student performance' correlated highly with vocabulary test results.

'Parental support', as observed by the teachers, correlated significantly only with recall tests unlike with recognition test results. The possible interpretation of this finding might be that those children who were motivated extrinsically were better focused and could better retrieve information. Performance in recall tests might be related to conscious and voluntary learning, whereas performance in recognition test could be related to incidental and involuntary learning.

The fact that 'motivation to learn English' and a positive 'attitude to English classes' correlated well with vocabulary test results might indicate that affective variables were also important determinants of lexical achievement.

The teacher variable appeared to be an important factor in the data analysis. The students' test results appeared to be related to the teaching contexts. The group taught by the teacher with the least experience and no qualifications (AB) achieved the lowest scores in all the three vocabulary sets. The scrutiny of the results at the level of groups showed that they had differing results. The teacher whose students obtained different results in all three sets taught the largest group (MG), so perhaps the number of learners in the group also influenced the outcomes. Although all the teachers adopted the same experimental technique their individual teaching styles, personality and attitude might have influenced the results. The informal classroom observation during the study revealed that general class atmosphere and teacher energy made the presentation more or less attractive, thus possibly more or less memorable.

Another possible explanation of the differing results in different groups, apart from the teacher's qualifications, experience and personality, are the learners' individual language learning abilities. This factor was not taken into account in this study, but might be an interesting source of information in the final interpretation. This aspect had not been considered for two reasons. The previous research project (Szpotowicz, 2000), which was of qualitative nature and examined eight case studies in a similar experiment, indicated that motivation and focus on learning had greater influence on vocabulary retention than memory capacity and intelligence. Secondly, it was difficult for teachers who had been teaching their students for a few months to assess their students' language learning potential in an objective way. However, if this experimental design was to be replicated with another group of young learners, who would have had learnt English with the same teacher for approximately one year, than it would be interesting to take this factor into account.

Conclusion

The results of the present study show that the words which evoke associations with Polish words are best remembered. Especially, if they are easy to pronounce for Polish learners, that is, consist of sounds which exist in the Polish phonological system. The research also confirmed a common tendency that English words which sound very similar to their Polish equivalents are commonly mispronounced. It can be assumed that they are subsumed to the same category in the mental lexicon and thus the pronunciation differences are ignored. The implication for teaching would be to pay special attention to accuracy in the oral production of these words.

The difference between recall and recognition in the test results revealed a consistent discrepancy between active and passive vocabulary stores of young learners of English. This information is important for young learners' teachers, as they should ensure testing both recognition and recall to get the whole picture of their students' vocabulary size.

In the teachers' opinions, voiced both in informal interviews and expressed in the questionnaires, the vocabulary teaching technique used in the research project proved to be effective. It helped the children who had problems with concentration on the tasks and allowed them to focus on the learning material for longer than usual, that is, before the technique was used. The teachers reported that the concentration level of the children participating in the experimental study was not lower than in other lessons; it was often higher.

It is also important to remember that those students who were focused on the presentation and practice activities scored better in both recall and recognition tests. This means that they eventually remembered the lexical material better. The implication for teachers is to organise the presentation phase of the lesson in the most attractive way and ensure that all students' attention is focused on the task.

References

Cameron, L. (2001) *Teaching Languages to Young Learners*. Cambridge: Cambridge University Press.

Dickinson, D. (1984) First impressions: Children's knowledge of words gained from a single exposure. *Applied Psycholinguistics* 5, 359–373.

Moon, J. and Nikolov, M. (eds) (2000) *Research into Teaching English to Young Learners*. Pecs: University Press Pecs.

Nation, P. (1990) *Teaching and Learning Vocabulary*. New York: Heinle and Heinle.

Szpotowicz, M. (2008) Second language learning processes in lower primary children. Vocabulary Acquisition. Warszawa: Wydawnictwa. Uniwersytetu Warszawskiego.

Szpotowicz, M. (2000) Young learners: How do they remember vocabulary? In J. Moon and M. Nikolov (eds) *Research into Teaching English to Young Learners* (pp. 360–373). Pecs: University Press Pecs.

Verhallen, M. and Schoonen, R. (1993) Lexical knowledge of monolingual and bilingual children. *Applied Linguistics* 14 (4), 344–363.

Yoshida, M. (1978) The acquisition of English vocabulary by a Japanese-speaking child. In E. Hatch (ed.) *Second Language Acquisition* (pp. 91–100). Rowley, MA: Newbury House.

Chapter 15

An Eye on Target Language Use in Elementary English Classrooms in China

JING PENG AND LILI ZHANG

Introduction

Researchers in second language acquisition field agree that input of the target language (TL) is crucial for successful second and foreign language learning. As foreign language (FL) learning usually takes place in classroom environments, teachers' use of the TL becomes an important source for students to obtain input in the TL. The present study aims to explore how teachers use the TL in elementary school English classes in China. Participants in the study were 54 English teachers of elementary schools and 203 students of the four teachers under observations. A naturalistic inquiry approach was adopted, and the results were analysed statistically. Totally, the investigation, including classroom observation, interviews and questionnaire studies spanned three months. The results of the study revealed that there were considerable variations in the amount of teachers' TL use. For most of the teachers, the amount of TL use was not more than 60% of their talk. This may not be sufficient enough for students' foreign language learning. Furthermore, from the viewpoint of pragmatics, teachers' TL use was not varied enough and was often found inappropriate. The findings of the study indicate that the current use of TL in FL classes of elementary schools in observed class is far from satisfactory.

Since the entry of China to WTO, English has become very popular in the country. Parents and society have exerted a huge demand for teaching English. Therefore, in 2001, the Ministry of Education of the People's Republic of China launched a new English Teaching Program: young children start to learn English in Grade 3 in elementary schools and teachers are encouraged to use the target language in the young learners' classrooms.

However, everything is new to the teachers. This is why we set out to examine how teachers use the TL in real classrooms in China. The participants selected for the study were 54 elementary-school teachers of English (four were involved in classroom observations and 50 filled in a questionnaire) and 203 students of the four teachers whose classrooms we observed. A naturalistic inquiry approach was adopted, and the results were analyzed statistically. The study, including classroom observations, interviews and filling in questionnaires, lasted three months. In the present chapter we aim to find out how teachers use the TL in English classes at elementary schools. We are particularly interested in the amount and appropriateness of TL use in the hope that our data may generate some findings and suggestions for teachers of English to further understand the importance of using TL in their classes, and for the current education system concerning how we can facilitate teachers' effective TL use in elementary-school foreign language (FL) classes.

Research into Teachers' TL Use in Class

That input is crucial for successful language acquisition to occur has been supported in a body of studies. Researchers such as Ellis (1984: 121) agree that it is crucial for learners to be exposed to the TL as much as possible in order to develop their language skills. Likewise, Chaudron (1988) emphasizes that it is important for teachers to expose learners to as many language functions as possible in the TL. After reviewing some research (e.g. Ellis *et al.,* 1994; Gass, 1997; Gass & Varonis, 1994, all cited in Turnbull, 2001), Turnbull (2001) concludes that exposing learners to TL input provides the strongest theoretical rationale for maximizing teachers' TL use.

Some empirical studies have gathered strong evidence on how teachers' use of TL could affect student language proficiency positively. A study conducted by Turnbull (2001) reviews four experimental studies concerning the impact of teachers' use of TL on student proficiency conducted by Carroll *et al.* (1967), Carroll (1975), Wolf (1977) and Burstall *et al.* (1974) respectively, in the 1960s and 1970s, all cited in Turnbull (2001). These studies all reflected the positive impact of teachers' use of TL on student's foreign language proficiency. Mayfield (2005) conducted an experiment in her own class and found that most of the students agreed that they could understand the benefits and felt that they learned more when the class was taught almost entirely in Spanish and the students preferred it, though they were sometimes frustrated. She also noticed that students started speaking spontaneously earlier than in her previous classes where she had difficulty using the target language.

Generally speaking, most of the existing studies focusing on teachers' TL use were conducted in the context of college foreign language (FL) classes (e.g. Duff & Polio, 1990; Polio & Duff, 1994) or in secondary schools (e.g. Franklin, 1990; Turnbull, 1999). Very little research has been carried out in a context where teachers use the target language, the mother tongue (MT), or a mixture of both languages with young beginners whose TL proficiency is very low. Thus, we will depart from the previous studies by investigating how teachers use the TL in English classes of elementary schools in China.

The Study

The present study aims to explore how the TL is used by Chinese teachers of English in elementary school EFL classrooms and to shed some light on what the current status of English education is in elementary schools. To be more specific, the present study addresses the following questions:

- How much English do teachers use in their total teacher talk in elementary-school English classes?
- How appropriate is their use of the TL?

The answers to these questions are based on classroom observations in four teachers' English classes and data collected with the help of two sets of questionnaires: one filled in by the students taught by the teachers under observation and one sent to teachers of English in Shapingba District, Chongqing.

Participants

Four teachers of English were involved in classroom observations at four different elementary schools in the main city areas of Shapingba District in Chongqing: Teacher A, from Yuying Primary school (a key elementary school), Teacher B, from an Affiliated Primary School of Chongqing University (an affiliated school), Teacher C, from Bing Jiang Primary School (a typical elementary school), and Teacher D, from Lie Shi Mu Primary school (a typical elementary school). Generally speaking, compared to typical elementary schools, key elementary schools and affiliated schools of Universities set high requirements to their teachers and students, and they usually attach more importance to English teaching than other elementary schools.

Besides the four teachers, their 203 fifth-grade pupils (age 10–11) also participated in the study: they filled in a questionnaire enquiring into their attitudes toward their teachers' use of English in class.

In order to gain further information and to make the findings easier to generalize, 50 more teachers, chosen randomly from primary schools in Shapingba district, also filled in a questionnaire concerning their professional background, their teaching practice relevant to the use of TL in class, the way they used English, as well as their attitudes toward using it.

Data collection instruments and procedures

Non-participant classroom observation and audio-recording

In the present study, the authors aimed to explore teachers' TL use in EFL classes of elementary schools instead of testing a cause-and-effect relationship. Thus, this study falls in the category of a descriptive study. In order to collect first-hand material in the classroom, the authors adopted the non-participant classroom observation approach and followed a kind of naturalistic enquiry research method. In the study, the classroom activities were observed by the authors (see Appendix A: the classroom observation checklist) and recorded with an MP3. The teacher talk recorded in the classroom was then transferred and kept in the computer for later replaying and retrospection as well as data analyses. After the recorded discourses were transcribed, the TL use in the teacher talk was analyzed with regard to the two research questions which the study set out to address.

During the first period of time the authors familiarized themselves with the learners and teachers in order to establish a comfortable rapport with them. Then, observations of the classes took place over seven weeks. During this period, all teachers used the same thematic units, interpreting and implementing them in a way typical of their daily teaching. Their talk was recorded on a MP3; thus resulting in 16 class hours for later study and analysis with the permission of the teachers. In addition, a classroom checklist was also filled in during and after each observation.

Interviews with teachers

In order to explore the teachers' attitudes and views on using the TL in class and to know more about some of their teaching behaviors concerning TL use, semistructured individual interviews were conducted. During the interviews some open-ended and closed questions were asked (see Appendix B), such as 'What do you think about the feasibility of using only the TL for teaching?', 'Do you usually use the same words for classroom organization?', 'How do you pay attention to the accuracy of your TL use in class?', 'What factors do you think may influence your effective use of English in class?' The open-ended questions were designed to allow for more freedom of response in order to know more about the thinking, opinions and problems of the interviewees. Also, teachers' answers were hoped to allow us to triangulate our data collected in observations.

Questionnaires

Obviously, the sample size of 16 class hours and four teachers was small and did not represent all teachers of English in elementary schools. Therefore, to triangulate other data with classroom observations, two questionnaires were administered in Chinese as subsidiary research tools for data collection. One questionnaire was designed for 50 teachers and consisted of 30 items; the other, consisting of 10 items, was designed for the students (see Appendix C and Appendix D).

The questionnaire for teachers consisted of two parts. The first 15 questions enquired into respondents' professional information and the teaching environment relevant to their use of the TL in class. These items were based on Franklin's (1990) study on the reasons why teachers do not use the TL in their classes with some modifications according to findings of the classroom observations and interviews with the four teachers. The other 15 questions concerned how teachers actually used English in class and their attitude toward TL use. These 15 questions were designed based on the research questions of the present study, aiming to make it more complete and informative.

The questionnaire designed for students also consisted of two parts: the first seven questions concerned students' after-class English learning environment, whereas the other eight items concerned students' perception of their teachers' use of the TL in class, for example, the amount of TL use and translation. Students' perceptions of these issues highly concerned both the authors and the observed teachers.

A pilot study was conducted with five teachers and 20 students before the main study in order to check the clarity of the questions, the format, and the range of the questions. Based on the findings of the pilot phase, the authors modified the questions that might cause misunderstanding and simplified some sentences that were too complicated for the learners.

In the main questionnaire study a total of 203 students were asked to respond to the questionnaire. Finally, 199 students' responses were considered valid and adopted for statistical analyses. As to the questionnaire designed for teachers, all the 50 copies of responses were considered valid.

Data analysis

Statistical analyses were carried out with the help of SPSS10.0. First, the data were input in the SPSS10.0. The participants' responses to the questionnaire items following the five-point Likert scale form were recorded like this: for a choice of A, 1 point was given, and B: 2 points, C: 3 points, D: 4 points and E: 5 points.

Results and Discussion

Amount of TL use in total teacher talk in elementary school English class

The amount of teachers' TL use indicates how much English is used in the total teacher talk in class. In the present study, each class under observation lasted about 40 minutes. Altogether four classes were observed, recorded and transcribed with each teacher resulting in a total time of 160 minutes for each participant. Table 15.1 shows the total time of TL use in

Table 15.1 Total time of four teachers' use of English in minutes and percentage (%) in four observed classes

Teachers	Class 1	Class 2	Class 3	Class 4	Mean
Teacher A	10 (90%)	8 (81%)	6 (82%)	7 (80%)	8 (83%)
Teacher B	11 (92%)	11 (94%)	10 (90%)	11 (93%)	11 (92%)
Teacher C	4 (62%)	4 (70%)	5 (68%)	5 (87%)	5 (71%)
Teacher D	5 (66%)	4 (63%)	5 (71%)	4 (59%)	5 (64%)

minutes and percentages used in the four classes of four teachers (A, B, C and D). Each period of class lasted 40 minutes; however the total time of observed TL is shorter than 40 minutes, because teachers did not talk all the time.

If we take the first observed class of Teacher A as an example, 10 minutes refers to the total time for which teacher A spoke English in class, and which accounts for 90% of her total speaking time. She talked in Chinese for one minute (10%). During the 29 or so minutes, there were some activities students did among themselves: they listened to a tape, read after the tape or worked on some written exercise, while the teacher did not talk. The data in Table 15.1 show that in the observed English classes the percentages of TL use were all over 59%, as this percentage was the lowest of English use in class 4 with Teacher D. Teacher A and Teacher B used mostly English in the observed classes: an average percentage of 83 and 92, respectively, whereas Teacher C and Teacher D used less English: 71% and 64%, respectively (see Table 15.1).

Interview data with teachers

Interviews with the four teachers and their students' answers to the questionnaire were analyzed to get more information about teachers' opinions and students' assessments of the amount of TL use in their EFL classes. When asked about the feasibility of using English exclusively for teaching, all of the teachers expressed their worries. The study shows the same results as those of Mayfield's (2005) study. The teachers' opinions can be categorized in the following groups:

(a) Students will get frustrated since they can not understand some of the teachers' English.
(b) Students' anxiety level will increase, which will impede their subsequent learning.
(c) It is not feasible to teach grammar in the TL.
(d) Too much time would be spent on explaining and paraphrasing.
(e) Without Chinese, teachers may lose control over class.

As the answers illustrate, teachers stated that they were afraid that much use of English would make their students frustrated, and thus would make them anxious. Some stated that when it came to teaching grammar and controlling class, English could not work. Some teachers were afraid that they could not be understood if they did not use Chinese, and some insisted that only Chinese could help students understand the essential features of English.

Results of questionnaire data

According to 50 teachers' answers to the questionnaire, although 92% of the respondents recognized the inherent importance of using English in practice, most of them used a limited amount of TL in their classes. Only 20% of the respondents reported that more than 80% of their talk was in English, and 42% admitted that they used English less than 60% of their total teacher talk, while 12% of the respondents reported their TL using was even less than 20%.

As far as the amount of teachers' TL use is concerned, Turnbull (2000) argues that the teachers who spoke the TL in less than 25% of class time were relying too heavily on the mother tongue and were depriving their students of valuable TL input. Concerning the appropriate amount of TL, in a study of elementary core French classes in western Canada, Shapson *et al.* (1978) stipulated 75% as the acceptable level of TL use by teachers. They found 'considerable variations amongst the teachers they observed; interestingly, only 26% of teachers used French (TL) for at least 75% of class time' (cited in Turnbull, 2001: 535).

Students' views

In order to know students' assessment of the amount of TL used by their teachers, students taught by the four teachers were asked to respond to a questionnaire. The results seem to stand in sharp contrast with what we expected (see Table 15.2). More than 60% of the students in each class reported that TL use by their teachers was relatively scarce. Even in Teacher B's class, where the teacher used English most frequently, only 5% of the students believed that the teacher often used English. No student thought that TL use was 'too much'. The results are in accordance with outcomes

Table 15.2 Students' assessment of the amount of English used by their teachers

Students	*Too little*	*Little*	*Just OK*	*Much*	*Too much*
Teacher A's students	15%	52%	29%	2%	2%
Teacher B's students	27%	43%	25%	5%	0%
Teacher C's students	17%	53%	25%	2%	3%
Teacher D's students	15%	51%	23%	9%	2%

of Mayfield's (2005: 5) study where 'students actually preferred that the class be taught almost exclusively in Spanish (TL), even though they were sometimes frustrated'. It could also be noted that in Teacher D's class, where the amount of English use was the least frequent, 11% of the students thought that the teacher's TL use was much or too much, ranking the highest among all the observed students.

Nevertheless, as the answers in the interviews tell us, the four observed teachers believed that too much English tended to make their students more anxious and frustrated. Also, they thought it could be a waste of time if teachers could not make themselves understood. Thus, their TL use was sometimes followed by Chinese explanations, or they chose to switch to Chinese and continue in the mother tongue. However, according to the students' feedback, the four teachers may have underestimated students' comprehension level as well as the ability to accept new things.

Data from classroom discourse

Staab (1986) further elaborated the two language functions of Halliday (1973), namely ideational and interpersonal, into four language functions including social needs, controlling, informing and reasoning (quoted in Liang & Mohan, 2003: 41). However, in early stages of language learning, there are few occasions when teacher talk involves the informing or reasoning functions which usually happen in high-level academic discourses. In elementary school English as a foreign language classes teachers use language for social needs and the needs of controlling as they lead their students to do a lot of language practice and drills on pronunciation, new words and simple sentence patterns. Therefore, the function category of 'academic' based on Turnbull (2000) was used to replace the two function categories of 'ideational' and 'reasoning' in the present study, and the classroom discourse was analyzed according to academic function, social function and controlling function.

In the transcribed datasets most of the four teachers' utterances in the TL were used for academic function (see Table 15.3). These utterances were used mainly for conducting language drills and for practising

Table 15.3 Distribution of teachers' TL use in three function categories in percentages

Teachers	Academic	Social needs	Controlling
Teacher A	84%	4%	12%
Teacher B	86%	4%	10%
Teacher C	79%	2%	19%
Teacher D	73%	4%	23%

pronunciation of words. For example Teacher B spent quite a lot of time asking learners to repeat her words and correcting students' pronunciation.

Excerpt 1

T:	Ok, what's this? (Shows a ping pong ball)
Ss:	Ping pong ball!
T:	Play Ping pong ball.
Ss:	Play Ping pong ball
T:	Play Ping pong ball (miming).
Ss:	Play Ping pong ball (miming).
T:	Yes, very good. Ping pong ball.
Ss:	Ping pong ball.
T:	Play Ping pong ball (miming).
Ss:	Play Ping pong ball (miming).
T:	Now I want someone read it. Play Ping pong ball (miming).
S23:	Play Ping pong ball (miming).
T:	Yes, good, you please.
S24:	Play Ping pong ball (miming).
T:	Play Ping pong ball (miming) you please.

Social discourse in teachers' talk, a kind of real communication between the teacher and students, was relatively rare (no more than 4%). In the datasets most of the teachers' feedback was simply 'yes', 'no', 'OK', 'good' or no feedback at all. However, according to students' answers to the questionnaire, the majority (91.5%) of the learners hoped the teacher could say something, especially some words of praise or encouragement. The teachers' neglect of giving feedback to the students may be caused by learners' limited size of vocabulary or teachers' lack of awareness of their need.

As for the function of controlling, about 12% of Teacher A's and 10% of Teacher B's TL use were for controlling, and sometimes body language and other visual measures were also applied. As Ellis (1984: 133) claims, classroom management and organization, as well as more obvious pedagogic goals, should be carried out in the TL. He further argues that when teachers use the L1 for regular classroom management, '... they deprive the learners of valuable input in the L2'.

Appropriateness of TL use from the pragmatic viewpoint

To have a closer look at teachers' TL use, a pragmatic analysis was carried out on several episodes of observed teacher talk. One of the differences between teacher talk and 'real talk' is that teacher talk is 'actually a kind of pedagogical talk, which is related to teaching, displaying knowledge of what one has learned or understands, and/or knowledge construction' (Hauser, 2006: 93). Such pedagogical discourse usually follows the form of a three-part sequence of turns, labeled as Initiation-Response-Feedback or

Initiation-Response-Follow up (IRF) by Sinclair and Coulthard (1975). In the IRF move, teachers usually know the answers to the initiated questions, and they use these display questions as a method of testing students' knowledge and understanding. In our observation datasets, we also found plenty of examples for such moves.

Excerpt 2

Teacher A is eliciting answers to 'Where are you from?'

T: Are you from England?

S1: No.

T: No, I'm not (corrects student).

S1: No, I'm not.

T: I'm from ...? (modelling next utterance, expected answer).

S1: From China.

T: No, I'm not. I'm from China.

S1: No, I'm not. I'm from China.

T: Great!

Excerpt 3

Teacher B working on the same structure

T: Where are you from?

S1: I am from China.

T: Yes.

T: Where are you from?

S2: I am from China.

T: Good.

Excerpt 4

Teacher D practising the same structure

T: Are you from England?

Ss: No!

T: Are you from China?

Ss: Yes, I am (together with the teacher).

T: Ok, follow me. Yes I am.

Ss: Yes, I am.

T: Yes I am.

Ss: Yes, I am.

T: Are you from China? (to one student).

S: Yes, I am.

T: Good.

An important question is whether these sequences are facilitative of or counter-productive for learning? As we can see, during these pedagogical episodes, in each of the IRF sequences, the teacher uses the F-component to confirm or correct students' R-component. It also presents the adequate answer to the class. However, too much feedback on correcting students' answers to make them speak phonologically, grammatically, lexically correctly may discourage students' activity and may even cause misunderstandings, as in the next example.

Excerpt 5

Teacher C drilling structure

T: Where are you from?

S: I from Chongqing.

T: No.

S: (confused) Oh, I from China.

T: No, I *AM* from Chongqing.

S: I am from Chongqing.

T: Good, sit down.

We also found that repetitive feedback and blanket evaluation were adopted in the observed classes. Short, simple and unchangeable feedback, such as 'Yes', 'No' and 'Good' were rather popular among teachers. Teachers' arbitrary judgments as feedback and failure to give students an opportunity to further continue the conversation made students lose the opportunity to take control of the interaction, as total control was in the teachers' hand. According to Hauser (2006: 97), 'in this sense, the degree to which students can be active participants in the pedagogical episode is limited, which in turn may limit opportunities for learning'.

To summarize the findings, to facilitate students' language learning, the teachers should, on the one hand, encourage students to self-evaluate their answers, or try to give them more opportunities to guess or expand their answers, or try to stimulate students to focus on the content and the subject matter of the questions, instead of the language structure of the question itself. They should try to encourage students to express their own idea about the question, even with the simplest language rather than force them to drill sentence patterns. Thus, they could create a friendly environment for communication in the classroom. Teachers' repetitive feedback or blanket evaluation may do no good to students' language learning. Take Teacher A as an example: although the average percentage of TL use amounts to 92%, most of her feedback is repetitive, she used mechanical drills, which are inappropriate to students' language learning especially the internalization of sample sentences.

Conclusion

The results of the study revealed that there were considerable variations in the amount of teachers' use of English. For most of the teachers, the amount of TL use was small, no more than 60% and it characterized very short periods of time in the 40-minute classes. This may not be sufficient enough for students' foreign language learning. Furthermore, from the viewpoint of pragmatics, teachers' TL use was not varied enough and was often found inappropriate. The findings of the study indicate that the current use of TL in FL classes of elementary schools in Shapingba district is far from satisfactory.

The study has a number of implications for elementary-school English classes, especially for teachers and current English teaching programs. Teachers' awareness of effective TL use in the English classes must be raised. In addition, course coordinators may provide more workshops and teacher training courses that focus on strategies in order to help teachers facilitate students' learning by means of more varied uses of English.

However, to have a closer look into the influence of teachers' use of TL to students' English learning outcome, more pragmatic analysis of teacher talk could be done to see whether teacher's input of TL could be 'taken in' by the students.

The study is of significance to Programs of Foreign Language Teaching in Elementary Schools in that it can provide us an opportunity to see the real status of teachers' TL use in English classes and propose some suggestions to improve the effectiveness of teachers' TL use in classes.

References

Chaudron, C. (1988) *Second Language Classroom: Research on Teaching and Learning.* Cambridge: Cambridge University Press.

Duff, P.A. and Polio, C.G. (1990) How much foreign language is there in the foreign language classroom? *Modern Language Journal* 74, 54–166.

Ellis, R. (1984) *Classroom Second Language Development.* Oxford: Pergamon.

Franklin, C.E.M. (1990) Teaching in the TL: Problems and prospects. *Language Learning Journal* 2, 20–24.

Halliday, M.A.K. (1973) *Explorations in the Functions of Language.* London: Edward Arnold.

Hauser, E. (2006) Teacher reformulations of students' answers during an episode of pedagogical talk. *Bulletin of the University of Electro-Communications* 19 (1–2), 93–99.

Liang, X. and Mohan, B.A. (2003) Dilemmas of cooperative learning and academic proficiency in two languages. *Journal of English for Academic Purpose* 2, 35–51.

Mayfield, J. (2005) Speak it and they WILL learn. *Pacific Northwest Council for Languages* 5 (2), 3–5.

Polio, C.G. and Duff, P.A. (1994) Teacher's language use in university foreign language classrooms: A qualitative analysis of English and TL alternation. *Modern Language Journal* 78, 313–326.

Shapson, S., Kaufman, D. and Durward, L. (1978) A study of elementary French programs in British Columbia. *Interchange* 12 (4), 23–34.

Sinclair, J.M. and Coulthard, R.M. (1975) *Towards an Analysis of Discourse: The English Used by Teachers and Pupils.* Oxford: Oxford University Press.

Staab, C.F. (1986) Eliciting the language of forecasting and reasoning in elementary school classrooms. *The Alberta Journal of Educational Research* 32, 109–126.

Turnbull, M. (1999) Multidimensional project-based second language teaching: Observations of four grade 9 core French teachers. *Canadian Modern Language Review* 56, 3–35.

Turnbull, M. (2000) Analyses of core French teachers' language use: A summary. On WWW at http://www.unb.ca/. Accessed 7.7.07.

Turnbull, M. (2001) There is a role for the L1 in second and foreign language teaching, but ... *Canadian Modern Language Review* 57 (4), 531–540.

Appendix A

Classroom observation checklist

(1) School: _____
(2) Time: _____
(3) Date: _____
(4) Teacher: _____
(5) Years of teaching: _____
(6) Number of students in class: _____
(7) Class subject: _____
(8) Resources used: _____
(9) What classroom activities are conducted by teachers?

( ) Classroom organization	( ) Disciplining
( ) Explaining meaning of words	( ) Explaining meaning of phrases
( ) Explaining meaning of sentences	( ) Explaining grammar
( ) Giving instructions to activities	( ) Teaching cultural background
( ) Instructions to exercise	( ) Small talk
( ) Correcting written work	( ) Others

(10) General comments:

_____

_____

(11) Brief evaluation of the quantity of the TL used by teachers in different activities based on the five-point Likert scale

Percentage of the TL activity	1 (0–20%)	2 (21–40%)	3 (41–60)%	4 (61–80%)	5 (81–100%)
Classroom organization					
Explaining meaning of words					
Explaining meaning of phrases					
Explaining meaning of sentences					
Activity instructions					
Disciplining					

Correcting written work					
Teaching background					
Teaching grammar					
Others					

(12) Measures taken

Measures ╲ Frequency	
Repetition	
Substitution	
Translation	
Visual measures (e.g. cards, body language, etc.)	
Others	

(13) Accuracy of using the TL

Mistakes ╲ Frequency	
Pronunciation	
Spelling	
Grammar	
Others	

Appendix B

Interview questions for teachers

(1) What do you think about the feasibility of using only the TL for teaching?
(2) Do you usually use the same words for classroom organization?
(3) How do you pay attention to the accuracy of your TL use in class?
(4) What factors do you think may influence your effective use of English in class?

Appendix C

Questionnaire for teachers

(1) What is your education qualification?
    A. Normal School Graduate   D. M.A.
    B. Academy Graduate   E. Others_____
    C. College Graduate

(2) Which certificate of the following have you got? (If there is more than one, please choose the one of higher level)
A. CET-3   B. CET-4   C. CET-6   D. TEM-4   E. TEM-8   F. None

(3) Are you confident with your English?
A. Not confident at all   B. Not confident   C. So so   D. Confident
E. Quite confident

(4) In your opinion, are you good at English?
A. Not good at all   B. Not good   C. So so   D. Good
E. Very good

(5) How many times have you been abroad?
A. 0   B. 1   C. 2   D. 3   E. ≥4

(6) Have you even take part in any training about English or teaching English?
A. Never   B. Occasionally   C. Sometimes   D. Often   E. Always

(7) Do you keep a teaching log?
A. Never   B. Occasionally   C. Sometimes   D. Often   E. Always

(8) Your school is a_____.
A. Typical elementary school (suburban)   B. Typical elementary school (urban)   C. Key elementary school   D. Private school   E. Other

(9) How many English teachers are there in your school?

(10) How is the expectancy from authorities toward English teaching in your school?
A. Very low   B. Low   C. So so   D. High   E. Very high

(11) How many periods of classes are you supposed to finish every week?
A. <10   B. 10–15   C. 16–20   D. 21–25   E. ≥26

(12) How many students are there in your class?
A. <30   B. 30–39   C. 40–49   D. 50–59   E. ≥60

(13) How is the diversity of students' English aptitude in your class?
A. Very small   B. Small   C. So so   D. Big   E. Quite big

(14) How about the discipline of the class you teach?
A. Very bad   B. Bad   C. So so   D. Good   E. Very good

(15) How is the expectancy from students' parents toward English teaching in your school?
A. Very low   B. Low   C. So so   D. High   E. Very high

(16) Do you agree to maximize teachers' TL use in class?
A. Not at all   B. No   C. Don't care   D. Yes   E. Very much

(17) Are you willing to maximize your TL use in class?
A. Not at all   B. No   C. Don't care   D. Yes   E. Very much

(18) What do you think is the percentage of your TL use in the whole teacher talk?
A. <20%   B. 20–40%   C. 40–60%   D. 60–80%   E. >80%

(19) What do you think about the amount of your TL use in class?
A. Too few   B. Few   C. Just OK   D. Much   E. Too much

(20) What do you think is the accuracy rate of your TL use?
A. <70%   B. 70–80%   C. 80–90%   D. 90–95%   E. >95%
(21) Do you pay attention to the accuracy of your TL use?
A. Never   B. Occasionally   C. Sometimes   D. Often   E. Always
(22) Do you use some verbal aids (such as repetition, paraphrase) to facilitate students' understanding?
A. Never   B. Occasionally   C. Sometimes   D. Often   E. Always
(23) Do you use some nonverbal aids (such as body language, sketch) to facilitate students' understanding?
A. Never   B. Occasionally   C. Sometimes   D. Often   E. Always
(24) If you find the aid measure can not work, will you try to use another one?
A. Never   B. Occasionally   C. Sometimes   D. Often   E. Always
(25) Do you use simple words to replace difficult words to facilitate students' understanding?
A. Never   B. Occasionally   C. Sometimes   D. Often   E. Always
(26) Do you translate your English to Chinese in order to make yourself understood?
A. Never   B. Occasionally   C. Sometimes   D. Often   E. Always
(27) You turn to Chinese in class because
A. You are afraid that students can not understand you
B. You believe that Chinese should be used for teaching English
C. You are not aware of the use of Chinese
D. You are not confident with your English
E. Others_____
(28) Are you satisfied with your English teaching?
A. Not satisfied at all   B. Not satisfied   C. So so   D. Satisfied
E. Quite satisfied
(29) Are you satisfied with your TL use in class?
A. Not satisfied at all   B. Not satisfied   C. So so   D. Satisfied
E. Quite satisfied
(30) Have you got some suggestions about improving teachers' TL use in class?

Appendix D

Questionnaire to students

(1) Do you like English class?
A. Yes, very much   B. Yes   C. Don't care   D. No   E. Not at all
(2) Do you spend a lot of time in learning English?
A. Yes, very much   B. Yes   C. Don't care   D. No   E. Not at all
(3) Have you got some tools for learning English such as computers, MP3?
A. Yes   B. No

(4) Have you got someone at home who could help you learning English?
A. Yes   B. No

(5) How much can you understand your teacher when she is speaking English?
A. Almost all of it   B. A majority of it   C. A half of it   D. A small part of it   E. Barely nothing

(6) How do you think about the amount of your teachers' TL use?
A. Too few   B. Few   C. Ok   D. Much   E. Too much

(7) If the teacher use a lot of verbal or non-verbal aids (such as repetition, miming, sketch) to help you understand her English, how much can you understand it?
A. Almost all of it   B. A majority of it   C. A half of it   D. A small part of it   E. Barely nothing

Chapter 16

What Primary School Pupils Think About Learning English as a Foreign Language

KRISZTINA NAGY

Introduction

This chapter explores how 10–11-year-old children think about their motivation to learn English in a foreign language context. The small-scale study was conducted as part of a larger research project into teachers' language use in the classroom. It was prompted by the need to hear not only the teachers' but also their pupils' voices. A special data collection method was designed to interview the children in pairs in groups of six. The results show that the children rely heavily on the teacher and the learning materials. They see a real need to learn the English language for placement exams in order to be able to study at a good secondary school. They also see English as an opportunity to travel or to get a job abroad as adults. However, they do not see a need for real communication at this stage. It is hoped that the findings will contribute to a better understanding not only of children's thinking and motivation, but also of the washback effect of the widespread use of exams at this young age.

In the last few years political changes have had a marked impact on language teaching and learning in Hungary. Since the political developments at the end of the 1980s, major changes have taken place in many areas of life. English has become a vital tool for economic development, tourism and entertainment. These developments have focused greater attention on how English is learnt in schools (Petzold & Berns, 2000). The effect of becoming a member of the EU and the resulting increase in the opportunity to study and work abroad and with foreign companies in Hungary all add to the demand for learning English. These factors have had a major impact on the education sector; English has become extremely popular, and is now the most popular foreign language in Hungary, taking over in this role from German, which was the key foreign language in Hungary for many years.

Starting foreign language study in the lower primary years has been part of the tradition for decades. Children are required to study a foreign language from Grade 4 (age nine); earlier it was Russian, but in 1989 Russian stopped being compulsory (Medgyes & Miklosy, 2000). Although the official start of foreign language learning in the curriculum is age nine, many children begin their study of a foreign language from as early as Grade 1 rather than from Grade 4. In some cases they even start in kindergarten because of parental pressure to succeed.

Primary schools find themselves competing for pupils, since the birth rate is falling. As parents can choose which schools their children attend, the programme offered can mean life or death for the survival of the school. They may offer English in the afternoon, during spare time, as well as making it part of the curriculum. So, young children find themselves studying a foreign language at school, while outside the classroom there is limited contact with the language. Hungary is mostly monolingual, films are dubbed and this age group rarely meets a foreigner with whom to converse.

The *National Core Curriculum* (NCC, 2003) states that the main aim of language learning is to develop learners' communicative competence. Learners study a foreign language to be able to use it in practice in real situations. At the same time, assessment, marks, points and tests (mostly written) are used in schools from a very early stage.

As a result of a research project into code-switching in the primary language classroom, and the associated beliefs and attitudes of teachers (Nagy & Robertson, forthcoming), it seemed important to ask what the pupils thought about their teachers' language choices and classroom practices for a balanced picture. Besides the main question about the teachers' language choices and use, two other questions were also asked. The children's answers to these questions serve as the basis of this chapter. The specially designed technique makes it necessary to describe how all three questions were presented, but only two will be analysed here.

Researching Pupils' Motivation and Thinking

In recent years a number of research papers have explored young students' motivation and attitudes to learning a foreign language (for a summary, see e.g. Elliott & Hufton, 2003; Nikolov, 1999). Most of these studies use conventional questionnaires and the analysis focuses on the associations between the young learners' attitudes and their motivation for learning. These studies provide opportunities for the pupils to think about their motivation for learning in general, but they were not designed to explore if there was a reason for learning it at any particular time.

Research questions

The research questions addressed in this chapter relate to the pupils' thinking and motivation for learning English. They are as follows:

(1)   What do pupils think helps or hinders them most while learning English?
(2)   What do pupils think the aims of learning and knowing English are at different stages in their lives?
(3)   Is there a difference between the perceptions of early beginners and late beginners?

Participants

The participants in this study are young learners of English from four primary schools in Budapest. The author observed them many times and talked to pupils at break times over two years. After a good rapport had been established with the children, permission was sought and given to interview them. Participation in the study started with classroom observation when they were in Grade 4. In Grade 5 the same learners were interviewed after the summer holidays in September 2006. Table 16.1 shows the distribution of learners according to their schools. In Hungary classes are divided into smaller groups for language learning so with the exception of one school two groups from each school participated in the study.

A total of 49 fifth-grade pupils (age 10–11) participated in the study. There were seven groups, with each group taught by a different teacher. Two schools (Kikerics and Ibolya) have a good reputation; their teachers are known as very capable language teachers and their resources are also exceptionally good. In these schools, English lessons begin at Grade 1 (age six). This early start fulfils the expectations of parents that their children should begin the study of English as early as possible. The children in these groups will be referred to as 'early beginners'. In the other two schools (Levendula and Gerbera) English lessons begin at Grade 4

Table 16.1   Participants in study from four schools

Name of school	Grade	Number of groups	Number of pupils	Level
Kikerics	5	2	12	Early beginners
Ibolya	5	2	12	Early beginners
Levendula	5	2	18	Late beginners
Gerbera	5	1	7	Late beginners

(age nine) in line with the recommendations of the curriculum. The children in these schools will be referred to as 'late beginners'.

A typical class in these schools has about 30 pupils. The classes are divided into two groups for language lessons, so there were between seven and 18 pupils in the groups participating in this study. As there was not enough time to interview all the pupils using the new technique, six pupils were chosen from each group. The teachers were asked to choose two very good and articulate pupils, two pupils from the middle range, and two pupils who were struggling with the language to represent each group.

At Gerbera school the Grade 5 class was divided into an English language group and a German group. The school used to specialize in German but now their teachers of German are retraining to teach English, following a huge demand for English. At this school seven permissions were given out by accident and the teacher insisted on working with all seven pupils, as it would have been awkward to deny one of them the honour of participating, as that pupil would have been heartbroken. This is why there are seven pupils in the late beginner Gerbera group (see Table 16.1). It was not possible to get permission to interview pupils again from the Gerbera school to balance the numbers; therefore, from one of the late beginner groups in Levendula school double numbers (12 pupils) were chosen; thus, 24 pupils were early beginners and 25 pupils came from late beginner groups.

Data Collection Instrument

A special instrument was designed to elicit the pupils' opinions and attitudes to the learning situation. A paper-based instrument (see description below) was used instead of a face-to-face interview with the researcher so as to minimise the unequal power relationship and to encourage the pupils to express their opinions freely. They were also asked to indicate how they usually feel during the English lessons by choosing from a range of different smileys.

In each elicitation session, six children were involved. They chose their own pairs, and each pair was assigned to a table on which there was a specially designed elicitation instrument. Once a pair finished answering the questions, they had a break while another pair finished and then they moved on to the next questionnaire and finally to the third. Each pair therefore completed three questionnaires.

It was assumed that working in pairs and being able to discuss their answers would help the children to think about these issues together. In Hungary children are hardly ever asked to give their opinions in class about why they think they are learning something or about their teacher's teaching, therefore this was an innovative task for them to do and I expected them to be more successful in pairs.

Questions 1a & 1b

Question 2

Question 3

Smileys

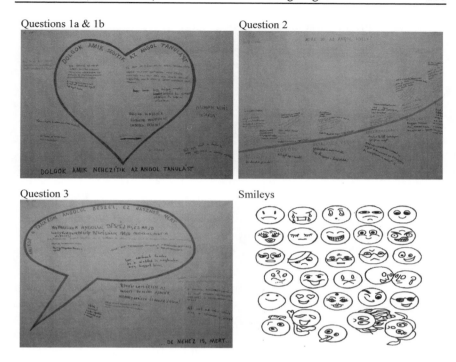

Figure 16.1 Photos of the three questionnaires completed by the children, and picture of the smileys

The elicitation instrument took the form of three big sheets of paper (size: 80cm × 58cm) prepared beforehand (see Figure 16.1). Each instrument contained a number of open-ended questions and the children were asked to write down their answers to the questions on the sheet of paper. All the questions were presented in Hungarian, their mother tongue (see Appendix) and the pupils were asked to respond in their mother tongue. The format of the elicitation instrument was designed to allow the pupils to write as much as they wished, and also to enable those in the same group to see the answers of the other pairs. The big pieces of paper also made the activity less like a test or the kind of form which they usually fill in and get marks for.

The children were given differently coloured felt tip pens, so in most cases it is possible to follow who wrote which answer. For example, one pupil wrote that English is 'not good for anything' for now, at the end of primary, in secondary, and at university. It is clear that the same pupil also wrote 'we can go to America' finishing the sentence: 'When you have grown up …'.

The tasks on the large pieces of paper were as follows:

Question 1a: On the first sheet of paper a big red heart was drawn and inside the heart the following words were written: 'Things that help me to learn English . . .'

Question 1b: Outside the heart shape, along the bottom was written: 'Things that make it more difficult for me to learn English . . .'

Question 2: On the second sheet of paper a time-line was drawn from left to right with the words: 'Knowing English is good, because . . .' Then, from left to right, just underneath the line the following times were given: 'Now', 'next year', 'at the end of primary', 'in secondary school', 'at university' and 'when you are a grown up'.

Question 3: On the third sheet of paper the questions were presented in a bubble: 'When my teacher only speaks English, it is good, because . . .' and outside the bubble: 'but it is also difficult, because . . .' The responses to this question are not presented in this chapter for reasons of lack of space.

The participants were also given a sheet with different smileys, and asked to choose and cut out two or three from them, stick them onto another piece of paper and write underneath them how they usually felt during English lessons. This task was planned to fill in time they had before going on to the next task. The results of the learners' responses to this task are also not included in this chapter because of lack of space.

Procedures

First, permission was obtained from the head teachers of the schools to interview the pupils at the beginning of the following school year (September). The six Grade 5 pupils selected from each class were asked to take home a form to be signed by their parents, so that the parent or guardian would give permission for the interview.

The children selected for participation in the elicitation tasks were taken out of class and worked with the researcher in an empty classroom or some other convenient location such as the library, kitchen or in one case, a corridor. All these locations had tables and were quiet and without too many people walking in and out.

Originally it was anticipated that the elicitation task would take 20 minutes, but all the sessions took considerably longer, partly because of the time necessary for settling down, but also because the pupils were very keen to stay outside the classroom as long as possible, some even openly asking the researcher to let them stay for the duration of the whole lesson (45 minutes).

The questionnaires were put on separate tables and the pupils were shown all of them; then, the questions were read out and the children

Pupils working on question 2

Pupils working on questions 1a & 1b and 3

 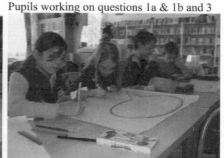

Figure 16.2 Pupils working on the questionnaires in the library

started working on their answers. The pupils were told that they could write as little or as much as they wished, and that even if somebody came up with the same answer, if they thought the same, they were asked to write it down again, so the researcher would know that there were more pupils thinking the same. The researcher explained to the participants that they would be working in pairs, they were to write their answers on one poster, and then wait till another poster was 'free'. Then, they would go there and work on that task.

Every group had separate sheets (Figure 16.2), allowing pupils to write as much as they wished, and also to avoid showing others their answers. Each pupil was allowed to choose who to work with. Only one group had a problem with pairing up, but after a short discussion a boy and a girl were happy to work together. Rotating from one question to the other did not seem to be as big a problem as had been anticipated, and the pairs who finished earliest were happily chatting with each other until the two other pairs were ready. Some of the pupils discussed the results with each other while moving to the next question, but in most cases they only discussed the questions with their partners. Instead of doing the extra activity separately, cutting out the smileys, they usually worked on the first three questions first, rotating without any instructions. Then they gathered together and did the last task as one group. The researcher tried to stay in the background, helping out only when asked and trying not to direct any responses.

Results

The written responses of the pupils were first translated into English and then grouped. This was not always easy to do; for example, the reasons for learning English at the end of primary school were: 'for exams', 'for entry exams', 'for getting to a secondary school'. Knowing the Hungarian context sometimes helped: pupils need to take two types of exams, external language proficiency exams and entrance exams designed by the secondary schools where they apply for admission. So, it was decided that entry exams at the end of primary school and entry exams to get to a good secondary school were the same category, but cases where a pupil wrote just 'exams' were treated separately, assuming that they meant external language proficiency exams. Tables 16.2–16.4 show the frequencies for each response. Early beginners are listed in the first column, late beginners in the second one and the third column shows the totals.

Pupils' Perceptions of Beneficial Factors

Table 16.2 shows the responses and their frequencies related to what the pupils perceived as supportive of their learning of English. The pupils who had been studying the language for four years (early beginners) thought that hearing the language helped them most (10 answers), but the books, exercise books and the teacher equally, were also very important and useful (seven answers, respectively). They also mentioned the dictionary (three times). The activities during the lessons (reading, speaking, writing, translating and practice) were viewed as helpful by some of the pupils, and four answered that learning lots also helps. Three pupils wrote that going abroad is useful.

The later beginners (who had started English a year prior to taking the task) seemed to rely on the books and exercise books most (15 answers). The teacher was very important for them (nine answers). They also used the dictionary (seven answers). Classroom activities were seen as very helpful, but for these pupils this meant mostly translating texts. Three learners referred to practice, two to studying hard, and three listed going abroad among priorities.

When these pupils were asked to consider how they learn the foreign language, both early and late beginners mentioned specific and classroom related factors first and most often. The most important factors for them were the textbooks, exercise books and dictionaries they used, the teacher and the classroom activities. The late beginners thought that the textbooks and exercise books were very important, while the early beginners realised that they needed to hear the language to be able to learn it. It is clear that the teacher holds the key to their learning, both by telling them what to learn, and also by helping with the pronunciation of words. This is especially important, as the Hungarian language is almost totally phonetic, so learning to read and write in Hungarian is much easier than learning to read and write in English. In English they need to be taught the pronunciation, spelling and written form of all the words separately in addition to their meanings.

As shown in Table 16.3, the early beginners thought that the teacher was the main factor in making learning more difficult (eight answers); two

Table 16.2 Pupils' perceptions of factors hindering them (summary of what pupils perceive as helpful in their learning of English)

Things that **help** *me to learn English*			
Answers	*Early beginners*	*Late beginners*	*All*
Books and exercise books	7	15	22
Teacher	7	9	16
Hearing the language	10	2	12
Dictionary	3	7	10
Studying a lot	4	2	6
Going abroad	3	3	6
Reading, speaking and writing in English	5	0	5
Translating texts	2	2	4
Practice	1	3	4
Paying attention	1	1	2
Correct material	1	0	1
If there are few pupils in the group	1	0	1
Exercises explained	1	0	1
Five lessons per week	1	0	1
When we translate the words in our head	1	0	1
We talk English not only in school, but also outside it	1	0	1
Learning it in kindergarten	0	1	1
Lots of room/space	0	1	1
To achieve a lot	0	1	1
Learning	0	1	1
Reading	0	1	1
Writing	0	1	1
Parents	0	1	1
Brothers and sisters	0	1	1

pupils said that if the teacher spoke only in English they found it hard to follow. The words themselves made it difficult for them to learn (four answers), whereas seven pupils from this group also realized that not paying attention may result in making progress harder.

The late beginners seemed to identify pronunciation as their biggest problem (12 answers). They also had problems with vocabulary (eight

Table 16.3 Summary of what pupils claim to make learning English difficult for them

Things that make it more difficult for me to learn English			
Answers	*Early beginners*	*Late beginners*	*All*
Teacher	8	4	12
The words	4	8	12
Pronunciation	0	12	12
If we don't pay attention	7	0	7
Equipment	3	0	3
If we don't practise	3	0	3
Texts	0	3	3
If the teacher speaks English only	2	0	2
Grammar	0	2	2
Language	0	2	2
Word order in question	1	0	1
If we speak almost only Hungarian during the lesson	1	0	1
Too many pupils in the group	1	0	1
If nobody talks to us	1	0	1
Too much to learn	0	1	1
Nothing	0	1	1
Other subjects	0	1	1
Completion of sentences	0	1	1
For me it is difficult to do	0	1	1

answers) and four pupils identified the teacher as the cause of difficulty. Three mentioned that the texts were really hard to understand.

For both groups most problems were related to the teacher and vocabulary learning. The early beginners gave some indication about at least one of the reasons why the teacher made their lives difficult; they found the teacher's use of English difficult to follow, as, most probably, the level is not tuned to their proficiency.

Words were difficult for both groups. On the one hand, their answers indicate that the main aim was to learn lots of words, as teachers used vocabulary tests frequently to make sure the pupils memorised vocabulary at home. On the other hand, pupils in the late beginner groups struggled with pronunciation, whereas none of the 24 early beginners mentioned problems with this aspect of learning. It is possible that as time goes by and the children learn more and more words, pronunciation is less of an issue for them. There is another plausible explanation: the late beginners started to learn from a particular coursebook without an oral period. This book introduces the printed word from the earliest stage; therefore, for these learners exposure to unknown words in print, reading texts and managing pronunciation may be more demanding than for those pupils who first became familiar with the language in spoken form in year one.

Goals in language study: From immediate future to adult needs

Table 16.4 shows what goals participants identified for the present time, near future, years later and for adult life. Generally, the early beginners and the late beginners gave very similar answers when asked why they thought knowing English was useful in the short and in the long run. The one marked difference is that six of the early beginners wrote that English 'is good if you go abroad right now', compared to a single late beginner, whereas six of the late beginners simply wrote 'to learn' and only one early beginner gave this reason. Later on, in secondary school and at universities, the most important things mentioned were to know more, to get to university, and to speak the language.

Both groups made it clear that the main reason for learning English for them was to get to a secondary school (11 answers from the early beginners and 12 answers from the late beginners). Both groups thought that they needed to take an exam at the end of the primary school (seven and six answers). The second most important aim for the children in both groups was to be able to travel abroad (nine and ten learners) and to work abroad (seven and 10 answers).

Discussion

When these pupils were asked to give their opinions about their foreign language learning, they took this task very seriously. They talked about the answers with each other, having obviously thought about them, and it seems that they tried to write down their own opinions, whether this meant that their answer was the only answer of its kind, or their answer was similar to those of their peers.

Their answers seemed to be strongly influenced by the classroom practices and the expectations of both the school and the parents. During the English lessons they frequently use texts, read and translate them, and they are also asked to learn the unknown words and often even memorise texts by heart. Their performances are measured by regular vocabulary

Table 16.4 Summary of reasons for learning English

Knowing English is good, because …				
	Answers	*Early beginners*	*Late beginners*	*All*
Now	If we go abroad	6	1	7
	To learn	1	6	7
	The earlier the better, easier	3	0	3
	To get good marks	2	1	3
Next year	To know more English, to learn	3	5	8
	To get to secondary school	4	0	4
	To pronounce the words	0	3	3
	If we go abroad	1	2	3
End of primary	Get to a secondary school (entry exams)	11	12	23
	Take an exam	7	6	13
In secondary	To get to university	1	6	7
	Take an exam	2	3	5
	To travel	3	0	3
At university	We would know everything, speak it	2	5	7
	To get a job	1	3	4
Grown up	To travel abroad	9	10	19
	Work abroad	7	10	17
	To be able to talk to people from abroad	1	3	4
	To get a good job (in Hungary)	2	1	3

tests, sentence translations (usually from Hungarian to English) and oral recitals of the texts, poems, songs, by heart. They get marks for these, in many classes one or even more marks per week. Their final mark at the end of the school year depends on these marks.

These final marks (along with those for their other subjects) at the end of the primary school may determine which secondary schools the pupils can get into. Secondary schooling is highly competitive in Hungary, and those secondary schools with a good reputation are in a position to design entry tests, and to select the best pupils from a large area. English language is highly valued, and many entrance tests include written questions, ensuring that the chosen pupils are already at an advanced level.

Pupils from a very young age find themselves learning English as a foreign language, and they are well aware that the competition for good schools, for places at university, and for a job, are all related to their English proficiency level and the exams they manage to pass. For them, learning English has become something to achieve, and for their teachers, getting their pupils through these exams rates far higher than communicative competence. But there is a contradiction, in that teachers are encouraged in the *National Core Curriculum* (2003) to teach everyday language, while the real focus, practically speaking, is on grammar teaching, learning words, reading and writing, answering questions from texts, to train pupils to pass tests and exams.

It is clear from the responses to the elicitation tasks that for future goals all the learners identified instrumental motives, as they expected proficiency in the English language to be something useful for some other purpose in adult life. Some mentioned the foreign language as a vehicle for communication with people abroad, suggesting an integrative motivation.

However, it is remarkable that none of the learners mentioned reasons related to any intrinsic motive: the pleasure of learning and knowing English. In fact, the opposite is true: many of the perceived problems relate to the language: vocabulary, pronunciation, grammar, and the lack of paying attention. This is a vicious circle, as if they do not find the actual language learning activities intrinsically motivating, they cannot consciously focus on tasks.

Another remarkable finding relates to the role of the teacher. Although many children listed the teacher as most helpful, the frequency of the teacher in the negative category requires some explanation. Most probably classroom practice is far from ideal if so many learners identify the teacher and her methodology as problematic. It is necessary to triangulate data from classroom observations with the answers of the children from the four schools to be able to analyse the reasons for the frequent negative evaluation of the teacher.

Conclusion

Teachers will be caught between two competing objectives, unless the situation as described above is openly acknowledged and either the aims of the curriculum or the use of entry exams changes. If asked to demonstrate a lesson for inspection purposes, they may well try to show pupils being free and communicative. But they and other teachers know very well what is probably normally happening in these classrooms – trying to get pupils through exams, mostly with the well-practised grammar translation method, memorising passages from texts, and vocabulary tests. The pupils are all well aware of this, and they would see some factors that are helping them to reach these aims as 'helpful', while others as 'making it more difficult to learn'. But these factors might have been very different if the aim was communicative competence.

The focus of the project of which this study forms a small part was not on the pupils' thinking or motivation, but the data presented in this chapter suggest that pupils' perceptions of their learning are important for an understanding of the state of English language teaching and learning in primary classrooms in Hungary. The study has some limitations. It is not possible to generalise from a relatively small number of answers and pupils from only one grade were sampled. In the future it would be useful to interview more pupils, from different grades, different schools, maybe from outside Budapest, to see if those pupils think in a similar way about learning a foreign language. It would also be interesting for the sake of comparison to carry out a similar study with learners of German.

References

Elliott, J. and Hufton, N. (2003) Achievement motivation in real contexts. *BJEP Monograph Series II*, 155–172.

Medgyes, P. and Miklosy, K. (2000) The language situation in Hungary. *Current Issues in Language Planning* 1, 148–242.

Nagy, K. and Robertson, D. (forthcoming) Target language use in English language classes in Hungarian primary schools. In M. Turnbull and J. Dailey-O'Cain (eds) *First Language Use in Second and Foreign Language Learning: Intersection of Theory, Practice, Curriculum and Policy*. Clevedon: Multilingual Matters.

National Core Curriculum (NCC) (2003) *Nemzeti alaptanterv*. Budapest: Ministry of Education.

Nikolov, M. (1999) 'Why do you learn English?' 'Because the teacher is short'. A study of Hungarian children's foreign language learning motivation. *Language Teaching Research* 3, 33–56.

Petzold, R. and Berns, M. (2000) Catching up with Europe: Speakers and functions of English in Hungary. *World Englishes* 19, 113–124.

Appendix

The questions in Hungarian:

(1a) Dolgok, amik segítik az angol tanulást
(1b) Dolgok, amik nehezítik az angol tanulást
(2) Mire jó az angol? (most, jövőre, középiskolában, egyetemen, felnőtt korban)
(3a) Amikor a tanárom angolul beszél ez hasznos, mert ...
(3b) De nehéz is, mert ...